Third Edition

Bernadine P. Branchaw, Ed. D.

Professor
Department of Business Information Systems
Haworth College of Business
Western Michigan University

GLENCOE
McGraw-Hill

New York, New York   Columbus, Ohio   Woodland Hills, California   Peoria, Illinois

This textbook has been prepared with the assistance of Visual Education Corporation, Princeton, New Jersey.

English Made Easy, Third Edition

Imprint 1997

Send all inquiries to:
Glencoe/McGraw-Hill
936 Eastwind Drive
Westerville, OH 43081

ISBN 0–02–800139–7

Printed in the United States of America.

7 8 9 10 11 12   066   02 01 00 99 98 97

Contents: *English Made Easy,* Student Edition

Lesson 1	A Brief Review Nouns, pronouns, adjectives, and verbs	1
Lesson 2	A Brief Review (Continued) Adverbs, prepositions, conjunctions, and interjections	5
Lesson 3	The Sentence Subjects and verbs; understood subjects	9
Lesson 4	Subjects and Verbs Main subjects and verbs; compound subjects and verbs	13
Lesson 5	Kinds of Sentences Declarative, interrogative, imperative, and exclamatory sentences	17
Lesson 6	Nouns Proper and common nouns	21
Lesson 7	More About Nouns Concrete and abstract nouns; compound and collective nouns	25
Lesson 8	Plural Nouns	29
Lesson 9	Possessive Nouns	33
Lesson 10	Pronouns Pronoun agreement with antecedents	37
Lesson 11	Forms of Pronouns Nominative, objective, and possessive forms of pronouns	41
Lesson 12	Pronoun Troublemakers Choosing the correct form of a pronoun	45
Lesson 13	*Who, Whom,* and Other Pronouns	49
Lesson 14	More About Pronouns Interrogative pronouns; pronouns ending in *-self;* indefinite pronouns	53
Lesson 15	Verbs Direct objects of verbs; verb phrases	57
Lesson 16	More About Verbs Helping verbs; principal parts of verbs; linking verbs	61
Lesson 17	Verb Tenses—Yesterday, Today, and Tomorrow	65
Lesson 18	The Regulars and the Irregulars	69
Lesson 19	*To Be* and *To Have*	73
Lesson 20	*To Do* and *To Go*	77
Lesson 21	Just *Perfect!* The Perfect Tenses	81
Lesson 22	Subjects and Verbs Must Agree!	85
Lesson 23	*Lie* and *Lay*	89
Lesson 24	*Sit* and *Set; Rise* and *Raise*	93
Lesson 25	More Troublesome Verbs *Learn* and *teach; leave* and *let; bring* to and *take* away; *affect* and *effect; borrow* and *lend*	97
Lesson 26	Adjectives Articles; descriptive, possessive, and limiting adjectives	101
Lesson 27	More About Adjectives Proper adjectives; double adjectives; commas and hyphens with adjectives	105

Lesson 28   Comparing Adjectives   109
             Descriptive, comparative, and superlative degrees of adjectives;
             irregular adjectives

Lesson 29   Really? Surely. Carefully!   113
             Adverbs; adjectives and adverbs with the same form

Lesson 30   Comparing Adverbs   117

Lesson 31   Some Troublemakers   121
             Placement of adjectives and adverbs in a sentence; double
             negatives; *sure* and *surely; bad* and *badly*

Lesson 32   More Troublemakers   125
             Using *other* or *else; real* and *really; well;* conjunctive adverbs

Lesson 33   *For, By,* and *Of*—The Preposition   129
             Prepositions and prepositional phrases

Lesson 34   Common Preposition Errors   133
             Between you and *me; among/between;* unnecessary prepositions;
             prepositions at the end of sentences

Lesson 35   Phrases   137
             Infinitive, participial, and gerund phrases

Lesson 36   Conjunctions Are Joiners!   141
             Conjunctions; pairs of conjunctions

Lesson 37   Clauses   145
             Independent and dependent clauses; noun, adjective, and adverb
             clauses

Lesson 38   Lost and Found Department   149
             Misplaced phrases; dangling participles; misplaced clauses

Lesson 39   Common Conjunction Errors   153
             Run-on sentences; comma splices

Lesson 40   Faulty Parallelism   157

Lesson 41   Using Punctuation Marks   161
             Periods, question marks, exclamation points, and hyphens

Lesson 42   Using Commas   165
             Commas used to separate

Lesson 43   Commas, Commas, and More Commas   169
             Commas used to set off

Lesson 44   The Versatile Comma   173
             More uses of commas

Lesson 45   The Semicolon and the Colon   177

Lesson 46   Dashes, Parentheses, and Brackets   181

Lesson 47   Quotation Marks, Underscores, and Apostrophes   185

Lesson 48   Capitals   189

Lesson 49   Numbers   193

Lesson 50   Word Usage   197
             Confusing word pairs

Index   201

Preface

THE GOALS OF *ENGLISH MADE EASY*   No matter what career you choose—accountant, attorney, banker, doctor, engineer, interior designer, marketing representative, secretary, teacher—you will need to know how to communicate effectively. In the world of business, you will communicate with a variety of people:

- Sales representatives and suppliers may call you for information.

- Supervisors and managers may ask you to prepare reports.

- Administrators and directors may discuss problems with you.

- Customers and visitors may ask you for directions or explanations.

In these and other business situations, you will take part in an exchange of information. Because the smooth flow of information is essential for every business, all companies value an employee who can communicate effectively, for this employee avoids misunderstandings, saves the company time and money, and keeps customers happy.

In every communication situation, your main tool for success is your command of the English language. To succeed in business, therefore, you need to improve your communication skills and to master standard English. *English Made Easy* will help you achieve these goals.

HOW *ENGLISH MADE EASY* REACHES ITS GOALS   The third edition of *English Made Easy* will help you master communication skills with a simple step-by-step approach to the correct use of the English language. This text-workbook describes and explains the basic principles of English and provides numerous illustrations of each principle. The third edition is designed to make learning not only easier but also more fun. This is a communication book that is both practical and enjoyable.

English Made Easy consists of 50 distinct lessons. Each four-page lesson presents you with two pages of instruction followed by two pages of exercises. The lessons follow a common format. Each one begins with a statement that introduces the lesson theme. This introduction is followed by one or more learning sections.

Within each lesson are several Checkup sections—usually one for each principle taught in that lesson. The Checkup exercises test your understanding of the text. They allow you to apply a principle immediately after it is presented in the text.

Because the answer to the first item in each Checkup is given, you have an opportunity to check yourself. Cover the text answer with a card and, following the directions for that Checkup, do the first item. Then check your answer against the text answer. If your answer is correct, continue doing the Checkup. If your answer is incorrect, review the text until you understand why you made an error. Only when you are sure that you will not repeat an error should you continue doing the Checkup.

Doing the Checkups conscientiously will help you to do better on the two-page exercises in each lesson, so do the Checkups carefully. When your instructor reviews the answers for the Checkups, make sure that you understand why each answer is correct. Again, review the text if necessary, or ask your instructor for help.

The two pages of exercises at the end of the lesson give you an opportunity to apply the principles learned in that lesson.

English Made Easy can help you develop the communication skills you will need for success in the business world. The time you invest now will pay dividends in the future.

ACKNOWLEDGMENTS   Many people—both teachers and students—contributed their ideas to this third edition of *English Made Easy*. Their helpful comments were much appreciated. Special thanks, however, must go to the following educators for their helpful comments and suggestions: Delores Anderson, Southwestern Technical College, Granite Falls, Minnesota; Jacqueline Hillis, Mansfield Business School, Dallas, Texas; Ruth Hogan, Pulaski State Area Vocational Technical School, Pulaski, Tennessee; Peter Newman, Sawyer Business School, Elizabeth, New Jersey; Gary Paulson, Willmar Technical College, Willmar, Minnesota.

My sincere appreciation goes to the editors at Glencoe—Stephanie Happer, executive editor, and Paula Martin, associate editor—who have made invaluable suggestions and improvements for the third edition of *English Made Easy*.

Bernadine P. Branchaw, Ed. D.
Professor, Haworth College of Business
Western Michigan University

A Brief Review

Do you remember all eight parts of speech? Let's review them in this lesson. In later lessons we will discuss each of these eight parts in greater detail.

NOUNS—PERSONS, PLACES, AND THINGS   A word that names a person, place, or thing is called a *noun*. The function of a noun in a sentence is to name something. If a word does not name something, it is not a noun.

Arlene prepares the *documents* in the computer *room.* *Arlene* is a noun; it names a person. *Documents* is a noun; it names things. *Room* is a noun; it names a place.

John presented his *paintings* at the *museum.* *John* is a noun; it names a person. *Paintings* is a noun; it names a thing. *Museum* is a noun; it names a place.

CHECKUP 1   Underline the nouns in the following sentences. Then write the nouns in the spaces at the right.

1. The computers were installed in the lab.
2. Several members of the committee revised the report.
3. Harold was transferred to the new plant.
4. Lisa taught classes during the day.
5. The damaged items were shipped in boxes.

1. **computers, lab** _____
2. _____
3. _____
4. _____
5. _____

PRONOUNS   A *pronoun* is a word that takes the place of a noun. We add variety to our speech and our writing when we use the following pronouns: *I, me, we, us, you, he, she, it, they, them, him, her, my, mine, yours, ours, their, his, hers, its, myself, himself, herself, ourselves, themselves, yourself, yourselves, itself,* and *theirs.* Imagine, for example, saying the following sentence without pronouns:

Tim and his brother Robert bought their computer from their uncle.

Without the pronouns, you would have to say:

Tim and Tim's brother Robert bought Tim and Robert's computer from Tim and Robert's uncle.

The pronouns make quite a difference! Let's look at another example:

The contract offered *them* many benefits. *Them* is a pronoun. The pronoun is used in place of the names of persons.

CHECKUP 2   Underline the pronouns in the following sentences. Then write the pronouns in the spaces at the right.

1. Once you start it, the machine will run by itself.
2. Sally and I appreciate your sending us the material.
3. We gave him a subscription to his favorite magazine.
4. Just between you and me, I think he is exaggerating.
5. Gena spells better than her cousin.

1. **you, it, itself** _____
2. _____
3. _____
4. _____
5. _____

ADJECTIVES—WORDS THAT DESCRIBE

An *adjective* modifies a noun or a pronoun. To *modify* means "to describe or limit the meaning of." In the first example below, you can see how the adjective *busy* modifies the noun *office*. The adjective tells "what kind of" office. Besides telling "what kind of," adjectives can also tell "which one" and "how many."

What kind of:	*busy* office	*happy* place	*good* record
Which one:	*this* one	*that* tax	*these* accounts
How many:	*one* year	*several* copies	*few* cents

This modeling agency has been recruiting models for *six* months.

The words *this, modeling,* and *six* are adjectives. *This* and *modeling* modify the noun *agency. Six* modifies the noun *months. This* tells "which one." *Modeling* tells "what kind of." *Six* tells "how many."

The words *the, a,* and *an* are also adjectives, but they are referred to as articles.

the text editor	*the* project	*the* assignment
an excuse	*a* survey	*an* application

CHECKUP 3 Underline the adjectives and articles in the following sentences. Then write the adjectives and articles in the spaces at the right.

1. Three credit customers were waiting in the line.
2. These machines have been cleaned several times.
3. Sam conducted the meeting of union officials.
4. Our friendly hosts welcomed us to their beautiful home.
5. Marked copies were distributed to the clients.
6. Where are the copies of the research proposal?
7. The company gave a bonus to all employees.
8. Use the margin on the right side for comments.
9. Brad wrote a detailed report for the manager.
10. They constructed a new shopping mall.

1. **Three, credit, the**
2. _____
3. _____
4. _____
5. _____
6. _____
7. _____
8. _____
9. _____
10. _____

VERBS—WORDS THAT "MOVE"

A *verb* is a word that tells what someone or something is or does. A verb expresses action.

Walt *anticipated* fewer changes in the program. The verb *anticipated* tells what *Walt* did.

Mark *painted* her portrait. The verb *painted* tells what *Mark* did.

CHECKUP 4 Underline the verbs in the following sentences. Then write the verbs in the spaces at the right.

1. They expanded the room several feet.
2. Sally listed her qualifications on the application.
3. Please purchase enough material to make two posters.
4. The company representative recommended her for a promotion.
5. Company officials offered us a substantial increase.
6. We canceled the order yesterday.
7. Yes, Mildred, we phoned the company early in the morning.
8. Our travel agent confirmed our flight plans.
9. They accepted her resignation with regret.
10. Rob went to the conference on Friday.

1. **expanded**
2. _____
3. _____
4. _____
5. _____
6. _____
7. _____
8. _____
9. _____
10. _____

EXERCISES

EXERCISE 1   Is the italicized word a noun (N) or a pronoun (P)? Circle the correct letter.

1. Where did she put the *manuals*?   1. N P
2. Our *supervisors* met all morning.   2. N P
3. Regardless of what *they* cost, buy them.   3. N P
4. First, we need to estimate our *expenses.*   4. N P
5. Where have all the *copies* gone?   5. N P
6. After the *convention,* we plan to tour the city.   6. N P
7. If I were *president,* I would recommend that we meet on Tuesdays.   7. N P
8. Have you seen the Anderson *files*?   8. N P
9. Patricia asked *her* for a copy of the speech.   9. N P
10. Did *you* read the label carefully?   10. N P
11. *Our* sales manager requested a survey of the new territory.   11. N P
12. With every *purchase* the customer receives a coupon.   12. N P
13. The captain of the team selected Sue and *me.*   13. N P
14. *He* handled several transactions at one time.   14. N P
15. Please replace the *bulb* in the overhead light.   15. N P
16. Whom have *you* recommended?   16. N P
17. The *speaker* kept us interested.   17. N P
18. *Her* interest in writing prompted her to become a journalist.   18. N P
19. After *your* meeting, what did you do?   19. N P
20. *Peter,* have you seen the new addition?   20. N P

EXERCISE 2   Underline the adjectives and articles in the following sentences. Then write the adjectives and articles in the spaces at the right.

1. Susan placed several lecture notes on the counter.   1. _____
2. Many people were present when the manager made the announcement.   2. _____
3. Local firms wanted a copy of the new manual.   3. _____
4. Low prices prompted us to buy five copies.   4. _____
5. The Friday session was canceled because of low enrollments.   5. _____
6. Bob, have you seen the new desks yet?   6. _____
7. Please destroy the old copies.   7. _____
8. She was hired because she had excellent English skills.   8. _____
9. Several applicants applied for the sales position.   9. _____
10. The new pricing schedule takes effect on Monday.   10. _____

EXERCISE 3   Underline the verbs in the following sentences. Then write the verbs in the spaces at the right.

1. Jennifer analyzed the data for Mr. Thompson.   1. _____
2. They acquired several parcels of land.   2. _____
3. She asked the retiring manager what his plans were.   3. _____
4. Please answer the phone immediately.   4. _____

5. Yes, Shirley, your order arrived today.   5. _____

6. The politician polled his constituents for their opinions about the bill.   6. _____

7. Interest rates increased 1 percent.   7. _____

8. Clerks and secretaries worked together on the project.   8. _____

9. Customers responded to our full-page advertisement in Sunday's paper.   9. _____

10. Please consider how much time it takes.   10. _____

11. Send the battery in for repairs.   11. _____

12. Pat Viard designed the office furnishings.   12. _____

13. The president and the vice president attended the meeting in San Antonio.   13. _____

14. They reorganized several departments over the years.   14. _____

15. At the convention we met several of our colleagues.   15. _____

16. We understood the deadline to be Saturday.   16. _____

17. Send the diskettes to me immediately.   17. _____

18. Individuals contributed money for flowers.   18. _____

19. Kathleen hopes to find a teaching position in Los Angeles.   19. _____

20. Jerry designed and built his own home.   20. _____

EXERCISE 4   Is the italicized word a noun (N), a pronoun (P), an adjective (A), or a verb (V)? Circle the correct letter. (*Note:* Some pronouns may also be used as adjectives.)

1. Yes, *Clark,* the report is finished.   1. N P A V

2. *You* should keep a copy for your files.   2. N P A V

3. The *goodwill* of our customers is important to us.   3. N P A V

4. The speaker *donated* his honorarium to the scholarship fund.   4. N P A V

5. Some of the equipment was stored in *her* basement.   5. N P A V

6. Susan received a *perfect* score for her performance.   6. N P A V

7. Our investments should give us a *sizable* profit.   7. N P A V

8. Her *thorough* reports received praise from her supervisor.   8. N P A V

9. Shareholders were asked to return the enclosed *proxy.*   9. N P A V

10. The *members* appointed Daniel as program chair.   10. N P A V

11. A *two-thirds* majority agreed with the proposed resolution.   11. N P A V

12. *Our* keynote speaker had us spellbound.   12. N P A V

13. *Complete* all the exercises on the first page.   13. N P A V

14. The *advisory* committee was composed of five people from the business sector and five people from the school system.   14. N P A V

15. Afternoon *breaks* should be taken by 3 o'clock.   15. N P A V

16. *His* loan was for 60 days only.   16. N P A V

17. The new billing *system* not only totals all balances but also provides daily reports.   17. N P A V

18. Please *announce* that we are here.   18. N P A V

19. Faye received a *bonus* for her efforts.   19. N P A V

20. *Call* Ms. Oldani for more information.   20. N P A V

21. *They* constructed a sturdy scaffold.   21. N P A V

22. Although they *shipped* the order several weeks ago, I still have not received it.   22. N P A V

23. Because a decision must be made by the end of the week, please *call* me and let me know what dates are available.   23. N P A V

24. A *service* fee of $5 will be charged to your account.   24. N P A V

25. Where have *you* placed the computer manuals?   25. N P A V

A Brief Review (Continued)

ADVERBS   An *adverb* is a word that modifies a verb, an adjective, or another adverb. Adverbs tell "how," "when," and "where."

How: Lift the box *carefully*. (Or: *slowly, quickly,* and so on.)

When: Return the manuscript *today*. (Or: *soon, tomorrow, immediately,* and so on.)

Where: Kyle went *home*. (Or: *upstairs, there, here,* and so on.)

The applicants did *well* on their qualifying exams. The adverb *well* modifies the verb *did*. The adverb tells "how." Did how? *Well.*

Today we received the blueprints. The adverb *today* modifies the verb *received*. It tells "when." Received when? *Today.*

CHECKUP 1   Underline the adverbs in the following sentences. Then write the adverbs in the spaces at the right.

1. The cost of the merchandise increased significantly.
2. We immediately accepted her resignation.
3. The box was attractively wrapped.
4. We finally received the instructor's manual.
5. The wallpaper was very expensive.
6. Word processing equipment is extremely expensive, but it is worth the money.

1. **significantly** _____
2. _____
3. _____
4. _____
5. _____

6. _____

PREPOSITIONS   A *preposition* is a word that shows the relationship of a noun or a pronoun to some other word in the sentence. Here are some commonly used prepositions:

at	under	on	before	until	of	through	for
in	over	by	after	between	to	during	with
about	since	up	upon	off	near	beside	beneath
along	below	into	from	like	except	among	behind
above	toward	within	without	onto	across	around	inside

Give the papers *to* Mr. Barnes. *To* is a preposition. It shows the relationship of the noun *papers* to the verb *give*.

We received electronic mail *from* several customers. *From* is a preposition. It shows the relationship of the noun *mail* to the noun *customers*.

CHECKUP 2   Underline the prepositions in the following sentences. Then write the prepositions in the spaces at the right.

1. During the afternoon session, we listened to Dr. Bournaous talk about nutrition.
2. Before noon, would you please get in touch with Mr. Karloff about the posters.
3. Harry and Margaret do not want the display above the bookshelves.

1. **During, to, about** _____
2. _____
3. _____

4. Under the desk there were several journals among the newspapers. 4. _____

5. What I told you must stay within these walls. 5. _____

6. You will find him around the corner with his friends. 6. _____

7. After work would you please stop by the store and buy some snacks for the party. 7. _____

8. Prior to granting approval of the contract, we want your comments by phone. 8. _____

CONJUNCTIONS

A *conjunction* is a word used to join words, phrases, or clauses. Some commonly used conjunctions are:

and   but   or   nor   for   yet   so

Joining words: Chris *and* Pat drafted the blueprints.

Use a pencil *or* a pen for filling in the squares.

Joining phrases: During the day *and* throughout the evening, Andrea worked.

Joining clauses: Our sales representative made the sale, *and* the secretary prepared the papers.

CHECKUP 3

Underline the conjunctions in the following sentences. Then write the conjunctions in the spaces at the right. (As you do so, try to determine whether the conjunction joins words, phrases, or clauses.)

1. Beth and Chris were married on Saturday. 1. **and (words)** _____

2. We will be happy to wrap and ship your order immediately. 2. _____

3. Andrew conducted the research, but Anthony gave the presentation. 3. _____

4. They waited two hours, but no one came to meet them. 4. _____

5. We could order a fruit basket or flowers. 5. _____

6. Please mail the manuscript by Monday or Tuesday. 6. _____

7. Please order orange juice and cereal for me. 7. _____

8. The researchers applied for grants from the government and from private foundations. 8. _____

INTERJECTIONS

An *interjection* is a word that expresses strong feeling.

We have the day off. *Hurray!*

Wow! Antoinette won the lottery.

Oops! I made a mistake.

Whoopee! We get to go to Hawaii for the week.

CHECKUP 4

Underline the interjections in the following sentences. Then write the interjections in the spaces at the right.

1. Yea! We were awarded the contract. 1. **Yea** _____

2. Whew! What a relief not to have to take the exam. 2. _____

3. Ouch! You hurt me. 3. _____

4. Yes! It's yours. 4. _____

5. Wow! It works. 5. _____

5. Wow! It works. 5. _____

6. Congratulations! You gave an excellent speech. 6. _____

7. Hurray! We won the contest. 7. _____

8. Help! I lost my pet. 8. _____

EXERCISES

NAME _____ DATE _____ SCORE _____

EXERCISE 1   Underline the adverbs in the following sentences. Then write the adverbs in the spaces at the right.

1. The boxes were conveniently out of reach.   1. _____
2. Daniel reacted negatively to all of our suggestions.   2. _____
3. After serving in the Persian Gulf War, he was honorably discharged.   3. _____
4. They would have bought more copies, but they were too expensive.   4. _____
5. After several weeks of waiting for the document, we finally received it.   5. _____
6. Please clean the floor quickly.   6. _____
7. The company readily agreed to the union's demands.   7. _____
8. When you proofread, proofread carefully so we don't have any mistakes on the
   final copy.   8. _____
9. After a careful examination of the books, we found several items listed
   incorrectly.   9. _____
10. Mr. Harrington is an exceptionally well-mannered young man.   10. _____
11. Are you sure they are not working too hard?   11. _____
12. Jennifer typed not only accurately but also rapidly.   12. _____
13. I believe he is much more intelligent than her former boss.   13. _____
14. May we have your reply tomorrow?   14. _____
15. I would like answers to my questions soon.   15. _____

EXERCISE 2   Underline the prepositions in the following sentences. Then write the prepositions in the spaces at the right.

1. Jack is now head of production for the company.   1. _____
2. The papers are either on my desk or in the files.   2. _____
3. During the last three years we have had over 500 applications.   3. _____
4. We walked along the beach until dark.   4. _____
5. Several members of the management team met and agreed with our recommendations.   5. _____
6. After thinking about it, we signed the letter.   6. _____
7. The partners voted in favor of a bonus.   7. _____
8. That same story was told to me after lunch.   8. _____
9. Without help from Cecilia, we could not have finished the project.   9. _____
10. The site is on a hill near Highway 24 about a mile from here.   10. _____
11. Over 15 percent of the people voted in favor of the nominees.   11. _____
12. On June 1 we will move into our new headquarters in New Orleans.   12. _____

EXERCISE 3   Underline the conjunctions in the following sentences. Then write the conjunctions in the spaces at the right.

1. Stella is exhausted, yet she continues to work.   1. _____
2. Everyone was in the office, so Richard felt he could leave.   2. _____
3. Hank or Brad will be the one to work overtime tonight.   3. _____

4. Eileen and I were competing for the same position in the department.   4. _____
5. The room was empty, for the wedding party had left hours ago.   5. _____
6. This morning is a convenient time for the delivery, but this afternoon is not.   6. _____
7. Our broker is responsible for buying and selling stocks.   7. _____
8. We'll learn today whether our proposal will be accepted or rejected.   8. _____
9. Jill ordered sweet and sour pork for her entrée.   9. _____
10. She was working quickly yet carefully.   10. _____

EXERCISE 4

Underline the interjections in the following sentences. Then write the interjections in the spaces at the right.

1. You're the winner of the grand prize. Congratulations!   1. _____
2. Wow! That was an outstanding performance by the pianist.   2. _____
3. Oops! I didn't mean to do that.   3. _____
4. We have front-row seats to the rock concert. Hooray!   4. _____
5. Oh! I meant to tell you about that sooner.   5. _____

EXERCISE 5

What part of speech is the italicized word? Write your answers in the spaces at the right.
(*Note:* Some pronouns may also be used as adjectives.)

1. Eileen *and* Oliver both had promising careers.   1. _____
2. We hoped to be finished by 2 p.m., *but* it was closer to 4 p.m. when we stopped.   2. _____
3. *Irene* agreed to recommend Myles for the position of vice president.   3. _____
4. *Your* applications for promotion will be reviewed by the committee.   4. _____
5. *Whew!* That was a close call.   5. _____
6. Several people were willing to attest *to* his loyalty.   6. _____
7. The dissertation will be *revised* to include faculty recommendations.   7. _____
8. *We* initiated the idea, but the officers carried it out.   8. _____
9. *Outspoken* critics were not in agreement with the rest of the reviewers.   9. _____
10. The twins worked *energetically* for the first few hours.   10. _____
11. After hearing the president's report, they *immediately* went to work.   11. _____
12. Marion's *supervisor* approved the design for the new building.   12. _____
13. Give *them* the merchandise they requested.   13. _____
14. Please walk *toward* the door quickly.   14. _____
15. The *glaring* error appeared on the front page of the company newsletter.   15. _____
16. On his résumé, he *stated* that he supervised ten employees.   16. _____
17. Rebecca will *not* sing in the school's choir.   17. _____
18. The new *system* is working out nicely in our office.   18. _____
19. The inspectors *wandered* through the plant looking for safety violations.   19. _____
20. Most of the goods received were of top quality, *but* some articles were not.   20. _____
21. The *exclusive* report was prepared by Victor Adams.   21. _____
22. Walking *toward* the door, he noticed the announcement on the bulletin board.   22. _____
23. The *extremely* fragile vase was sitting very close to the edge of the desk.   23. _____
24. *Glenda* was the number one choice for the position.   24. _____
25. Construction on the new administration building *began* last week.   25. _____
26. Members *of* the committee voted in favor of a bonus.   26. _____
27. Theresa *and* Brian went to the theater.   27. _____
28. *Oh!* I forgot to make that change.   28. _____
29. The directions were *very* difficult to follow.   29. _____
30. We will address *their* concerns at the meeting.   30. _____

The Sentence

THE SENTENCE—A COMPLETE THOUGHT   A *sentence* is a group of words expressing a complete thought. If a group of words does not express a complete thought, it is not a sentence.

Mr. Alteria, who is chairman of the Board of Directors. This is not a sentence. It does not express a complete thought. You need to know more. Did Mr. Alteria do or say something? Did someone say something *about* Mr. Alteria? By themselves, the words *Mr. Alteria, who is chairman of the Board of Directors* make no sense. You need more information.

Mr. Alteria, who is chairman of the Board of Directors, announced an increase in stock dividends. This is a sentence. It expresses a complete thought. What did Mr. Alteria do? Mr. Alteria announced an increase in stock dividends.

CHECKUP 1   Decide whether each of the following word groups is a sentence. If the group of words is a sentence, circle *S*. If the group of words is not a sentence, circle *NS*.

1. The letter, which is on his desk.
2. Everyone in the office was invited to the company's open house on Sunday.
3. The files on the Smith manufacturing proposal are gone.
4. Now that we have completed the report.
5. We invite all the employees to attend the installation of the newly elected union officials.

1. S Ⓝ︎Ⓢ︎
2. S NS
3. S NS
4. S NS
5. S NS

THE SUBJECT—A NOUN OR A PRONOUN   Every sentence has two parts, the subject and the predicate. The *subject* of a sentence names a person, place, or thing about which something is being said. The subject shows who is speaking, who is spoken to, or the person or thing spoken about.

Who is speaking: *Eleanor* became the new manager of the store. The subject is *Eleanor,* the person who is speaking. This subject names a person.

Who is spoken to: *You* have a month to finish the report. The subject is *you,* the person spoken to. This subject names a person.

Who is spoken about: *Barbara Rivera* is qualified to be our next president. The subject is *Barbara Rivera,* the person spoken about. This subject names a person.

What is spoken about: *Springfield* is the capital of Illinois. The subject is *Springfield,* the thing spoken about. This subject names a place.

What is spoken about: Her *enthusiasm* is contagious. The subject is *enthusiasm,* the thing spoken about. This subject names a thing.

CHECKUP 2   Underline the subjects in the following sentences. Then write the subjects in the spaces at the right.

1. <u>Freedom</u> is precious to all of us.
2. George studied the case well before briefing us on it.
3. The senators voted to give themselves a pay increase.
4. Alberta can do the work a lot faster than anyone else.

1. **Freedom** _____
2. _____
3. _____
4. _____

5. The Browns had to be excluded from the contract.   5. _____
6. He will definitely learn from his mistakes.   6. _____
7. My secretary is the one whom I would recommend for the job.   7. _____
8. The individuals assigned to the task had prior experience.   8. _____
9. Bart designed the cover for the new textbook.   9. _____
10. Her attorney filed the necessary papers.   10. _____

THE UNDERSTOOD SUBJECT

In sentences that give a command or make a request, the subject is always understood to be *you*. But the word *you* frequently does not appear in such sentences. It does not appear because the *you* is understood when one person is speaking directly to another.

Please write a report on motivation. The sentence makes a request. The subject is understood to be *you:* (You) Please write a report on motivation.

Assign points to each item on the scale. The sentence gives a command. The subject is understood to be *you:* (You) Assign points to each item on the scale.

CHECKUP 3

Write the subjects for the following sentences in the spaces at the right. If the subject is understood to be *you*, write *(you)*.

1. The format for the report includes the introduction, body, and conclusion.   1. **format** _____
2. Were you interested in going to the convention in Dallas?   2. _____
3. Use secondary sources of information for your report.   3. _____
4. The questions asked in an interview determine the kind of information gathered.   4. _____
5. The bars in a bar chart are sometimes vertical and sometimes horizontal.   5. _____
6. Discuss the factors contributing to traffic flow at some specific location.   6. _____
7. Write a report using figures and tables.   7. _____
8. Analyze the courses required by your school for a degree in your major.   8. _____
9. The procedures manual contains useful information.   9. _____
10. Research the topic at the local library.   10. _____

THE VERB—THE ACTION WORD

Just as every sentence must have a subject, so every sentence must have a predicate. (The predicate contains the verb and its modifiers.) The *verb* is a word that tells what the subject does, what the subject is, or what happens to the subject.

Tells what the subject does: Our manager *visited* the new building. The verb *visited* tells what the manager did.

Tells what the subject is: Ms. Carlyle *is* our department chairperson. The verb *is* tells what Ms. Carlyle is.

Tells what happens to the subject: Robert *was initiated* into the fraternity. The verb *was initiated* tells what happened to Robert. Note that this verb has *two* words.

CHECKUP 4

Underline the verbs in the following sentences. Then write the verbs in the spaces at the right.

1. Everyone looked tired at the meeting this afternoon.   1. **looked** _____
2. Call me with the sales figures for July.   2. _____
3. The visitors from France toured our plant and offices.   3. _____
4. They equip the office with new computers when necessary.   4. _____
5. We had expected them on Monday.   5. _____
6. The company replaced the damaged items.   6. _____
7. Ann recognized the new employee immediately.   7. _____
8. Read the user's manual first.   8. _____
9. Our company publishes sports equipment catalogs.   9. _____
10. They contacted the airline for ticket information.   10. _____

EXERCISE 1

Decide whether each of the following word groups is a sentence. If the group of words is a sentence, circle *S*. If the group of words is not a sentence, circle *NS*.

1. Although there have been many manufacturers of the car.   1. S NS
2. We will consider the consultant's advice.   2. S NS
3. While you were shopping at the mall yesterday.   3. S NS
4. Being there with him.   4. S NS
5. Plan to work on the project with Darrell Clark.   5. S NS
6. A decrease of 5 percent.   6. S NS
7. All orders are to be filled by the end of the day.   7. S NS
8. Place the emphasis on accuracy.   8. S NS
9. Because of the challenge it offers.   9. S NS
10. The facts did not reveal the fundamental problem.   10. S NS
11. Whom we all admired and respected for his loyalty.   11. S NS
12. An individual who can work well with others.   12. S NS
13. We received your estimates yesterday.   13. S NS
14. A number of elements in the proposal were modified.   14. S NS
15. A single remaining task to be completed.   15. S NS
16. Another frustrating situation that may occur.   16. S NS
17. If a suitable place is conveniently available.   17. S NS
18. Each employee will discover his or her own set of problems.   18. S NS
19. Standards need to be established before proceeding with the plan.   19. S NS
20. The work ethic is deeply ingrained in us.   20. S NS
21. Review each chapter before taking the test.   21. S NS
22. The painters completed the job on Friday.   22. S NS
23. Before we make a public announcement.   23. S NS
24. That we have a meeting to discuss the plans.   24. S NS
25. Several of us were working late that day.   25. S NS
26. Before we went to the theater.   26. S NS
27. We will ship that package before the end of the day.   27. S NS
28. We received estimates from three contractors.   28. S NS
29. Considering the length of your proposal.   29. S NS
30. Norma scheduled the meeting for Tuesday.   30. S NS

EXERCISE 2

Underline the subjects and the verbs in the following sentences. Then write the subjects and the verbs in the spaces provided.

1. Several representatives exhibited their products at the convention.   1. _____
2. Sound strategy works.   2. _____
3. You purchased too much paper.   3. _____
4. They negotiated a contract with the company.   4. _____
5. Respect the customer's wishes.   5. _____
6. Introduce yourself first to the host.   6. _____

7. We ordered a limousine for our drive to the airport.

8. The bakeries in our neighborhood make fantastic pastries.

9. She submitted her resignation yesterday.

10. The interest on the mortgage was $30,000.

11. Telephones were installed in the new offices on Tuesday.

12. Enter the beneficiary's name on all the insurance forms.

13. Allen graduated from college with honors.

14. They mailed the letter to the Arizona address.

15. The director scheduled me for overtime twice this week.

16. Bob purchased three franchises in Texas last year.

17. The veterinarian helped with the delivery of the new calf.

18. Peg retired at the end of the year.

19. Everyone made a contribution to the flower fund.

20. Each year all committees submit a report to the president.

21. Proofread the letter carefully before lunch.

22. Approval was given by Mr. Andreas.

23. The contract goes to the lowest bidder.

24. Lamar is the new head of our human resources department.

25. The advertisements featured hair products.

26. Settlement of the strike appears imminent.

27. It is extremely warm in this office today.

28. Yes, we raised our prices on all our products.

29. Traffic moves slowly after 5 p.m.

30. Ask for a certified check.

31. All were asked to complete a questionnaire on etiquette.

32. Stay late to complete the inventory of our stock.

33. Three reasons for his transfer were given.

34. The reports need more specific information.

35. Retailers published a catalog of our products.

36. The judge called a recess after 2 p.m.

37. The list was revised twice in three years.

38. A number of applicants submitted applications for the job.

39. The advertisement featured Gilmore's latest dress fashions.

40. Listen carefully to the directions.

41. Christopher prompted the speaker.

42. The proceeds of the fund-raiser exceeded $12,000.

43. This apple tastes sour.

44. The cover looks very similar to the previous one.

45. We mailed the invoices on Friday.

46. Please accept this gift as a token of our appreciation.

47. Terry received a letter from his attorney.

48. The card measures 5 by 7 inches.

49. The lowest bid was under $20,000.

50. The store announced its annual sale.

51. Revise the sales figures for March and April.

52. Cheryl organized the monthly status reports.

53. Their offer included a price reduction.

54. Her service record is outstanding.

55. We invited the mayor to our business seminar.

Subjects and Verbs

THE MAIN SUBJECT   The *main subject* is the most important word, or words, in the subject. Modifiers—adjectives and adverbs—are not part of the main subject.

> Large educational *grants* were awarded to top researchers. The main subject is *grants*. The words *large educational* are modifiers; they are not part of the main subject.

> The assertive young *woman* won the election. The main subject is *woman*. The words *The assertive young* are modifiers; they are not part of the main subject.

CHECKUP 1   Underline the main subjects in the following sentences. Then write the main subjects in the spaces at the right.

1. Short-term <u>loans</u> benefit young homeowners.   1. **loans** _____
2. The confident worker submitted his ideas in the suggestion box.   2. _____
3. His shiny red car was parked near the curb.   3. _____
4. The well-known author had written several books.   4. _____
5. A ten-story building was erected across the street from our complex.   5. _____
6. Fortunately, high-performance computers were ordered for our office.   6. _____
7. Forty-four contestants arrived for the audition.   7. _____
8. The poorly designed photocopier lasted only a year.   8. _____
9. Our energetic engineer had proposed several good ideas.   9. _____
10. The executives prefer to read a summary of the report.   10. _____

THE MAIN VERB   The *main verb* is the most important word that expresses the action. When the verb has more than one word in it, the main verb is always the *last* word.

> Darlene *bought* the flowers. There is only one verb—*bought*. It is, of course, the main verb.

> Charles *answered* the telephone. There is only one verb—*answered*. It is, of course, the main verb.

> You *should rejoice* over your good fortune. The main verb is the last verb, *rejoice*. The other verb, *should*, is a helper.

> The orders *had been received* earlier. The main verb is the last verb, *received*. The other verbs, *had* and *been*, are helpers.

CHECKUP 2   Underline the main verbs in the following sentences. Then write the main verbs in the spaces at the right.

1. The inspectors had been <u>examining</u> the orders.   1. **examining** _____
2. Where have you been all this time?   2. _____
3. Several resolutions were adopted by committee members.   3. _____
4. I could have worked all week on the manuscript.   4. _____
5. Audrey has been reading for two hours.   5. _____
6. You might have called me with the results.   6. _____
7. All the workers are being informed of the change.   7. _____
8. Has Rose filed all the letters yet?   8. _____
9. The rumor is being heard by everyone.   9. _____
10. The new computers will have been installed by that time.   10. _____

THE COMPOUND SUBJECT

Compound means two or more parts. A subject is compound when two or more nouns or pronouns are joined by a conjunction (*and*, *or*, or *nor*). The nouns or pronouns have the same verb.

Louise and *Helen* are attorneys. The nouns *Louise* and *Helen* form the compound subject. The two parts of this compound subject are joined by the conjunction *and*. They have the same verb, *are*.

She or *Sam* will visit you. The pronoun *she* and the noun *Sam* form the compound subject. These words are joined by the conjunction *or*. They have the same verb, *will visit*.

CHECKUP 3   Underline the compound subjects in the following sentences. Then write the compound subjects in the spaces at the right.

1. <u>Joanne</u> and <u>he</u> asked for the same week off in December.

1. **Joanne, he**

2. Ms. Roebuck and Mr. Wiseman are both making presentations at the same time.

2. _____

3. Papers and pencils are necessary to take the qualifying exam.

3. _____

4. Men and women were needed as volunteers for the Red Cross.

4. _____

5. Health, happiness, and wisdom were her dreams.

5. _____

6. Charlene or I will supervise the installation of the computers.

6. _____

7. Our computers and printers should arrive by the end of the month.

7. _____

8. Churches and schools will benefit most from the Governor's plan.

8. _____

9. The president or vice president will be coming to our open house.

9. _____

10. Teachers and students worked on the syllabus for the semester.

10. _____

11. Myra or Joe will complete the order.

11. _____

12. Friends and relatives attended the farewell party.

12. _____

THE COMPOUND VERB

A *compound verb* consists of two or more verbs that are joined by a conjunction (*and*, *or*, or *nor*). The verbs have the same subject.

The clerk *sings* or *whistles* when she is in the warehouse. The words *sings* and *whistles* form the compound verb. These words are joined by the conjunction *or*. They have the same subject, *clerk*.

The manager *organizes* and *directs* the project. The words *organizes* and *directs* form the compound verb. These words are joined by the conjunction *and*. They have the same subject, *manager*.

CHECKUP 4   Underline the compound verbs in the following sentences. Then write the compound verbs in the spaces at the right.

1. The new manager <u>received</u> and <u>welcomed</u> our suggestions for the work schedule.

1. **received, welcomed**

2. Greg, as human resources director, hired and fired employees.

2. _____

3. Jane opened and distributed the mail to all departments in the company.

3. _____

4. Clarence edited and proofread the report that went to the marketing manager.

4. _____

5. Please sign and return the enclosed contract by Monday.

5. _____

6. Print or type the information on the application for employment.

6. _____

7. You may write or type your responses.

7. _____

8. He bought and sold stocks for a living.

8. _____

9. She plays cards and knits at the same time.

9. _____

10. Dean Westbrook interviewed and hired three new instructors.

10. _____

11. Ms. Sobel reviewed and adopted the new guidelines.

11. _____

12. They painted and polished the new fixtures.

12. _____

EXERCISES

NAME _____ DATE _____ SCORE _____

EXERCISE 1   Underline the main subjects in the following sentences. Then write the main subjects in the spaces at the right.

1. A major source of income will be from the Grant Foundation.
2. All branches of the bank will be remodeled.
3. Our largest department store in town is Hudson's.
4. Miller Investment executives are conducting a seminar this afternoon.
5. Student members were recognized for their achievements at the banquet.

1. _____
2. _____
3. _____
4. _____
5. _____

EXERCISE 2   Underline the main verbs in the following sentences. Then write the main verbs in the spaces at the right.

1. She may have called you yesterday.
2. Is Deborah studying at the library this evening?
3. The student might have been he.
4. Does this new car require a specific grade of oil?
5. You must decide today whether to take the job or not.

1. _____
2. _____
3. _____
4. _____
5. _____

EXERCISE 3   Underline the compound subjects in the following sentences. Then write the compound subjects in the spaces provided.

1. Herb or Louis will be coming to check our new electronic mail system.
2. Brackets, dashes, and apostrophes are all punctuation marks.
3. The author and publisher were meeting in New York City.
4. Management or marketing will be Kaye's major.
5. Letters and memos need to be proofread before they are transmitted.

1. _____
2. _____
3. _____
4. _____
5. _____

EXERCISE 4   Underline the compound verbs in the following sentences. Then write the compound verbs in the spaces provided.

1. Gloria spoke and wrote French fluently.
2. We washed and dried the dishes before putting them back on the shelf.
3. Mr. Eisenbard proposed and supported the amendment to the club's constitution.
4. The assistant composes and types his own letters.
5. Ruth will read and study the proposal before making a decision.

1. _____
2. _____
3. _____
4. _____
5. _____

EXERCISE 5   Decide whether each of the following groups of words is a sentence. If the group of words is a sentence, write the subject and the verb in the space provided. If the group of words is not a sentence, write *no sentence*.

1. An individual who cares about the company and what happens to it.
2. Dictionaries vary greatly in size, purpose, and reliability.
3. Our marketing director who was on sabbatical last year.

1. _____
2. _____
3. _____

4. Everyone needs help sometimes with the spelling and pronunciation of
   a particular word.   4. _____

5. John pretended that he had given a lecture on space travel.   5. _____

EXERCISE 6

Either a subject or a verb is missing from the following sentences. For each sentence, underline *S* if a subject is needed in place of the question mark; underline *V* if a verb is needed. Then in the spaces at the right write a subject or a verb that would complete each sentence.

1. Many (?) responded to our advertisement.   S V   1. _____
2. Important (?) were difficult to locate in the files.   S V   2. _____
3. Ingrid (?) how to use the computer manual.   S V   3. _____
4. The (?) entered the bay and headed toward the dock.   S V   4. _____
5. If employees want to keep their jobs, (?) will work hard.   S V   5. _____
6. When Michael (?) his own business, he had to borrow over
   $20,000.   S V   6. _____
7. (?) asked what time she could take her break.   S V   7. _____
8. Angelo (?) that he could type 75 words a minute.   S V   8. _____
9. This afternoon (?) want to begin our advertising campaign.   S V   9. _____
10. Will you be (?) to the computer workshop on Excel?   S V   10. _____
11. Researchers (?) many samples of fabric for their experiment.   S V   11. _____
12. Ms. Olsten, our office manager, (?) new stationery and
    envelopes.   S V   12. _____
13. The announcement (?) that 200 workers were to be hired by the
    new company.   S V   13. _____
14. Friends and (?) attended her graduation party.   S V   14. _____
15. News of the company merger (?) all the employees.   S V   15. _____
16. Have (?) seen the latest report on the new product?   S V   16. _____
17. The Sales Department (?) its highest goal last month.   S V   17. _____
18. (?) was able to finish the letter in less than five minutes.   S V   18. _____
19. By taking the shortest route, (?) arrived early.   S V   19. _____
20. All (?) receive a copy of the annual report from the company.   S V   20. _____

EXERCISE 7

In each of the following sentences, make the subject compound by adding another subject in place of the question mark. Write your answers in the spaces at the right.

1. Dan and (?) will be attending the wedding in the fall.   1. _____
2. Cars and (?) filled the company parking lot.   2. _____
3. Teachers and (?) who attended the book fair were pleased with the selections.   3. _____
4. The King and (?) of Spain were in the United States for a five-day visit.   4. _____
5. Ladies and (?) were invited to the gala party after the performance.   5. _____

EXERCISE 8

In each of the following sentences, make the verb compound by adding another verb in place of the question mark. Write your answers in the spaces at the right.

1. The sales representatives exhibited and (?) samples of their products.   1. _____
2. Proofread and (?) the letter before you mail it.   2. _____
3. Prices rise and (?) depending on the economy.   3. _____
4. The prospective applicants were interviewed and (?).   4. _____
5. The Minute Men cleaned and (?) the furniture.   5. _____

Kinds of Sentences

Sentences are classified according to what they do. Observe what the following sentences do so that you'll be able to recognize and classify sentences.

Reports present information to someone who will make a decision. This sentence states a fact. It is a declarative sentence. *Remember:* A declarative sentence *declares.*

Who has the report? This sentence asks a question. It is an interrogative sentence. *Remember:* An interrogative sentence *interrogates*—asks a question.

Proofread the report. This sentence gives a command. It is an imperative sentence. *Remember:* An imperative sentence *commands* or gives an order.

Wow! That's an impressive report. This sentence shows emotion. It is an exclamatory sentence. *Remember:* An exclamatory sentence *exclaims.*

CHECKUP 1   Identify the following sentences as declarative (D), interrogative (I), imperative (IMP), or exclamatory (E) by circling the proper symbol.

1. Have you seen the latest edition of the book?
2. Oh! I didn't know that before.
3. Insure your house against fire and theft.
4. The applications arrived this morning.
5. Place the books on the top shelf in the cabinet.
6. When will the shipment of computers arrive?

1. D Ⓘ IMP E
2. D I IMP E
3. D I IMP E
4. D I IMP E
5. D I IMP E
6. D I IMP E

DECLARATIVE SENTENCES   A *declarative sentence* makes a statement. It states a fact, a belief, or an opinion. A declarative sentence ends with a period.

Fact: Mary Alice Freeman is our new office manager.

Belief: I'm sure that she will do a good job in preparing the report.

Opinion: That meal was simply delicious.

CHECKUP 2   Write three declarative sentences using the words given below as the subjects of the sentences. *Remember:* End your sentences with periods.

1. stationery _____

2. catalog _____

3. employees _____

INTERROGATIVE SENTENCES   An *interrogative sentence* asks a question. An interrogative sentence ends with a question mark.

Have they been here yet?   Where is the proposal?

As you can see, an interrogative sentence asks a *direct* question, such as "What is your name?" A sentence that asks an *indirect* question, such as "She asked me my name," is *not* an interrogative sentence; it is a declarative sentence.

DIRECT QUESTION	INDIRECT QUESTION
Is it here?	Bob asked if it were here.
Did you go?	Diana asked if I wanted to go to lunch.

When an interrogative sentence makes a request, use a period (not a question mark) at the end of the sentence.

Will you please give me the report. A request—not really a question.

Will you please answer the telephone. A request—not really a question.

CHECKUP 3   Write four interrogative sentences that start with the words listed below. End your sentences with question marks.

1. When _____
2. Where _____
3. How _____
4. Why _____

IMPERATIVE SENTENCES
An *imperative sentence* makes a request or gives a command. The subject of the imperative sentence is generally the pronoun *you*, even though it does not appear in the sentence.

Request: Please answer the letter as soon as possible.

Command: Search the files until you find the copy.

An imperative sentence ends with a period—unless it makes a strong command, in which case it may end with an exclamation point.

Strong command: No!   Stop it!   Hurry!   Go!

CHECKUP 4   Write four imperative sentences. End your sentences with periods. If a sentence makes a *strong* command, however, end it with an exclamation point.

1. _____
2. _____
3. _____
4. _____

EXCLAMATORY SENTENCES
An *exclamatory sentence* expresses strong feeling. It is a declarative sentence stated with great emotion or excitement. An exclamatory sentence always ends with an exclamation point.

Yes!   That's right!   You can do it!   You won the race!

CHECKUP 5   Write four exclamatory sentences. End your sentences with exclamation points.

1. _____
2. _____
3. _____
4. _____

EXERCISES

NAME _____ DATE _____ SCORE _____

EXERCISE 1   Identify the following sentences as declarative (D), interrogative (I), imperative (IMP), or exclamatory (E) by circling the proper symbol.

1. Members of the Board of Governors are debating the issue.
2. Have you seen the new recruits?
3. Just a minute now!
4. Where did you place the new sign?
5. Watch where you step.
6. The owner and the manager were not available for questions.
7. A copy of the letter was lying on her desk.
8. Are you sure it is true?
9. Make sure that the office is locked when you leave.
10. Yes, Mr. Tucker approved the transfer.
11. What do you intend to do about it?
12. Give the note to Ms. Powers before she leaves.

1. D I IMP E
2. D I IMP E
3. D I IMP E
4. D I IMP E
5. D I IMP E
6. D I IMP E
7. D I IMP E
8. D I IMP E
9. D I IMP E
10. D I IMP E
11. D I IMP E
12. D I IMP E

EXERCISE 2   Write five declarative sentences using the words listed below as the subjects of the sentences. *Remember:* End your sentences with periods.

1. experience _____
2. traffic _____
3. tours _____
4. assistant _____
5. terminal _____

EXERCISE 3   Write five interrogative sentences that start with the words listed below. *Remember:* End your sentences with question marks.

1. What _____
2. Why _____
3. Where _____
4. Who _____
5. When _____

EXERCISE 4   Write five imperative sentences. *Remember:* End your sentences with periods. If a sentence makes a strong command, end it with an exclamation point.

1. _____
2. _____
3. _____
4. _____
5. _____

EXERCISE 5

Write five exclamatory sentences. *Remember:* End your sentences with exclamation points.

1. _____
2. _____
3. _____
4. _____
5. _____

EXERCISE 6

Change the following sentences from indirect questions to direct questions. *Remember:* Use a question mark after each direct question.

1. I asked him his name.

_____

2. I asked her the name of her company.

_____

3. I asked if he had been hired.

_____

4. I asked what time it was.

_____

5. I asked the secretary if she believed the story.

_____

EXERCISE 7

Change the following sentences from direct questions to indirect questions.

1. Bob asked, "Will you complete the report?"

_____

2. Diana said, "Where are the proposals?"

_____

3. Joni asked, "Did you have any difficulty with the directions?"

_____

4. Ms. Brown said to the applicant, "How much experience do you have?"

_____

5. Mr. Watts said, "Where is the Wilson file?"

_____

EXERCISE 8

Punctuate the following sentences by placing a period (.), question mark (?), or exclamation point (!) in the spaces at the right.

1. Handle the package with care   1. _____
2. What were his motives   2. _____
3. Hurry   3. _____
4. She was careless with the computations   4. _____
5. When is the mortgage payment due   5. _____
6. The original freight bill should accompany the damage claim   6. _____
7. That's marvelous   7. _____
8. What are you thinking   8. _____
9. That's neat   9. _____
10. We ordered three styles: men's, women's, and children's   10. _____

Nouns

A NOUN   A *noun* names something. Let's call it a name word. A noun may name a *person, place, thing, idea,* or *quality.*

A person:	Sue	Carl	woman	child
A place:	London	Detroit	town	Muir Woods
A thing:	computer	printer	vehicle	building
An idea:	capitalism	freedom	patriotism	democracy
A quality:	freshness	richness	love	joy

Managers, supervisors, and *directors* attended the *convention* in *New Orleans. Managers, supervisors, directors, convention,* and *New Orleans* are all nouns. Each word names something.

Our *assistant* ordered *computers, printers,* and *diskettes. Assistant, computers, printers,* and *diskettes* are all nouns. Each word names something.

The *employees* at *Haines Hospital* had the *conviction* and *courage* to express their *grievances. Employees, Haines Hospital, conviction, courage,* and *grievances* are all nouns. Each word names something.

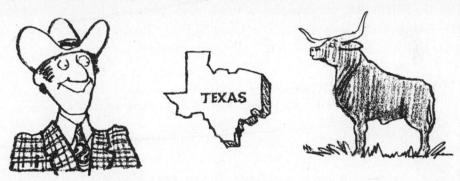

CHECKUP 1   Underline the nouns in the following sentences.

1. Over a thousand shares of stock were traded on Wall Street this afternoon.
2. You can send Brown Brothers a copy of the invoice.
3. The goods were shipped from our plant in Chicago.
4. Please order supplies for Ms. Rinehard.
5. Henry, please take this tray down to the cafeteria.
6. Ms. Armstrong will visit our offices in New York, Illinois, and Ohio.
7. Terry will forward two copies of the report to the manager.
8. The report is lying on your desk, Mr. Graves.

CHECKUP 2   The words at the left tell what kind of noun to look for in each line. Underline the correct noun for each line. Then write that noun in the space at the right.

1.	Person:	manager	office	computer	1.	**manager**
2.	Place:	book	San Francisco	lighting	2.	
3.	Thing:	Ms. Martin	analyst	folder	3.	
4.	Quality:	city	smoothness	chair	4.	
5.	Idea:	machine	country	freedom	5.	

PROPER NOUNS

A *proper noun* names a *particular* person, place, or thing. Proper nouns are capitalized.

Names of persons:	Denise	David	Mr. Shoemaker	Ms. VanHofstra
Names of places:	Columbus	Seattle	Australia	Kenya
Names of things:	Lake Erie	Empire State Building	Rocky Mountains	Jefferson Memorial

Myles and *Patrick* purchased a *Range Rider* in *May. Myles, Patrick, Range Rider,* and *May* are all proper nouns. They are all capitalized.

Tourists from *Illinois* flew to *Washington, D.C.,* to see the *Jefferson Memorial. Illinois, Washington, D.C.,* and *Jefferson Memorial* are all proper nouns. They are all capitalized.

CHECKUP 3 Underline the proper nouns in the following sentences.

1. Calvin Null is a professor of social sciences at the School of Medicine at Southwestern University.
2. It took Ken Burns five years to film a documentary on the Civil War.
3. The ecologist, Paul R. Ehrlich, has been one of the better-known scientists since publishing his book.
4. The National Archives plans to release excerpts from five videotapes.
5. Earlier in April, the two countries agreed to open offices in Chicago.
6. Investors Trust isn't sure what it will do with the Grand Hotel in midtown Manhattan.
7. The family moved from one town to another in eastern North Carolina.
8. Glen was an admissions officer at Rutgers University in New Brunswick, New Jersey.
9. Sarah learned patience on a trip to Gettysburg with her son's fifth-grade class.
10. His solo flight across the Atlantic in a single-engine plane was hailed as a feat of incredible endurance.
11. Her first challenge as principal of the James G. Blaine Public School came the night she arrived.
12. That was the year the New York Giants won the Super Bowl.

COMMON NOUNS

A *common noun* does not refer to a particular person, place, or thing. Common nouns refer to *general* persons, places, or things. They are not capitalized.

Name of persons:	woman	man	student	adult	professor
Name of places:	city	state	county	country	theater
Name of things:	telephone	basket	magazine	desk	chair

An *executive* in our *office* received many *awards. Executive, office,* and *awards* are all common nouns. They refer to any one of a class of persons, places, or things. They are not capitalized.

The *students* toured several *states* and returned with many *memories. Students, states,* and *memories* are all common nouns. They refer to any one of a class of persons, places, or things. They are not capitalized.

The *president* wants *managers* and *supervisors* to attend the *session.* The words *president, managers, supervisors,* and *session* are all common nouns. They refer to any one of a class of persons, places, or things. They are not capitalized.

CHECKUP 4 Underline the common nouns in the following sentences.

1. The treasurer of the company told us about the bonus.
2. The doctor will give your wife the results of the test.
3. The agreement was between the two gentlemen.
4. The auditor and director encouraged Emilia to interview for the position.
5. Officers did not want to publicize the accident.
6. Our customers are young working couples.
7. When will Daniel return to the office?
8. Our main objective is to increase profits by 5 percent.

EXERCISES

NAME _____ DATE _____ SCORE _____

EXERCISE 1   Identify the nouns in the following sentences by underlining proper nouns once and common nouns twice. *Remember:* Identify only nouns.

1. Leo Rosten believes that the purpose of life is to be useful, to be responsible, and to be compassionate.

2. Japan has more American fast-food franchises than any country outside North America.

3. Jayne was driving from Chicago to Wisconsin when she passed a sign for Lambs Farm and decided to stop in.

4. A former Hungarian musician, he found the road to riches in Europe.

5. Replacements were brought in from Scotland, Wales, and England.

6. Tom graduated from Central University Medical School in Chicago in June.

7. The next year I was elected president of this branch of the National Honor Society.

8. Catherine was vacationing at Lake Powell, Utah, in August when she learned about her promotion.

9. Just up the road, Mark and Joe had been searching the area for an unusual spiral-grain wood.

10. During his speech at the Democratic National Convention, Michael Lears referred to his family.

11. When he was only a boy, his parents rented a house in Albany, New York.

12. The ambassador to the United Nations was on the telephone.

13. He was in Prague as ambassador to Czechoslovakia.

14. From Florida to Alaska, 19 states contain about 460 million acres of federal land.

15. Loopholes in mining laws and regulations must be corrected.

16. Scientists at the U. S. Department of Agriculture in Athens, Georgia, have developed a device that takes the guesswork out of buying melons.

17. As Christmas approached, we decided to buy presents at the mall.

18. Laughing and weeping Germans chipped away at the Berlin Wall.

19. Several politicians left the meeting early.

20. Vera attended a convention in San Antonio, Texas.

21. Brokers receive a commission on every bond they sell.

22. The miners had achieved a great victory.

23. The workers formed themselves into a nationwide movement called the Confederation of Workers.

24. Some artists and writers left the region to find artistic freedom.

25. The General Accounting Office learned that the government could cut its costs in half.

26. Every July the Defense Department receives about 5,000 inquiries from Capitol Hill.

27. As long as the Republicans control the White House, and the Democrats control the Congress, the veto is a partisan issue.

28. He's writing a book on political corruption.

29. After World War II, Americans, many of them with young children, began to think more about their health.

30. Columnist William Sellars described the low point in his career as a journalist.

31. After five seasons, Jerry Rose of the San Francisco 49ers was the greatest deep-threat wide receiver in professional football.

32. The Johnsons were in Hawaii for their first vacation in years.

33. After a day of working over kilns, the potter looked forward to an evening of fine food.

34. Jim Hines and his colleagues created life-size puppets.

35. The best time to buy a new car is at the end of the month because salespeople want their monthly reports to look good.

36. People touring attractions at national parks usually go during the summer months.

37. The distance from your elbow to your wrist equals the length of your foot.

38. The rise in the price of gasoline, brought on by political tensions in the Mideast, has prompted consumers to seek ways to cut fuel consumption.

39. For Joe Oldani, the grandson of Greek and Italian immigrants, his patriotism began when he first visited the Statue of Liberty.

40. Dan and Ian went to City Gardens to practice basketball.

41. An 8-ounce glass of milk has about as much potassium as the average banana.

42. The driver just called a second time to say he can't find my house.

43. Robert L. Barrington is a dermatologist at Mount Sinai Medical Center in New York City.

44. The White Sox opened a new ballpark in Chicago, Illinois.

45. His career spanned 43 years at Brown and Associates.

46. His films won 28 Academy Awards.

47. Susie Smith has long been a fan of the music of Bob Marley.

48. The Indianapolis 500 is always on Memorial Day weekend.

49. Cindy and Will watched a movie after they ate their pizza.

50. Sarah remembered that the typewriter in the main office needed to be repaired.

EXERCISE 2

The nouns listed below are commonly used in business. Use each noun correctly in a sentence. Use a dictionary to check the meaning of any noun you do not know. (Note that some of these nouns are singular and others are plural.)

1. workers _____
2. letter _____
3. office _____
4. shareholders _____
5. contract _____
6. wholesalers _____
7. discount _____
8. computers _____
9. consultants _____
10. advertisements _____
11. production _____
12. attorney _____
13. investments _____
14. company _____
15. agent _____
16. memo _____
17. description _____
18. broker _____
19. prices _____
20. property _____

More About Nouns

CONCRETE NOUNS   A *concrete noun* is a common noun that names something you can see, hear, smell, touch, or taste. The following are examples of concrete nouns:

computer   A *computer* is a concrete noun because it can be seen and touched.

hamburger   A *hamburger* is a concrete noun because it can be seen, touched, tasted, and smelled.

noise   *Noise* is a concrete noun because it can be heard.

CHECKUP 1   One concrete noun is in each group of three words below. Identify the concrete nouns by writing them in the spaces at the right.

1. acorn   adjust   action
2. beard   beautiful   belief
3. cooperation   cost   curtain
4. deceptive   decibel   dictionary

1. **acorn** _____
2. _____
3. _____
4. _____

CHECKUP 2   List four concrete nouns. Tell why each noun is concrete. *Remember:* A concrete noun can be seen, heard, smelled, touched, or tasted.

1. **telephone**   **It is a concrete noun because it can be seen and touched.** _____
2. _____
3. _____
4. _____

ABSTRACT NOUNS   An *abstract noun* is a common noun that names an idea or a quality. Abstract nouns cannot be seen, heard, smelled, touched, or tasted. The following are examples of abstract nouns:

oversight   joy   peace   emotion   wisdom   beauty

courage   love   strength   character   happiness   personality

CHECKUP 3   One abstract noun is in each group of three words below. Identify the abstract nouns by writing them in the spaces at the right.

1. kangaroo   freedom   knapsack
2. liability   boat   lumber
3. book   enthusiasm   marble
4. nail   natural   forest

1. **freedom** _____
2. _____
3. _____
4. _____

CHECKUP 4   List four abstract nouns. Use each in a sentence.

1. **justice**   **Justice prevailed in the courtroom.** _____
2. _____
3. _____
4. _____

COMPOUND NOUNS
Compound nouns are formed from two words that may be written as one word, as two separate words, or as a hyphenated word.

ONE WORD	TWO SEPARATE WORDS	HYPHENATED WORD
goodwill	home run	mother-in-law
trademark	sea gull	life-style
halftime	money order	attorney-at-law

Do you have a *life insurance* policy?
It's the law in Michigan to wear your *seat belt*.

Some proper nouns contain a compound noun.

Edison *High School*   Tourist *Airlines*
The Penguin *Bookstore*   Mountain *Community College*

We're flying out of Chicago on Midpoint *Airlines*.

Several of the students attend Harper *Community College*.

CHECKUP 5   Identify the compound nouns in the following sentences. Underline the compound nouns, and write them in the spaces at the right.

1. The open house was scheduled to take place from 2 p.m. until 5 p.m.   1. **open house**
2. I had never seen so many oil wells in my life.   2. _____
3. Several of the files were used as cross-references.   3. _____

CHECKUP 6   Make compound nouns using the one-word nouns listed below. Write the compound nouns in the spaces at the right.

1. base   1. **baseball**   4. night   4. _____
2. day   2. _____   5. head   5. _____
3. home   3. _____   6. check   6. _____

COLLECTIVE NOUNS
A *collective noun* names a group or collection of persons, places, or things. The collective noun considers the group of persons, places, or things as *one* person, *one* place, or *one* thing.

Group of persons: crew   team   navy   people   committee
Group of places: republic   nation   federation
Group of things: herd   bunch   flock   swarm   litter

Collective nouns may be either singular or plural. They usually take singular verbs because the group is acting together as one unit. A collective noun takes a plural verb when the members of the group act as individuals.

Our *team* is practicing three nights a week. (The team is acting as one unit.)

The *team* were talking among themselves. (The members of the team are acting as individuals.)

The *audience* applauds the performer. (The audience is acting as one unit.)

The *audience* took their seats. (The members of the audience are acting as individuals.)

CHECKUP 7   Write a collective noun for each of the words listed below.

1. musicians   1. **orchestra**   4. trees   4. _____
2. cattle   2. _____   5. wolves   5. _____
3. banana   3. _____   6. sailors   6. _____

EXERCISES

NAME _____ DATE _____ SCORE _____

EXERCISE 1   Identify the concrete nouns in the following sentences by writing the concrete nouns in the spaces at the right.

1. Has Mary Ann picked up the tickets for the show yet?   1. _____
2. Several envelopes were lying on the desk.   2. _____
3. Paychecks were distributed on Tuesday.   3. _____
4. We ordered computers, printers, and desks.   4. _____
5. The boxes held about 20 books.   5. _____
6. She said the letters were by the telephone.   6. _____
7. Doug wanted us to go to the store to buy supplies for the office. 7. _____
8. Where are my notes?   8. _____
9. Many of the students were going to study at the library.   9. _____
10. Please order three new cabinets for the workroom.   10. _____

EXERCISE 2   Identify the abstract nouns in the following sentences by writing the abstract nouns in the spaces at the right.

1. For her, happiness meant having a job she liked.   1. _____
2. What was his personality like?   2. _____
3. Jake has an excellent memory.   3. _____
4. Always tell the truth when you are applying for a job.   4. _____
5. Because of his fairness in dealing with others, he was well-liked. 5. _____
6. What's your greatest fear?   6. _____
7. Many books have been written about how to achieve success.   7. _____
8. We have the freedom to do what we want.   8. _____
9. Morale was high because of the recent pay raises.   9. _____
10. Her friendship meant a lot to me.   10. _____

EXERCISE 3   Identify the compound nouns in the following sentences by writing the compound nouns in the spaces at the right.

1. We received an invitation to attend the meeting of stockholders. 1. _____
2. Our manager has five granddaughters.   2. _____
3. The headlines did not tell the entire story.   3. _____
4. Please use the handrail when you go down the stairs.   4. _____
5. Our international students liked to travel throughout the United States. 5. _____
6. Mr. Willis and Ms. Wharton were the new chairpersons.   6. _____
7. Mr. Burke asked for an investigation of the trademark law.   7. _____
8. His son wanted to attend Baker Community College.   8. _____
9. We needed a new design for our letterhead.   9. _____
10. Maryland is in the Eastern time zone.   10. _____

EXERCISE 4   Identify the collective nouns in the following sentences by writing the collective nouns in the spaces at the right.

1. Is United Chemical a company or a corporation?   1. _____
2. The mob was disbursed by the police officers.   2. _____

3. The faculty was meeting to discuss class schedules.   3. _____
4. The majority voted to approve the new ruling.   4. _____
5. Myron sat on several important boards within the community. 5. _____
6. The firm he worked for was noted for its bonus at Christmastime. 6. _____
7. Betty's family greeted her upon her return from Africa.   7. _____
8. Our team won the regional championship.   8. _____
9. Cecilia was asked to be a member of the jury.   9. _____
10. The choir sang several songs and then took requests.   10. _____

EXERCISE 5   List ten concrete nouns. Tell why each noun is concrete.

1. _____
2. _____
3. _____
4. _____
5. _____
6. _____
7. _____
8. _____
9. _____
10. _____

EXERCISE 6   Name ten abstract nouns.

1. _____   7. _____
2. _____   8. _____
3. _____   9. _____
4. _____   10. _____
5. _____   11. _____
6. _____   12. _____

EXERCISE 7   Make compound nouns using the one-word nouns listed below. Write the compound nouns in the spaces provided.

1. door _____   7. rain _____
2. earth _____   8. tooth _____
3. knee _____   9. house _____
4. life _____   10. foot _____
5. mail _____   11. news _____
6. pay _____   12. team _____

EXERCISE 8   One concrete noun is in each group of three words below. Identify the concrete nouns by writing them in the spaces at the right.

1. freedom carpet love   1. _____
2. truth sadness lamp   2. _____
3. door spirit quietness   3. _____
4. reliability keyboard softness 4. _____
5. gaiety stapler devotion   5. _____
6. electricity employee employable 6. _____

Plural Nouns

NUMBER A noun may be singular or plural. A noun that refers to *one* person, place, or thing is *singular* in number. A noun that refers to *more than one* person, place, or thing is *plural* in number.

Singular: case   ax   tooth   box   lady   **Plural:** cases   axes   teeth   boxes   ladies

Here are some general rules for forming the plural of nouns: Most nouns form the plural by adding *s* to the singular.

Singular: board   manager   employee   **Plural:** boards   managers   employees

Nouns ending in *s, x, z, ch,* or *sh* form the plural by adding *es* to the singular.

Singular: pass   branch   waltz   push   **Plural:** passes   branches   waltzes   pushes

How nouns ending in *y* form their plurals depends on the letters before the *y*. If the letter before the *y* is a consonant (that is, *not* a vowel), change the *y* to *i* and add *es*.

Singular: fly   tally   copy   duty   fifty   **Plural:** flies   tallies   copies   duties   fifties

If the letter before the *y* is a vowel (*a, e, i, o,* or *u*), then simply add *s* to make the noun plural.

Singular: trolley   holiday   attorney   key   **Plural:** trolleys   holidays   attorneys   keys

CHECKUP 1   Identify the following nouns as singular or plural by writing *S* or *P* in the spaces at the right.

1.	churches	bush	computers	1. **P, S, P**
2.	bus	employers	term	2. _____
3.	day	bank	parks	3. _____
4.	cities	replies	box	4. _____

When a noun ends in *o* and the *o* is preceded by a vowel, form the plural by adding *s* to the singular.

Singular: radio   portfolio   cameo   **Plural:** radios   portfolios   cameos

When a noun ending in *o* relates to music, form the plural by adding *s*.

Singular: piano   soprano   banjo   **Plural:** pianos   sopranos   banjos

In other instances, the plural is generally formed by adding *es*.

Singular: hero   echo   tomato   potato   **Plural:** heroes   echoes   tomatoes   potatoes

Nouns ending in *f* or *fe* often form the plural by changing the *f* or *fe* to *ve* and adding s.

Singular: leaf   self   knife   life   **Plural:** leaves   selves   knives   lives

Some nouns ending in *f* or *fe* form the plural by just adding *s*.

Singular: belief   chef   staff   cliff   sheriff   **Plural:** beliefs   chefs   staffs   cliffs   sheriffs

CHECKUP 2   Write the plurals of the following nouns in the spaces at the right.

1. veto, ego
2. hero, safe
3. memo, piccolo
4. wolf, thief
5. reef, zero
6. shelf, tornado
7. mosquito, video
8. contralto, proof
9. giraffe, logo
10. bluff, solo

1. __vetoes, egos__
2. _____
3. _____
4. _____
5. _____
6. _____
7. _____
8. _____
9. _____
10. _____

Some nouns form their plurals in irregular ways. It is best to just memorize these nouns.

Singular:	child	mouse	woman	ox
Plural:	children	mice	women	oxen

Some nouns have one form for both the singular and the plural.

Singular:	trout	fish	series	deer	sheep
Plural:	trout	fish	series	deer	sheep

Some nouns are always singular. Some nouns are always plural.

Singular:	music	honesty	news	measles
Plural:	scissors	oats	thanks	pliers

Compound nouns generally form the plural by adding *s* to the most important word.

Singular:	father-in-law	notary public	letter of credit	right-of-way	runner-up
Plural:	fathers-in-law	notaries public	letters of credit	rights-of-way	runners-up

Remember: When you are in doubt about forming the plural of a noun, check the dictionary. You'll always find the correct spelling there.

CHECKUP 3   Review the plurals you have studied in this lesson by correcting the following sentences. Underline any incorrect plurals, and write them correctly in the spaces at the right. If a plural is correct, write *OK*.

1. The tailor rechecked all the stitchs.
2. Several loafs of bread were on the table.
3. Have you seen the beautiful grottos in France?
4. The sleeves were way too short on his suit coat.
5. The chief of staffs were having a meeting at the White House.
6. Many of the womens in the audience wore long gowns.
7. Raymond still needed two classes to graduate.
8. The premiums on the insurance policys are due next week.
9. We'll need matchs for starting the campfire.
10. Hundreds of business-reply envelopes had to be opened before the sales conference at noon.

1. __stitches__
2. _____
3. _____
4. _____
5. _____
6. _____
7. _____
8. _____
9. _____
10. _____

EXERCISES

NAME _____ DATE _____ SCORE _____

EXERCISE 1   Write the plurals for the following nouns in the spaces at the right. If the plural is the same as the singular form, write *same*.

1. turkey		38. desk	
2. automobile		39. checkbook	
3. file		40. telephone	
4. chairman		41. alto	
5. deer		42. violin	
6. railway		43. half	
7. staff		44. wrench	
8. cashew		45. mouse	
9. trout		46. bunch	
10. child		47. scissors	
11. cassette		48. tweezers	
12. flock		49. hundred	
13. berry		50. eagle	
14. country		51. paragraph	
15. ax		52. emergency	
16. coach		53. fiasco	
17. studio		54. attorney	
18. cameo		55. gully	
19. portfolio		56. gravy	
20. kangaroo		57. bylaw	
21. letter		58. calf	
22. sheep		59. butterfly	
23. brush		60. cafe	
24. pen		61. supervisor	
25. computer		62. hotel	
26. business		63. economics	
27. combo		64. image	
28. security		65. injury	
29. wife		66. cuff	
30. wolf		67. bush	
31. goose		68. series	
32. brief		69. goods	
33. hobby		70. class	
34. sister-in-law		71. stretch	
35. banjo		72. miss	
36. aircraft		73. nicety	
37. statistics		74. number	

75. officer _____
76. certificate _____
77. peony _____
78. pitcher _____
79. planet _____
80. site _____
81. ski _____
82. kiss _____
83. tax _____
84. yacht _____
85. zone _____
86. lullaby _____
87. kidney _____

88. journey _____
89. bus _____
90. judge _____
91. junior _____
92. insert _____
93. infantry _____
94. occasion _____
95. ox _____
96. granary _____
97. agreement _____
98. man-of-war _____
99. notification _____
100. arm _____

EXERCISE 2   Write singular nouns that end in *s, x, z, ch,* and *sh* in the first column. Then write the plurals of these nouns in the second column.

SINGULAR   PLURAL

_____   _____
_____   _____
_____   _____
_____   _____
_____   _____
_____   _____
_____   _____
_____   _____
_____   _____
_____   _____
_____   _____
_____   _____
_____   _____
_____   _____

EXERCISE 3   Write singular nouns that end in *y* and are preceded by a consonant in the first column. Then write the plurals of these nouns in the second column.

SINGULAR   PLURAL

_____   _____
_____   _____
_____   _____
_____   _____
_____   _____
_____   _____
_____   _____
_____   _____
_____   _____
_____   _____
_____   _____
_____   _____

Possessive Nouns

A *possessive noun* shows ownership or possession. The apostrophe (') is used to show the possessive form of a noun.

the client's file   the company's policy   Nathan's book

the supervisor's report   one person's opinion   our nation's flag

a month's rent   a day's rest   a week's salary

Helen's office   the court's ruling   the cat's meow

Note that the word following the possessive is always a noun: *file, report, opinion,* and so on.

POSSESSIVES OF SINGULAR NOUNS

To form the possessive of a singular noun, we usually add *'s* (an apostrophe and *s*) to the noun.

the instructor's manual   the company's charter   the boss's desk

Gus's plane   Dr. Burns's office   Rex's bike

the team's coach   the union's officers   the doctor's report

As you can see, we have added *'s* to *Gus* and to *boss* and to other words that end in *s*. But we do not always add *'s* to a singular word that already ends in *s*. If the *'s* makes a possessive that is awkward to pronounce, then add *only* the apostrophe ('). Usually add only the apostrophe when the noun has two or more syllables and ends with an *s* or a *z* sound.

Carol Simmons' computer (*Simmons's* would be too awkward to pronounce.)

Mr. Rodriguez' office (*Mr. Rodriguez's* would be too awkward to pronounce.)

POSSESSIVES OF PLURAL NOUNS

Forming the possessive of a plural noun is simple, but be sure to change the singular noun to its correct plural form first. To form the possessive of a plural noun that does *not* end in *s*, add an apostrophe and *s('s)*.

SINGULAR	PLURAL	PLURAL POSSESSIVE
child	children	children's games
woman	women	women's fashions
mouse	mice	mice's food

Avoid using the possessive form for inanimate objects. Use the *of* phrase instead.

the hood of the car (NOT: the car's hood)   the color of the dress (NOT: the dress's color)

It is correct to use the possessive form for time, distance, quantity, and celestial bodies.

SINGULAR	PLURAL	PLURAL POSSESSIVE
week	weeks	weeks' salary
year	years	years' experience
dollar	dollars	dollars' worth
sun's warmth (only one sun)		
today's schedule (only one today)		

To form the possessive of a plural noun that ends in *s*, add only an apostrophe *(')*.

SINGULAR	PLURAL	PLURAL POSSESSIVE
lady	ladies	ladies' coats
baby	babies	babies' blankets
Jones	Joneses	Joneses' yard

CHECKUP 1   Write the singular possessive, the plural, and the plural possessive for each of the nouns listed below.

	SINGULAR POSSESSIVE	PLURAL	PLURAL POSSESSIVE
1. seller	1. **seller's**	**sellers**	**sellers'**
2. customer	2. _____	_____	_____
3. stockholder	3. _____	_____	_____
4. man	4. _____	_____	_____
5. lady	5. _____	_____	_____

POSSESSIVES OF COMPOUND NOUNS

For compound nouns, form the possessive by adding an apostrophe and *s ('s)* to the end of the word.

COMPOUND NOUN	SINGULAR POSSESSIVE	PLURAL POSSESSIVE
sister-in-law	sister-in-law's	sisters-in-law's
father-in-law	father-in-law's	fathers-in-law's

SEPARATE POSSESSION

When two or more nouns are used to show *separate ownership,* write *each* noun in the possessive form.

Here, both Eddie and Nora have cars. Eddie owns his car. Nora owns hers. Therefore, we must say *Eddie's and Nora's cars.* Do you see that you repeat the word *car* after *Eddie's?* Because you say *Eddie's car, Eddie* must also have an apostrophe and *s ('s): Eddie's* and *Nora's* cars.

JOINT POSSESSION

When two or more nouns are used to show *joint ownership,* write only the *last* noun in the possessive form.

This car is not Eddie's; this car is not Nora's. The car belongs to both Eddie and Nora. Therefore, we use one apostrophe and *s ('s)* to show ownership by one group: *Eddie and Nora's car.*

CHECKUP 2   Correct any errors in the use of possessives in the following sentences. Underline each error. Then write your corrections in the spaces at the right.

1. Gerald and Jane's offices are on the tenth floor.
2. Dick's and Pat's business was near the airport on South Street.
3. Peter and Rachel's teaching contracts were renewed for another year.
4. Her son's-in-law apartment had a lovely view of the lake.
5. Kathy and Judy's bikes were purchased from Riley's Cycle Shop.

1. **Gerald's** _____
2. _____
3. _____
4. _____
5. _____

EXERCISES

NAME _____ DATE _____ SCORE _____

EXERCISE 1   In the spaces provided, write the singular possessive, the plural, and the plural possessive for each of the nouns listed below.

	SINGULAR POSSESSIVE	PLURAL	PLURAL POSSESSIVE
1. sister-in-law	1. _____	_____	_____
2. client	2. _____	_____	_____
3. purchaser	3. _____	_____	_____
4. saleswoman	4. _____	_____	_____
5. athlete	5. _____	_____	_____
6. county	6. _____	_____	_____
7. senator	7. _____	_____	_____
8. son	8. _____	_____	_____
9. cameraman	9. _____	_____	_____
10. reporter	10. _____	_____	_____
11. class	11. _____	_____	_____
12. community	12. _____	_____	_____
13. secretary	13. _____	_____	_____
14. accountant	14. _____	_____	_____
15. Brown	15. _____	_____	_____
16. vice president	16. _____	_____	_____
17. dollar	17. _____	_____	_____
18. Wells	18. _____	_____	_____
19. broker	19. _____	_____	_____
20. boss	20. _____	_____	_____

EXERCISE 2   Write the correct possessive form for each of the italicized expressions below. (*Hint:* Rewrite only the *italicized* words.)

1. The *game of the child* was interrupted by friends.

_____

2. *The memo of Mr. Brown* clarifies the situation.

_____

3. Today it is a *market of the buyer* in real estate.

_____

4. The *letter of the president* was received with delight.

_____

5. The *votes of the citizens* were counted and verified.

_____

6. *A friend of Ms. Block* provided the snacks for the party.

_____

7. Our *office of the accountant* overlooked the Hudson River Valley.

_____

8. The *opinion of the mayor* was that we should support Harry's idea.

9. The *writing of the author* needed no editing.

10. The *brief of the lawyer* was prepared well in advance of the case.

11. *The business of Mack and Jeff* earned over $10,000 the first year.

12. The *address of the sender* appeared on the envelope.

13. *The pen of Ross* was lying on his desk.

14. *The clientele of Jake* came from the other side of town.

15. *A friend of Myra* helped her get the job.

16. *The catalog of Spears* weighed about five pounds.

17. The *decision of the supervisor* was based on new information.

EXERCISE 3

Underline the nouns that should be written in the possessive form. Then write the correct possessive forms in the spaces at the right. If a sentence is correct, write *OK*.

1. Ms. Morrison son is getting married on Saturday.   1. _____
2. Nadia sells men clothing in a large department store.   2. _____
3. Krista office needs a painting.   3. _____
4. Martha indicated on her résumé that she had five years experience.   4. _____
5. The attorneys fees were extremely high.   5. _____
6. The hunters approached the fox den with caution.   6. _____
7. Jacobson advertisement appeared in the Sunday edition of the newspaper.   7. _____
8. The Meyerses car was left unlocked overnight.   8. _____
9. David Probes documentaries are very educational.   9. _____
10. Jack and Lorry took several months vacation last year.   10. _____
11. Rita's room was a mess.   11. _____
12. The papers were lying on the boss desk.   12. _____
13. The lady hat matched her dress.   13. _____
14. Allen agreed to do the work for a week salary.   14. _____
15. Winning the board game was just beginner luck.   15. _____
16. Now is the best time to buy the company preferred stock. 16. _____
17. Timothy's and Mark's computers were being delivered Tuesday.   17. _____
18. The author manuscript had been reviewed for publication. 18. _____
19. The photographer camera needed to be replaced.   19. _____
20. Did you get your money worth?   20. _____
21. The stockholders' votes would determine whether the sales proposal would be implemented.   21. _____
22. Several of the children's drawings were on display in the library.   22. _____
23. The consultant's seminars were well attended by the company employees.   23. _____
24. Six month interest had to be paid.   24. _____
25. The five foremen responsibilities were to supervise other employees.   25. _____

Pronouns

As you know, a pronoun takes the place of a noun. In Lesson 1, to show how pronouns help us to avoid repeating nouns, we compared the following sentences:

Tim and his brother Robert bought their computer from their uncle.

If we left out the pronouns, this sentence would be quite awkward:

Tim and Tim's brother Robert bought Tim and Robert's computer from Tim and Robert's uncle.

Obviously, pronouns add variety to our speech and our writing! In fact, you probably use the following pronouns every day.

I, me, my	we, us, our, ours
you, your, yours	you, your, yours
he, him, his; she, her, hers; it, its	they, them, their, theirs

Notice how the pronouns in the following sentence are used as replacements.

Christopher asked Karen to give *him* a copy of *her* letter. The pronouns *him* and *her* are used to avoid saying "to give *Christopher* a copy of *Karen's* letter."

CHECKUP 1   Underline the pronouns in the following sentences. Then write the pronouns in the spaces at the right.

1. You have my permission to use our copier.
2. Roger's sailboat was purchased from his friends in Vancouver.
3. Their dog was playing with its tail.
4. Have you had a chance to speak with them about your retirement?

1. **You, my, our**
2. _____
3. _____
4. _____

FOLLOW THE LEADER!   Often a pronoun "follows the leader." That is, a pronoun often follows a noun, so we can consider pronouns as followers and nouns as leaders. (Perhaps you have already learned to call leaders *antecedents*.)

Mr. Thompson promoted *his* assistant. *Mr. Thompson* is the leader—the noun that comes first. *His* is the follower—the pronoun that refers to the noun *Mr. Thompson*.

CHECKUP 2   Underline the pronouns and their leaders (the antecedents) in the following sentences. Then write the pronouns and their leaders in the spaces at the right.

1. Has Jean submitted all her expense forms?
2. The president wanted her assistant to work overtime.
3. Ivan entered the data into his computer.
4. The corporation paid its stockholders a healthy dividend on their investments.

1. **Jean, her**
2. _____
3. _____
4. _____
   _____

AGREEMENT—SINGULAR OR PLURAL?

Pronouns, like nouns, can be either singular or plural. It is simple to decide whether a pronoun should be singular or plural: simply *follow the leader!* If the pronoun refers to a singular noun, the pronoun must be singular. If the pronoun refers to a plural noun, the pronoun must be plural.

The *owners* evaluated *their* employees every six months. *Owners* is plural, and *their* is plural.

The *owner* evaluated *her* employees every six months. *Owner* is singular, and *her* is singular.

CHECKUP 3   Do the pronouns in these sentences follow their leaders? Underline any incorrect use of singular or plural pronouns. Write your corrections in the spaces at the right. (*Hint:* The leaders are in italics.)

1. The newspaper's *editorials* were well written because it had been edited by a grammarian.
2. *Karl* managed their own business.
3. The *Barker Hotel* improved their reputation by providing better service.
4. *Cheryl* had their application completed that same day.

1. **they** _____
2. _____
3. _____
4. _____

AGREEMENT—MALE, FEMALE, OR NEUTER?

The pronouns *he, him,* and *his* are, of course, masculine in gender. The pronouns *she, her,* and *hers* are feminine in gender.

Clyde Rodman bought *his* sister's business. The masculine pronoun *his* is used to agree with *Clyde Rodman,* the name of a man.

Amy replaced *her* sedan with a sports car. The feminine pronoun *her* agrees with *Amy,* clearly a feminine word.

Each *doctor* must submit *his or her* report. Is *doctor* masculine, or is it feminine? Of course, it can be either. Thus we say *his or her* to agree with *doctor.*

Words like *supervisor, employee, accountant, president,* and *person* are called *common nouns;* they can be either masculine or feminine. Let's look at a few more examples:

Each *employee* in the company was asked for *his or her* advice. An employee may be male or female. Thus *his advice* would not be correct, and *her advice* would not be correct. *His or her* is correct.

Every *member* in our fraternity gave *his* suggestion. In a particular case where all the members are men, *his* is correct.

Each *member* in our sorority gave *her* support to the clothing drive. In a particular case where the members of the group are all women, the pronoun *her* is correct.

The pronouns *it* and *its* are used to agree with *neuter nouns*—that is, nouns that are neither masculine nor feminine. Examples of neuter nouns are *company, computer, printer,* and *desk.*

When you find my *expense report,* put *it* on my desk. *It* agrees with *expense report.*

CHECKUP 4   Do the pronouns in these sentences follow their leaders? Underline any incorrect use of pronouns. Write your corrections in the spaces at the right. If a sentence is correct, write *OK.*

1. The company plans to reward their employees.
2. A doctor is trained to heal his patients.
3. The Outdoor Club wanted their members to vote on the issues.
4. Each office assistant said she would be willing to work on the report.
5. Every participant was requested to submit his or her evaluation of the presentation.

1. **its** _____
2. _____
3. _____
4. _____
5. _____

EXERCISES

NAME _____ DATE _____ SCORE _____

EXERCISE 1   Identify the pronouns in the following sentences by writing them in the spaces at the right. (*Hint:* There may be more than one pronoun in a sentence.)

1. Where have you seen them recently?
2. At the piano recital, we saw many of our neighbors.
3. Dale and Leslie went to visit their uncle in New Hampshire.
4. Her manager agreed to help him and his assistant with the work.
5. They said that their corporation received its charter several years ago.
6. Ann Marie promised us that we could have the tennis court by noon.
7. He and I plan to attend the open house on Saturday.
8. We wish we could attend the opening ceremony, but we are already committed to another engagement.
9. My car was picked up by John and his friend.
10. Yes, I will buy several of your tickets tomorrow.
11. Can you give me a ride to the airport?
12. You and your sisters have given me much comfort during my hospital stay.
13. They both have excellent jobs.
14. They can give you all the help you need.
15. Give the papers to them.
16. Shall we have the meeting at your place or at mine?
17. Several of them were broken in shipment.
18. Was he the one your supervisor wanted to hire?
19. You and I will be asked to make presentations at our annual seminar.
20. Give us an account of what you did when you were in Washington, D.C.
21. Their company will be moving its corporate headquarters.
22. He agreed to assist her in her research.
23. After we retire, Robert and I hope to travel.
24. Our associates were impressed by what their consultants said.
25. She realized that she was not responsible for his actions.

1. _____
2. _____
3. _____
4. _____
5. _____
6. _____
7. _____

8. _____
9. _____
10. _____
11. _____

12. _____
13. _____
14. _____
15. _____
16. _____
17. _____
18. _____
19. _____
20. _____
21. _____
22. _____
23. _____
24. _____
25. _____

EXERCISE 2   Replace the word or words in parentheses with a pronoun. Write the pronouns in the spaces at the right.

1. Return the envelope to *(Lorraine)* by noon tomorrow.
2. *(Sue and Larry)* bought their home in Shorewood, Illinois.
3. *(Joe's)* car was in the garage for repairs.
4. *(Employees)* wanted to start working on the project immediately.
5. *(Jane and Richard)* reviewed the plans for the new building.
6. Zane gave *(Zane's)* version of the meeting between him and his boss.
7. *(You and I)* organized the entire event.
8. *(Ms. Rochar and she)* were responsible for preparing the brochure.
9. Only *(Kathleen and Joe)* know the date for the merger.

1. _____
2. _____
3. _____
4. _____
5. _____
6. _____
7. _____
8. _____
9. _____

10. Are these papers *(Frank's and Mary's)*?   10. _____

11. May I see *(Beth's)* copy of the program.   11. _____

12. Have you given *(him and her)* your opinion?   12. _____

13. Is this manuscript *(Glen's)*?   13. _____

14. The assistant told *(Dawn)* about the meeting.   14. _____

15. Please call *(Ricardo and Carmen)* before noon.   15. _____

16. Our supervisor promised to notify *(Lois and me)* of any change.   16. _____

17. The clerk mailed *(the book)* on Monday.   17. _____

18. If that machine is defective, we will have to replace *(the machine)*.   18. _____

19. Give these copies to *(Jo and Jake)*.   19. _____

20. No, Sam did not explain *(Sam's)* absence.   20. _____

21. *(Mrs. O'Neill and her staff)* created a new design for the ad.   21. _____

22. Only the attendees know of *(the competitors' and the supporters')* proposals.   22. _____

23. Stan Targowski reminded *(Stan Targowski's)* clients about the luncheon
    meeting.   23. _____

24. If I have the time, I would like to review *(Rita's)* manuscript.   24. _____

25. Gertrude included *(Gertrude's)* recommendations in the report.   25. _____

EXERCISE 3 Identify the leaders (the antecedents) of the pronouns in the following sentences by writing the leaders in the spaces at the right. (*Hint:* The pronouns are in italics.)

1. Give the customers what *they* want.   1. _____

2. The car was selected for *its* color.   2. _____

3. Farm Insurance Co. has *its* headquarters in Bloomington, Illinois.   3. _____

4. Dr. Hastings explained the surgery to *his* patient.   4. _____

5. May I please have my manuscript back after you have read *it*.   5. _____

6. Neither Norman nor Nathan has given *his* review.   6. _____

7. Heather and Milt opened *their* gifts at the awards banquet.   7. _____

8. Have Mr. Shaw and Mr. Patel seen *their* new offices?   8. _____

9. Sitting at *her* desk, Ann read the day's mail.   9. _____

10. The two Senators eventually had *their* bill approved.   10. _____

11. When Gary and Al heard about the merger, *they* were concerned.   11. _____

12. A middle-aged couple bought *their* first house.   12. _____

13. She and I will make *our* presentation on Thursday.   13. _____

14. Legends live on for *their* entertainment and educational value.   14. _____

15. The President says *he* is eager to become accountable.   15. _____

16. Congress will continue *its* current session until July 4.   16. _____

17. Mr. Wilson said, "Please give *me* the sales figures for April."   17. _____

18. Please sign the form and return *it* in the enclosed envelope.   18. _____

19. He and I have *our* work scheduled for the month.   19. _____

20. Representative Wolf and he were asked to submit *their* questions about the
    proposed bill.   20. _____

21. You and she should have requested *your* travel funds earlier.   21. _____

22. Ms. Kostner explained *her* absence from the meeting.   22. _____

23. Few were happy with *their* appointments.   23. _____

24. Dr. Peake and I presented the results of *our* research.   24. _____

25. Many salespersons excel at the human relations aspects of *their* work.   25. _____

26. Cheryl decided to reschedule *her* afternoon meeting.   26. _____

27. After you review the proposal, forward *it* to Mr. Hart.   27. _____

28. We guarantee that you will be satisfied with *our* work.   28. _____

Forms of Pronouns

The pronouns *he*, *his*, and *him* represent three different forms of one pronoun. The pronoun *he* is a nominative form. The pronoun *his* is a possessive form. And the pronoun *him* is an objective form.

Here is a list of pronoun forms:

Nominative: I   we   you   he   she   it   they
Objective: me   us   you   him   her   it   them
Possessive: my   our   your   his   her   its   their

NOMINATIVE FORMS OF PRONOUNS

We use the nominative forms *I, we, she,* and so on, as subjects of verbs.

They demonstrated the use of the photocopier. *They* is the subject of the verb *demonstrated.*

Ranjin and *she* prepared the report. Here the pronoun *she* is part of the compound subject *Ranjin and she,* which is the subject of the verb *prepared.*

Notice that the forms *you* and *it* can be either nominative or objective.

As *you* know, *I* gave it to Mr. Hammer. *You* is the subject of the verb *know,* and *I* is the subject of the verb *gave.* (Later you will see that in this sentence, *it* is an objective form.)

CHECKUP 1

Underline the nominative-form pronouns in the following sentences. Then write the nominative-form pronouns in the spaces at the right.

1. He said that she could have the letter.
2. Both she and he are living in Florida.
3. Will you please submit your résumé and letter of application.
4. When they saw the pictures, they wanted copies.

1. **He, she** _____
2. _____
3. _____
4. _____

IT IS I!

We also use nominative pronouns following the verbs *am, is, are, were, was, be, been,* or any form of the verb *to be.*

It is *I*. (NOT: It is me.)

Imagine: The two winners were Rhonda and she! (NOT: Rhonda and her.)

CHECKUP 2

Select the correct pronoun from each pair in parentheses, and write it in the space at the right.

1. Deborah and *(her, she)* witnessed the accident.
2. It is *(me, I)* who called you yesterday.
3. That is *(her, she)* on the front cover of the magazine.
4. Our manager and *(him, he)* reviewed the plans for the new addition.

1. **she** _____
2. _____
3. _____
4. _____

OBJECTIVE FORMS OF PRONOUNS

The objective pronouns *(me, us, you, him, her, it,* and *them)* are used as direct objects of verbs. The direct object follows the verb and answers the question *what* or *whom.*

Heidi will sell *them* today. *Them* is the direct object of the verb *sell.* Sell *what?* Them.

Objective forms are also used as indirect objects. An indirect object follows the verb and answers the question *to whom, for whom, to what,* or *for what.*

The president will buy *him* a computer. Buy *whom?* No answer. (The president will not, of course, buy *him.*) Buy *what?* A *computer.* Thus *computer* is the direct object. *Him* is an indirect object.

He gave *her* a book. Gave *whom?* No answer. Gave *what?* A *book. Book* is the direct object. *Her* is the indirect object.

In addition, objective forms are used as objects of prepositions.

Give the report to *her*. *Her* is the object of the preposition *to.*

They need another person like *you* (NOT: *yourself*). *You* is the object of the preposition *like.*

Yes, I was asking about *them*. *Them* is the object of the preposition *about.*

CHECKUP 3   Select the correct pronoun from each pair in parentheses, and write it in the space at the right. Make sure you understand *why* your answer is correct.

1. The finance manager wants *(they, them)* to attend the workshop.   1. **them** _____
2. Check with *(she, her)* about the plans for the advertisement.   2. _____
3. *(He, Him)* and she were both chosen to be cosponsors.   3. _____
4. Several of us wanted to work with *(he, him)* on the brochure.   4. _____
5. Give *(they, them)* the resources they need to complete the task.   5. _____
6. *(I, me)* was selected to design the new company logo.   6. _____
7. Ask *(she, her)* for the access code.   7. _____

POSSESSIVE FORMS OF PRONOUNS   We use the possessive forms of pronouns to show ownership.

my printer	*his* idea	*our* firm	*its* quota
your office	*her* papers	*their* presentation	

As you see, these forms are used *before* nouns. The forms *mine, yours, hers, his, its,* and *theirs* can be used *in place of* nouns.

This book is *mine,* but that one is *yours*.

If that book is *theirs,* then where is *ours?*

Use a possessive-case pronoun to modify a gerund—a verb form ending in *ing* and used as a noun.

I appreciate *your* (NOT: *you*) **returning the book by Wednesday.** *Note:* Remember that *its* is a possessive pronoun. Do not confuse *its* with *it's,* which is the contraction meaning "it is."

CHECKUP 4   Replace the word or words in parentheses with a possessive pronoun. Write the pronoun in the space at the right.

1. The manager and supervisor made *(the manager and supervisor's)* decision.   1. **their** _____
2. You're right. The company decided to renew *(the company's)* lease.   2. _____
3. I'm sure that this is *(Mike's)* sweater.   3. _____
4. I look forward to *(Eileen's)* calling me for an interview.   4. _____
5. The committee members were aware of *(the committee members')* influence.   5. _____
6. Jake obviously wants to sell *(Jake's)* stock in the company.   6. _____
7. Did Hilda ask them to forward *(Hilda's)* mail?   7. _____

EXERCISES

NAME _____ DATE _____ SCORE _____

EXERCISE 1   Select the correct pronoun from each pair in parentheses, and write it in the space at the right.

1. It is *(I, me)* who asked for a copy of the user's manual.   1. _____
2. This one is *(my, mine)*; that one is *(your, yours)*.   2. _____
3. Between you and *(I, me)*, I would like to have the afternoon off.   3. _____
4. Bob said that *(she, her)* could buy the office supplies from the new vendor. 4. _____
5. Shirley, like *(yourself, you)*, has the ability to get along well with people. 5. _____
6. *(They, Them)* will listen to our concerns at the meeting.   6. _____
7. Mr. Hanecki and *(I, me)* conducted the seminar for all office employees.   7. _____
8. Please call *(he, him)* at his office before 3 p.m.   8. _____
9. Have you checked with *(they, them)* about their travel plans?   9. _____
10. All the workers except *(she, her)* reported on time.   10. _____
11. It's odd that someone like *(he, him)* would be elected to office.   11. _____
12. *(He, Him)* recommended several people for the job.   12. _____
13. Please give *(they, them)* the opportunity to speak at the meeting.   13. _____
14. *(I, Me)* have a plane to catch at two o'clock.   14. _____
15. Lerner & Sons reduced *(their, its)* furniture prices drastically.   15. _____
16. *(They, Them)* are arranging our schedules for *(we, us)*.   16. _____
17. The representatives taught *(we, us)* how to use the computer.   17. _____
18. Are you sure that is *(my, mine)*?   18. _____
19. *(He, Him)* is the one who made that suggestion.   19. _____
20. Donald and *(she, her)* will represent the company at the meeting.   20. _____
21. Please let *(me, my)* edit the newsletter before you mail it out.   21. _____
22. *(We, Us)* volunteered to stay late to finish the project.   22. _____
23. Tell *(she, her)* that we solved the problem.   23. _____
24. Stern Company announced that *(they, it)* would be moving on July 1.   24. _____
25. Was it *(my, mine)* typewriter or *(you, yours)* that was damaged?   25. _____
26. *(You, Your)* collected enough samples for *(we, us)*.   26. _____
27. Ask *(they, them)* how to install the new motor.   27. _____
28. It was *(he, him)* who solved the mystery for us.   28. _____
29. If this is *(my, mine)* manual, then that one must be *(her, hers)*.   29. _____
30. Would you please work for *(my, me)* tonight.   30. _____
31. It was *(they, them)* who processed the papers for *(her, hers)* visa.   31. _____
32. *(She, Her)* and *(he, him)* identified the culprit.   32. _____
33. When are you planning to give *(we, us)* the order?   33. _____
34. Have you seen *(he, him)* around the office lately?   34. _____
35. *(We, Us)* routed all shipments through Ohio.   35. _____

EXERCISE 2   Correct any pronoun errors in the following sentences. Underline each error. Then write your corrections in the spaces at the right. If a sentence is correct, write *OK*.

1. I assume that her will bring the manuscript with she.   1. _____
2. Them will proceed with theirs plans for a new office building.   2. _____

3. Someone like he should have the manager's job. 3. _____

4. It was I who reported the election results. 4. _____

5. Ours accountant said that us did not owe any taxes. 5. _____

6. Do you object to him being present at the departmental meeting? 6. _____

7. Many of we wanted to see the opening game at Hamilton Park. 7. _____

8. The company lost it lease when new owners bought the building. 8. _____

9. That book is their; this one is my. 9. _____

10. Have you heard they speak before? 10. _____

11. I appreciate you bringing the matter to my attention. 11. _____

12. It is me who established the scholarship fund for minority workers. 12. _____

13. Him and her photographed the new products for the fall catalog. 13. _____

14. Will you please hand I that letter on Tom's desk. 14. _____

15. Gerry said that she would finance the project. 15. _____

16. Are you relying on we to finish the work that you started? 16. _____

17. Them had an interesting story to tell when them returned from camp. 17. _____

18. Many of they had explored the possibility of printing a newsletter. 18. _____

19. Either her or him will arrange for a visiting scholar to come to ours university. 19. _____

20. Me promised she that me would serve as a moderator. 20. _____

21. The idea for a new procedure was their. 21. _____

22. Have you thought about promoting he? 22. _____

23. Is this package for I or for she? 23. _____

24. Check with they before you release the story. 24. _____

25. Our company plans to relocate it's headquarters to New York City. 25. _____

26. Have you heard that he will be our new president? 26. _____

27. It is us who will make the final selection. 27. _____

28. Where have them all gone? 28. _____

29. Her and me obtained permission to leave work at noon. 29. _____

30. Many of them had asked not to work over the Christmas holidays. 30. _____

31. Both of the contracts need to be signed by he. 31. _____

32. Yes, that book over there is my. 32. _____

33. If you wish, him will give you ours tickets. 33. _____

34. Theirs supply of stationery was very low. 34. _____

35. Is her the one who must approve our travel advances? 35. _____

36. Neither one of we will be able to furnish the names of the winners. 36. _____

37. Committee members were aware of theirs duties to the organization. 37. _____

38. The union resumed it's talks with the company representatives at noon. 38. _____

39. Both of they will receive merit pay because of their contributions to the company. 39. _____

40. Between you and I, I think that Henry will get the job. 40. _____

41. I thought it was she who called the meeting of the secretaries. 41. _____

42. Him and Mr. O'Riley will not be in the office today; they are at a convention in Dallas. 42. _____

43. Do you realize that the final decision is your? 43. _____

44. It was them who ordered the merchandise from Conrad Brothers. 44. _____

45. Please talk to they before you turn in your resignation. 45. _____

46. Us were unable to place our order on time. 46. _____

47. Which assignment is mine? 47. _____

48. We told they to conduct a tlelphone survey. 48. _____

49. The new computer workstation is located in theirs office. 49. _____

50. She asked me if that was one of mine ideas. 50. _____

Pronoun Troublemakers

WHEN WORDS ARE MISSING Choosing the correct form of a pronoun may be tricky in a sentence like this one:

Dawna likes basketball better than *(I, me)*.

Which would you choose, *I* or *me*? With *I*, the sentence would mean that Dawna likes basketball better than *I* like basketball. But with *me*, the sentence means that Dawna likes basketball better than she likes *me!* Quite a difference. The trick to such problems is simply to find the missing words. The words *than* and *as* are tip-offs; they warn you to be careful. For example:

Howard enjoys television more than *(I, me)*. With the missing words, this sentence can be either: Howard enjoys television more than (Howard enjoys) *me*. Or: Howard enjoys television more than *I* (enjoy television).

Usually, however, only one of the pronouns could be correct. For example:

They can edit the letter as well as *(she, her)*. *She* is correct: They can edit the letter as well as *she* (can edit the letter). It makes no sense to say "They can edit the letter as well as (they can edit) her."

David has more artistic talent than *(she, her)*. *She* is correct: David has more artistic talent than *she* (has). It makes no sense to say "David has more artistic talent than (David has) her."

CHECKUP 1 Select the correct pronoun from each pair in parentheses, and write it in the space at the right. Remember to say the missing words to yourself.

1. I enjoy going to the theater as much as *(she, her)*.
2. Mr. Hayata has been a manager longer than *(I, me)*.
3. Ms. Belcher is concerned about the reorganization more than *(he, him)*.
4. His talk motivated Charlie as much as *(I, me)*.
5. We enjoyed the game more than *(they, them)*.

1. **she** _____
2. _____
3. _____
4. _____
5. _____

WHEN THERE ARE TOO MANY WORDS Sometimes we must omit words to make a choice between pronouns. For example:

Ms. Peroni and *(I, me)* will revise this brochure.

Omit the words *Ms. Peroni and* and the choice then becomes simple: *I* will revise. (NOT: *Me* will revise.) A nominative pronoun is needed to be the subject of the verb *will revise*.
 Let's change the sentence as follows:

Two editors, Ms. Peroni and *(I, me)*, will revise the brochure.

I is still correct. Omit the beginning words, and you will get *I will revise*. . . . The nominative *I* is the subject of the verb *will revise*. Another example:

Please give the information to Mr. Donahue and *(I, me)*.

If you omit the words *Mr. Donahue and* the choice is clear: give the information to . . . *me*. An objective pronoun is needed to be the object of the preposition *to*.

CHECKUP 2

Select the correct pronoun from each pair in parentheses, and write it in the space at the right.

1. Ask Rita or *(he, him)* for the keys to the cabinet.
1. **him**
2. Either Kevin or *(they, them)* will be asked to prepare the bulletin.
2. _____
3. When you are finished with the journal, please give it to Phyllis or *(they, them)*.
3. _____
4. Leah and *(I, me)* are eager to try out the new equipment.
4. _____
5. Grace invited *(he, him)* to the grand opening of the new mall.
5. _____
6. Because of his experience, Scot knows the computer better than *(I, me)*.
6. _____
7. Friends like Dino and *(she, her)* are wonderful to have.
7. _____
8. Sylvia supervises the computer lab as well as *(he, him)*.
8. _____
9. Judith and *(I, me)* commented on the new policy.
9. _____
10. They mailed the questionnaires to Janice and *(I, me)*.
10. _____
11. The manager assigned *(she, her)* to the production team.
11. _____
12. She and *(I, me)* will learn how to use the new computer software.
12. _____

ANOTHER TROUBLEMAKER!

We must also omit words to choose pronouns correctly in sentences such as these:

(We, Us) managers are conducting training seminars.

They sent invitations to *(we, us)* managers.

Which would you choose, *we* or *us*? In both cases, the choice becomes clear when you omit the word *managers*.

(We, Us) are conducting training seminars. Of course, you would not say "*Us* are conducting"! *We* is correct.

They sent invitations to *(we, us)*. Of course, you would not say "sent invitations to *we*"! *Us* is correct here.

Do not be fooled when the pronoun is the object of a preposition:

All of *us* managers are conducting training seminars. Here, *us* is the object of the preposition *of,* and the object of a preposition is *always an objective form*.

CHECKUP 3

Select the correct pronoun from each pair in parentheses, and write it in the space at the right.

1. *(We, Us)* accountants will be extremely busy the weeks before April 15.
1. **We**
2. All of *(we, us)* were going to spend our free time doing as we pleased.
2. _____
3. Ms. Yeager said, "*(We, Us)* nurses need to attend classes to keep abreast of what is going on in the medical field."
3. _____
4. Ask *(we, us)* to do the job, and we will follow through for you.
4. _____
5. Several of *(we, us)* were invited to the reception.
5. _____
6. *(We, Us)* had the courage to say what we thought at the union meeting.
6. _____
7. They tried to give *(we, us)* samples, but we refused them.
7. _____
8. Some of *(we, us)* secretaries are attending the luncheon sponsored by the National Bank.
8. _____
9. Although both of *(we, us)* had been there before, we were eager to go again.
9. _____
10. *(We, Us)* finance majors are busy preparing our résumés.
10. _____
11. They asked *(we, us)* about the announcement.
11. _____
12. *(We, Us)* decided to withdraw our offer for the house.
12. _____

EXERCISES

NAME _____ DATE _____ SCORE _____

EXERCISE 1   Select the correct pronoun from each pair in parentheses, and write it in the space at the right. Remember to say the missing words to yourself.

1. No one was more appreciative than *(I, me)* about the award.   1. _____
2. The recently hired consultant, Jeff Meyerhoffer, is as enthusiastic as *(she, her)*.   2. _____
3. We walked as many miles in the race as *(they, them)*.   3. _____
4. As a vice president, Ina was more effective and competent than *(he, him)*.   4. _____
5. The land was surveyed by our engineer and *(he, him)*.   5. _____
6. My sister and *(I, me)* discussed the matter yesterday.   6. _____
7. Is the new purchasing agent younger than *(she, her)*?   7. _____
8. Ms. Babbit worked harder on the project than *(he, him)*.   8. _____
9. The keyboard operators typed more invoices in the last hour than *(they, them)*.   9. _____
10. I believe that Morris is a better analyst than *(she, her)*.   10. _____
11. Mike's departure from our office will hurt the company more than *(we, us)*.   11. _____
12. Because of the delay, the Olsens arrived much later than *(we, us)*.   12. _____
13. Mr. Parker, our office manager, lets Elaine work more hours than *(I, me)*.   13. _____
14. A progress report should be submitted by you and *(he, him)* before the end of the week.   14. _____
15. Our human resources director needs to remind the computer operators and *(she, her)* about the approaching deadline.   15. _____
16. Are you as hungry as *(I, me)*?   16. _____
17. The delivery was made on time because of the efforts by Lester and *(they, them)*.   17. _____
18. Workers like Mitzie and *(she, her)* are always in demand.   18. _____
19. His leaving the company posed more of a problem for *(he, him)* than for *(we, us)*.   19. _____
20. Are you as tall as *(I, me)*?   20. _____

EXERCISE 2   Select the correct pronoun from each pair in parentheses, and write it in the space at the right.

1. My brother and *(I, me)* plan to take a trip to Ireland this summer.   1. _____
2. We taught Arnie and *(she, her)* how to use word processing software on the office computer.   2. _____
3. After staying up late last night, Marilyn and *(she, her)* wanted to sleep longer in the morning.   3. _____
4. A complete report needs to be made by either you or *(he, him)*.   4. _____
5. Between Alicia and *(they, them)* I am sure the work will get done.   5. _____
6. Dr. Holman and *(he, him)* will advise us about the medical grant.   6. _____
7. Wilma and *(we, us)* plan to work on the financial report until it is finished.   7. _____
8. Three officers and *(they, them)* will investigate the problem and report back to us.   8. _____

9. In the future, prepare a copy for Mr. Galatin and (*I, me*).

9. _____

10. The judge called Marya and (*we, us*) to his chambers.

10. _____

11. Carolyn took Allison and (*I, me*) to her office in the World Trade Center.

11. _____

12. Ms. Tarrington, our boss, told Lee and (*they, them*) what to expect after the merger.

12. _____

13. The duties had to be divided between Althea and (*she, her*).

13. _____

14. Walt surprised (*we, us*) with his excellent suggestions for remodeling.

14. _____

15. The new director called Jill and (*he, him*) to the office.

15. _____

16. My friend and (*she, her*) plan to renew their friendship over dinner.

16. _____

17. Ms. Winston and (*he, him*) can tour our building any time.

17. _____

18. Between you and (*I, me*), I suggest that we suspend production for now.

18. _____

19. Eleanor and (*I, me*) wish to add our names to the list of donors.

19. _____

20. Simon and (*they, them*) recommended several proposals for the board of directors to consider.

20. _____

EXERCISE 3   Select the correct pronoun from each pair in parentheses, and write it in the space at the right.

1. (*They, them*) acknowledged our presence in the audience.

1. _____

2. Having heard our side of the story, do you think they will believe Bruce and (*I, me*)?

2. _____

3. (*We, Us*) aspiring artists would like to display our work at the art show.

3. _____

4. Invitations had to be sent to (*they, them*) within three weeks.

4. _____

5. Yes, (*we, us*) attorneys promise to let you know when the case comes up in court.

5. _____

6. The petitions were circulated among (*we, us*) voters.

6. _____

7. Because of (*he, him*), we received a bonus at the end of the month.

7. _____

8. (*She, Her*) and I will be working for a special agency this summer.

8. _____

9. If someone has to be present, then I recommend that (*he, him*) be our representative.

9. _____

10. Coauthors like Theresa and (*she, her*) prefer to work separately.

10. _____

11. (*I, Me*) now realize that we should have bid higher for the antique desk.

11. _____

12. Either (*she, her*) or I will stay to finish the minutes from the meeting.

12. _____

13. You can send the applications to (*we, us*) reviewers.

13. _____

14. The manager suggested that they send the manuscript to (*I, me*).

14. _____

15. (*We, Us*) librarians were happy to be members of the advising committee.

15. _____

16. No, not all of (*we, us*) chemists have been given the formula for the new product.

16. _____

17. Mr. Plank said that (*we, us*) workers were doing a fine job of assembling the motors.

17. _____

18. Ms. Davis explained that she had written to (*they, them*) about the new work schedule.

18. _____

19. Many of (*we, us*) finance officers have had over ten years' experience.

19. _____

20. (*We, Us*) were happy to receive the invitations to the grand opening.

20. _____

21. Several of (*we, us*) wanted to appear on the program.

21. _____

22. It was (*I, me*) who made that phone call from your office.

22. _____

23. Hazel claims that (*she, her*) sent the transcript to you last Friday.

23. _____

24. All of (*we, us*) were eager to read the auditor's report.

24. _____

25. Sarah and (*they, them*) had submitted their retirement letters.

25. _____

26. (*We, Us*) project managers are expected to work overtime.

26. _____

27. (*She, Her*) and I had supported the new program.

27. _____

28. Monica told (*they, them*) that she would interview the applicants.

28. _____

Who, Whom, and Other Pronouns

WHO AND *WHOM* ARE PRONOUNS TOO   *Who* is a nominative form; use it when a nominative is needed. *Whom* is objective; use it when an objective form is needed.

Ms. Ferguson, *who* is my administrative assistant, interviews the applicants.

The pronoun *who* is a follower; it refers to *Ms. Ferguson,* its leader (or antecedent). In the clause *who is my administrative assistant,* the pronoun *who* is the subject of the verb *is.* Thus the nominative form *who* is correct. (*Note:* A clause is a group of words that has a subject and a verb.)

Ms. Ferguson, *whom* you met yesterday, is my administrative assistant.

The pronoun *whom* refers to *Ms. Ferguson,* its leader. But the clause *whom you met yesterday* is out of normal order. Let's change it to *you met whom yesterday.* Now you can see that *whom* is the object of the verb *met;* thus an objective form is correct.
    A Shortcut: Let the *m* in *whom* and the *m* in *him* remind you that they both are in the objective form.

His brother, *(who, whom)* we hired as an attorney, will represent us in court.

First, put the *who/whom* clause in its normal order. The normal order for the clause in the preceding example would be *we hired (who/whom) as an attorney.* Now let's see what happens when we substitute *he* or *him:*

We hired *he* as an attorney (No!)   We hired *him* as an attorney (Yes!)

Him is correct, because the word we need is the object of the verb *hired.* Let *him* remind you of *whom,* and you get the correct answer:

His brother, *whom* we hired as an attorney, will represent us in court.

A TROUBLEMAKER!   As you know, the *who/whom* clause always begins with the word *who* or *whom,* so it's easy to find the clause. Look at how some troublemakers can cloud your choice:

Frederico recommended an individual *(who, whom)* I think is unqualified.

Don't let the words *I think* distract you! Put them in normal order and substitute *he/him:*

I think *(who, whom)* is unqualified = I think *(he, him)* is unqualified.

You wouldn't say *him* is unqualified. You would use a nominative. *Who,* the nominative form, is the subject of the verb *is.*

Frederico recommended an individual *who* I think is unqualified.

Please refer *(whoever, whomever)* you think is qualified for the job to Ms. Swartz.

What is the clause? It is *(whoever, whomever) you think is qualified for the job*. Put the clause in normal order and the choice becomes clear: *you think whoever is qualified for the job* (because a nominative is needed for the subject of the verb *is qualified*).

Give this project to *(whoever, whomever)* you want to give it to.

The clause is *(whoever, whomever) you want to give it to*. In normal order, it is *you want to give it to (whoever, whomever)*. Since the choice will be the object of the preposition *to*, the objective *whomever* is correct.

CHECKUP 1   Select the correct word from each pair in parentheses, and write it in the space at the right. If necessary, put the *who/whom* clause in normal order first.

1. *(Who, Whom)* did you recommend for the position?
2. *(Who, Whom)* will be our new supervisor in the finance department?
3. Mr. Steuhler, *(who, whom)* I saw at the convention, was talking with one of our competitors.
4. It is Gary Perry *(who, whom)* I hope will become our next chairman.
5. Julie and Louis are the ones *(who, whom)* I think should be hired.

1. __Whom_____
2. _____
3. _____
4. _____
5. _____

WHICH OR THAT?   Clauses can also be introduced by *that* or *which*. (*Who* refers to people; *which*, to animals and things. *That* can refer to people, animals, or things.)

The package, *which* arrived yesterday, was opened by Ms. Huang. The leader (or antecedent) of *which* is *package*. (**Note:** The commas separate the *which* clause from the rest of the sentence.)

The main idea in this sentence is *The package was opened by Ms. Huang*. The *which* clause gives us extra information—nonessential information. It says: "By the way, the package arrived yesterday." Let's assume for a minute that there are *several* packages, and only *one* was opened by Ms. Huang. If so, then the writer must supply some essential information to make it clear which of the packages Ms. Huang opened:

The package that arrived yesterday was opened by Ms. Huang. (**Note:** There are no commas and the word *which* has been replaced by *that*.)

The clause *that arrived yesterday* is not extra information in this case. It clearly identifies a particular package so that there will be no confusion. Because *that* clauses are essential, we do *not* separate them with commas. *That* is sometimes used in place of *who* or *whom*.

The applicants *that* we hired will do a good job. (**Note:** No commas with *that*.)

CHECKUP 2   Replace each blank in the sentences below with *that* or *which*.

1. The cat _____ you saw yesterday is called Spider.
2. One of the recommendations _____ she made was accepted by the board.
3. The shipment, _____ arrived by truck, had been damaged.
4. The appraisal _____ Hank made on the house was accurate.
5. Our office, _____ was painted five years ago, needs to be painted.
6. The merchandise _____ was shipped on Monday arrived early.
7. Her new contract, _____ contains revisions, is enclosed.
8. She tested the well water _____ was on their property.
9. Give me the updated sales reports _____ you compiled.
10. Our meeting, _____ was scheduled for today, has been cancelled.

1. __that_____
2. _____
3. _____
4. _____
5. _____
6. _____
7. _____
8. _____
9. _____
10. _____

EXERCISES

NAME _____ DATE _____ SCORE _____

EXERCISE 1   Select the correct pronoun from each pair in parentheses, and write it in the space at the right. If necessary, put the *who/whom* clause in normal order first.

1. To *(who, whom)* shall we mail the purchase order?

2. She is the attorney *(who, whom)* is representing Mr. Bartel.

3. Jennie DeVito, *(who, whom)* I told you about, is my cousin.

4. They are the ones *(who, whom)* are asking about our services.

5. We'll be happy with *(whoever, whomever)* you recommend.

6. The person *(who, whom)* they chose is Arlene Travers.

7. Give the award to the person *(who, whom)* receives the highest evaluations.

8. The repair person *(who, whom)* you called for is well-qualified to do the job.

9. He is the one *(who, whom)* will make the decision about the move.

10. *(Whoever, Whomever)* would like to take the bus tour should sign up by Friday.

11. Amanda and Jill are the ones *(who, whom)* really know how to write articles for publication.

12. Ms. Armstrong, *(who, whom)* you met in Dan's office, is the sales representative for Iron Works, Ltd.

13. *(Who, Whom)* do you think we should get to record the minutes?

14. The company will provide an all-expense-paid trip to Paris to *(whoever, whomever)* records the most sales for the month.

15. Nadia Riley, *(who, whom)* I talked to you about this morning, is transferring to the Accounting Department June 1.

16. *(Whoever, Whomever)* is planning to attend the conference should let me know by the end of the week.

17. They chose Barry Carter, *(who, whom)* has worked very hard for the company.

18. *(Who, Whom)* do you think will get the promotion to vice president?

19. *(Whoever, Whomever)* reaches the company quota by the end of the month will receive a $1,000 bonus.

20. He's the man *(who, whom)* I thought you would recommend.

21. *(Who, Whom)* do you think we should select for our chairperson?

22. Roger Michaels, *(who, whom)* Riley Brothers honored last month, is going to be here this afternoon.

23. Fran is the one *(who, whom)* is always available when we need her.

24. It was he *(who, whom)* we selected as our patron.

25. Do you know *(who, whom)* is the director of the research project?

1. _____

2. _____

3. _____

4. _____

5. _____

6. _____

7. _____

8. _____

9. _____

10. _____

11. _____

12. _____

13. _____

14. _____

15. _____

16. _____

17. _____

18. _____

19. _____

20. _____

21. _____

22. _____

23. _____

24. _____

25. _____

EXERCISE 2   Correct any errors in the usage of *who, whom, whoever,* and *whomever.* Underline each error. Then write your corrections in the spaces at the right. If a sentence is correct, write *OK.*

1. Unfortunately, none of the interviewees who we talked with has the qualifications we're looking for.

2. Give this manual to whoever is in charge of the computer lab.

1. _____

2. _____

3. Many of the celebrities who were from out of town stayed overnight at the Walton Plaza.

3. _____

4. Each manager should support whoever the committee members select as chair.

4. _____

5. Rick Williams, who you introduced us to at the conference, made a very good impression on Mr. Danforth.

5. _____

6. The man who is sitting next to the keynote speaker is Mr. Shull.

6. _____

7. Only Ms. Crawford, whom is the vice president of marketing, can verify those figures.

7. _____

8. It was she who we thought would be the new coach of our team.

8. _____

9. The question of whom should be responsible for the marketing strategies will be taken up at the meeting.

9. _____

10. The person who I met at the convention is a candidate for a position at Carson Corporation.

10. _____

11. Who would you suggest as a replacement?

11. _____

12. George is the one whom is always willing to help us.

12. _____

EXERCISE 3   Replace each blank with *which* or *that*. Write the correct answers in the spaces at the right.

1. Here is the study guide _____ was lying on Sue's desk.

1. _____

2. Our company, _____ was established 75 years ago, is about to close.

2. _____

3. The apartment complex, _____ is under new management, has over 100 units.

3. _____

4. The new journal, _____ contains articles by well-known authors, has a subscription rate of $50 for the year.

4. _____

5. The books _____ are on the table were donated yesterday.

5. _____

6. His article on the communication process, _____ was published in the company newsletter, won him an award.

6. _____

7. He wrote the song _____ we sang at commencement.

7. _____

8. Chicago, _____ is a large city, has several wonderful museums.

8. _____

9. Here is the application _____ the passport office sent.

9. _____

10. Our new building, _____ opened in January, was furnished by Howards.

10. _____

11. Her proposal is the one _____ we decided to accept.

11. _____

12. They sold the car _____ had the most mileage.

12. _____

EXERCISE 4   Correct any errors in the usage of *which* and *that*. Underline each error. Then write your corrections in the spaces at the right. If a sentence is correct, write *OK*.

1. The wheel which squeaks is at the back of the car.

1. _____

2. The petition that Judge Kraft received had more than enough signatures.

2. _____

3. Two of the letters, that he signed, did not go out in the morning's mail.

3. _____

4. The store which is owned by Mr. Easton is on Washington Road.

4. _____

5. They bought the house which was recommended by the real estate agent.

5. _____

6. Unlike most reports that are written at the request of management, recommendation reports are often initiated by the writer.

6. _____

7. The brief, that he sent to Judge Mason, had to be revised.

7. _____

8. Simon's report on health benefits, which I sent you last week, should answer all your questions.

8. _____

9. A price increase, that Linda suggested, did not go into effect.

9. _____

10. She is the type of student which will do well in math.

10. _____

11. The problem is one which can be resolved quickly.

11. _____

12. Our business, that is located in the suburbs, recently expanded.

12. _____

More About Pronouns

PRONOUNS IN QUESTIONS   Pronouns that we use in questions are called *interrogative pronouns: who, whom, whose, which,* and *what.*

Who do you think is best qualified for the job? *Who* is the subject of the verb *is.*

Whom should I call first? Normal order: I should call *whom* first. *Whom* is the object of the verb *should call.*

Whose report do you prefer? *Whose* is a possessive pronoun like *hers* or *theirs.*

What would you consider a good buy? *What* is indefinite—it refers to nothing in particular.

Which do you think is the better buy? *Which* refers to *one* particular person or thing.

The words *whose* and *which* are also used as adjectives.

Whose car will you be driving? *Whose* modifies *car.*

Which book did you like better? *Which* modifies *book.*

THIS and THAT; THESE and THOSE   Be sure to remember that *this* and *that* are singular; *these* and *those* are plural.

SINGULAR	PLURAL
this computer, this printer	these computers, these printers
that computer, that printer	those computers, those printers

Remember, too, to use *this* and *these* to indicate persons or things that are near. Use *that* and *those* for persons or things that are far.

This carton is for recycling newspapers. *That* carton (the one on the counter) is for magazines. *This* shows the carton that is closer; *that* shows the one that is farther away.

These cartons are for recycling newspapers. *Those* cartons (the ones on the counter) are for magazines. *These* indicates the cartons that are closer; *those* indicates the cartons that are farther away.

Notice that *this, that, these,* and *those* can be used as adjectives or pronouns:

ADJECTIVES	PRONOUNS
This book is mine. *That* book is yours.	*This* is mine. *That* is yours.
These books are mine. *Those* books are yours.	*These* are mine. *Those* are yours.

As you see, they are adjectives when they modify the noun *book* or *books.* They are pronouns when they stand alone.

SELF-ENDING PRONOUNS   The pronouns *myself, yourself, herself, himself,* and *itself* are singular. Their plural forms end in *selves: ourselves, yourselves, themselves.*

I will edit this letter *myself. Myself* refers to *I.*

We will answer these letters *ourselves. Ourselves* refers to *we.*

A *self*-ending pronoun *must* refer to something in the sentence. It cannot stand alone; it must have a leader (or antecedent).

Wrong: Mr. Beswick invited Bob and *myself*. What does *myself* refer to? Nothing!

Right: Mr. Beswick invited Bob and *me*.

In sentences where *you* is understood, *yourself* or *yourselves* may be perfectly okay.

Please file this *yourself*. *You* is understood: *(You)* please . . . .

Beware! On television or in conversation you may hear someone say *hisself*, but there is no such word! Say *himself*. *Theirselves* and *theirself* are also incorrect.

CHECKUP 1
Select the correct pronoun from each pair in parentheses, and write it in the space at the right. *Hint:* Make sure a *self*-ending pronoun has a leader!

1. He *(hisself, himself)* repaired the leaking faucet in the lounge.
2. *(Who, Whom)* is responsible for preparing the agenda for the meeting?
3. *(What, Which)* of the ideas presented do you see as the best solution to the problem?
4. *(Who, Whom)* should I recommend for the opening in the sales department?
5. Keep a copy of the contract for *(yourself, ourselves)*.

1. __himself_____
2. _____
3. _____
4. _____
5. _____

EACH and *EVERY*   *Each* and *every* are called *indefinite pronouns* because they refer to persons, places, or things *in general*. They do not refer to specific persons, places, or things. *Note: No one* is always two words. *Any one* and *every one* are written as two words only when the word *of* follows.

Any one of you can come. Every one of the books must be shelved.

The indefinite pronouns you use most frequently are:

SINGULAR				PLURAL		SINGULAR OR PLURAL	
anybody	either	everything	nothing	both	several	all	more
anyone	every	neither	one	few	many	any	most
anything	everybody	nobody	somebody			none	some
each	everyone	no one	someone				

The singular pronouns require singular verbs, and the plural pronouns require plural verbs:

***Anybody* who *wants* a copy of the report should ask Ms. Viera.** *Anybody* is singular; *wants* is singular.

***Everyone likes* his and her schedule.** *Everyone* is singular; *likes* is singular. Note: *Everyone* is masculine or feminine so we use *his* and *her* and not just the masculine pronoun.

We have two engineers; *both* he and she enjoy working overtime. *Both* is plural; *enjoy* is plural.

For those pronouns that can be either singular or plural, look at the key word following the pronoun to determine whether a singular or a plural verb is needed.

SINGULAR	PLURAL
None of the merchandise was shipped.	None of the cartons were shipped.
None (no one) was hurt.	None (of the people) were hurt.
Some of the information was accurate.	Some of the reports were accurate.

EXERCISES

NAME _____ DATE _____ SCORE _____

EXERCISE 1   Select the correct pronoun from each pair in parentheses, and write it in the space at the right.

1. *(Who, Whom)* seems interested in the job?   1. _____
2. *(What, Which)* have they done with the evaluations?   2. _____
3. *(Which, That)* copy is the one you need for your presentation?   3. _____
4. *(What, Which)* of the two plans do you suggest we use?   4. _____
5. *(Who, Whom)* is our representative in this area?   5. _____
6. *(What, Which)* did you learn from your historical study of letters?   6. _____
7. To *(who, whom)* did you speak about the telephone installation?   7. _____
8. *(That, Which)* partner in the firm is more reliable?   8. _____
9. *(Who, Whom)* should I say is calling?   9. _____
10. *(Which, What)* of you would like to work on the Feinberg account?   10. _____
11. *(Who, Whom)* wants to take credit for this project?   11. _____
12. *(What, Which)* has happened to all the supplies in the cabinet?   12. _____
13. *(What, Which)* one of the two boxes needs to be shipped to Ann Arbor?   13. _____
14. *(Who, Whom)* are you performing for this evening?   14. _____
15. *(Which, That)* brand of merchandise would you choose?   15. _____

EXERCISE 2   Select the correct pronoun from each pair in parentheses, and write it in the space at the right.

1. *(This, These)* are the qualifications she listed on her résumé.   1. _____
2. *(That, Those)* are the transparencies that I need for the presentation.   2. _____
3. *(This, These)* is the one that I would like you to buy.   3. _____
4. *(That, Those)* portraits of our founders need to be refinished.   4. _____
5. *(That, Those)* furniture needs to be repaired by an expert.   5. _____
6. *(This, These)* computers were purchased sometime in July.   6. _____
7. *(This, These)* is the job for which I was trained.   7. _____
8. *(That, Those)* are not the ones that we ordered.   8. _____
9. *(That, Those)* coupons were in yesterday's paper.   9. _____
10. *(That, Those)* window was replaced several times already.   10. _____
11. *(This, These)* clock runs about five minutes fast each day.   11. _____
12. *(This, These)* are the ones I would choose if I were you.   12. _____
13. *(This, These)* proposal is well-written and well-organized.   13. _____
14. *(That, Those)* packages on the counter need to be delivered today.   14. _____
15. *(These, This)* contracts required the signatures of the president and the vice
president.   15. _____

EXERCISE 3   Select the correct pronoun from each pair in parentheses, and write it in the space at the right.

1. Most of the applicants completed the application forms by *(itself, themselves)*.   1. _____
2. Since no one else was around to help, we had to do all the work by *(ourselves,
themselves)*.   2. _____

3. The engineer was able to fix the machine so that it would start by *(itself, themselves)*.   3. _____

4. Many of the participants wanted to try the new technique by *(ourselves, themselves)*.   4. _____

5. Are you sure you want to take the trip by *(yourself, ourselves)*?   5. _____

6. Allen saw *(himself, hisself)* on the videotape.   6. _____

7. To the amazement of her coworkers, Carmen invited *(herself, ourselves)* to the breakfast meeting.   7. _____

8. All of us enjoyed *(ourselves, yourselves)* at the centennial celebration.   8. _____

9. They said they could repair the machines by *(theirselves, themselves)*.   9. _____

10. Our manager wanted to finish the report by *(himself, hisself)*.   10. _____

EXERCISE 4   Decide whether a singular or a plural verb is needed to complete each of the following sentences. Select the correct verb from each pair in parentheses, and write it in the space at the right.

1. Both of the officers *(has, have)* over five years' experience.   1. _____

2. All of the participants *(was, were)* able to finish their projects.   2. _____

3. If someone *(need, needs)* a ride to the meeting, please let me know.   3. _____

4. Everyone *(want, wants)* to voice his or her opinion.   4. _____

5. Every worker *(is, are)* responsible for completing the insurance form.   5. _____

6. Each of the accountants *(has, have)* his or her own desk.   6. _____

7. Many of the people *(was, were)* ready to leave after the first act.   7. _____

8. Most of the afternoon *(was, were)* spent reading the guidelines.   8. _____

9. Neither of the brokers *(was, were)* willing to lower the commission rate.   9. _____

10. Every one of the employees *(is, are)* a registered voter.   10. _____

EXERCISE 5   Correct any pronoun errors in the following sentences. Underline each error. When you have a choice, correct the pronoun rather than another word. Then write your corrections in the spaces at the right. If a sentence is correct, write *OK*.

1. Derrick and myself were compiling a reading list for the new employees.   1. _____

2. Which of these computers has been repaired?   2. _____

3. Who should I call first when you are not available?   3. _____

4. This folders are the ones we should consider buying for our seminar participants.   4. _____

5. Each student should complete their project by Monday.   5. _____

6. Give the project to whoever you want.   6. _____

7. Would you please tell me whom is the owner of the company.   7. _____

8. He was eager to repair the machine by hisself.   8. _____

9. Bonnie and Sylvia wanted to organize the exhibit by theirselves.   9. _____

10. Every carpenter should use their own tools.   10. _____

11. Are these your keys?   11. _____

12. Whom would you like to see represent us at the union meeting?   12. _____

13. People like themself should be proud of themselves.   13. _____

14. Greg asked that he be allowed to work by hisself.   14. _____

15. The team discussed the plays among theirselves.   15. _____

16. This recycling drive is for a good cause.   16. _____

17. Each committee member is responsible for his actions.   17. _____

18. Whom is in charge of the maintenance department?   18. _____

19. Ms. Roberts promoted Rachel and myself.   19. _____

20. We will offer the job to whoever you recommend.   20. _____

Verbs

As you know, a sentence must have both a subject and a verb. Verbs are action words—they make sentences *move!* Notice how the verbs in the following paragraph move each sentence.

As a student at Midwestern State University, I *strengthened* my ability to get along well with others and to adapt to new friends and new environments. While a first-year student, I *participated* in the Student Volunteer Action Group. As a sophomore, I *organized* and *planned* the successful Fall Festival. During my junior and senior years, I *joined* several professional associations and *served* as president and treasurer for two of them. In addition to all these extracurricular activities, I *maintained* a 3.0 grade-point average throughout my four years.

CHECKUP 1   Underline the verbs in the following sentences. Then write the verbs in the spaces at the right.

1. Marvin distributed *The Wall Street Journal* to the officers of the bank.
2. Prepare employment correspondence on high-quality paper.
3. His demonstration clarified the procedure.
4. Many of them agreed to the new regulations.
5. The new manager demanded that we be on time for work.

1. **distributed** _____
2. _____
3. _____
4. _____
5. _____

USE OF VERBS

We use verbs to make statements and requests, to give commands, and to ask questions.

Make statements: Our agents *receive* commissions.

The managers *recommended* changes.

The verbs *receive* and *recommended* make statements about their subjects.

Make requests: Please *read* the enclosed bulletin.

Please *sign* these papers.

The verbs *read* and *sign* make requests of their subjects—*you* (understood).

Ask questions: *Is* it a modern office?

Who *returned* the documents?

The verbs *is* and *returned* ask questions about their subjects.

Give commands: *Send* Mr. LaRue a card.

Proofread the material carefully.

The verbs *send* and *proofread* give commands to their subjects—*you* (understood).

CHECKUP 2   Decide how the verbs are used in the following sentences. Underline each verb. Then state whether the verb is used in a statement, a request, a command, or a question.

1. The interviewer and the interviewee discussed the job requirements.
2. Who requested the Stoner file?
3. Use the elevators in the main lobby of the building.
4. People's needs fall into three categories: food, shelter, and clothing.
5. Please ask Will to see me in my office.

1. **statement** _____
2. _____
3. _____
4. _____
5. _____

THE HAVES and the HAVE-NOTS

Direct objects are receivers; they receive the action of the verb. Have you already noticed that some verbs have direct objects and others do not?

She **corrected** the **schedule**. *Schedule* is the direct object of the verb *corrected*. Corrected what? The *schedule*.

Ms. Fontaine **applauded**. No direct object. The action of the verb applauded begins and ends with the doer, Ms. Fontaine. There is no receiver.

Verbs that *have* direct objects are called *transitive verbs;* those that do *not have* direct objects are called *intransitive verbs.* The "haves" are transitive; the "have-nots" are intransitive.

CHECKUP 3

Underline the verb in each of the following sentences. Then write the direct object of the verb in the space at the right. If there is no direct object, write *have-not*.

1. Bartley retired.
2. Our auditor submitted a report.
3. Edit the proposal carefully.
4. Our hearts raced.
5. The mayor sought reelection.
6. Sue completed the schedule.
7. They practiced all night.
8. We accepted their apology.

1. **have-not** _____
2. _____
3. _____
4. _____
5. _____
6. _____
7. _____
8. _____

HELP!

Sometimes, a verb needs help. Together, a verb and its helpers make up a *verb phrase.* For example, *will be going* is a verb phrase. The main verb (always the last verb in the verb phrase) is *going;* the helpers are *will be.* Let's look at more verb phrases.

They **have written** several articles and books. *Have written* is the verb phrase. *Have* is the helper; *written* is the main verb.

She **should have been selected**. *Should have been selected* is the verb phrase. *Should have been* is the helper; *selected* is the main verb.

CHECKUP 4

Underline the helping verbs in the following sentences. Then write the *main* verbs in the spaces at the right.

1. We will have received the checks by then.
2. The secretary will take minutes of the departmental meeting.
3. The books are being displayed in the showcase in the lobby.
4. Donna will design visual aids for our presentation.
5. Several of us have been traveling during the summer.
6. They are planning a retirement party for him.
7. We could have gone to the movies last night.
8. Sam has been training the new recruits.

1. **received** _____
2. _____
3. _____
4. _____
5. _____
6. _____
7. _____
8. _____

Helpers are also called "auxiliary verbs." Here are some of the common auxiliary verbs.

be	am	is	was	were	been
did	have	has	had	may	might
will	would	are	can	could	must
do	should	shall			

EXERCISE 1   Identify the verbs in the following sentences. Write the verbs in the spaces at the right.

1. The committee members met yesterday morning.   1. _____
2. Our sales department contacts about 1,000 customers a day.   2. _____
3. Jan coordinated all the activities for her office.   3. _____
4. The sales representative demonstrated his products for us.   4. _____
5. The receptionist assisted the general manager.   5. _____
6. Please send a copy of the letter to the insurance agent.   6. _____
7. The company carpenters constructed a railing around the deck.   7. _____
8. Most of us face economic worries.   8. _____
9. Let us reconsider our decision to delay the project.   9. _____
10. Our character is a composite of our habits.   10. _____
11. I immersed myself in an in-depth study of Asian literature.   11. _____
12. We both acknowledged the problems in the company.   12. _____
13. They treated the customers with respect.   13. _____
14. Look upon the weaknesses of others with compassion.   14. _____
15. The experience taught me independence.   15. _____

EXERCISE 2   Decide how the verbs are used in the following sentences. Underline each verb. Then state whether the verb is used in a statement, a request, a command, or a question.

1. Lock the door after 5 p.m.   1. _____
2. Her department has permission to purchase its own word processing
   equipment.   2. _____
3. Who examined the merchandise?   3. _____
4. Please sell the 100 shares of stock.   4. _____
5. Where was the package?   5. _____
6. We stake our reputation on our service to customers.   6. _____
7. Provide a full explanation for your decision.   7. _____
8. Some messages combine more than one business objective.   8. _____
9. Please answer the letter within the next 48 hours.   9. _____
10. Proposal writers usually receive specific assignments.   10. _____

EXERCISE 3   Underline the verb in each sentence. If the verb *has* a direct object, write the direct object in the space at the right. If the verb *does not have* a direct object, write *have-not*.

1. They disagreed.   1. _____
2. Martha promised the results by the next day.   2. _____
3. The rock concert begins at 8 p.m. at Miller Auditorium.   3. _____
4. The clerk smiled pleasantly.   4. _____
5. Several of the employees played there yesterday.   5. _____
6. Give the paint to the workers on the second floor.   6. _____
7. He gave her a plant as a present.   7. _____
8. Joel David sold his collection of stamps.   8. _____

9. Several people called.

9. _____

10. While in Africa she bought many souvenirs.

10. _____

11. Darlene wanted a commitment to quality from her staff.

11. _____

12. The boat floated down the river.

12. _____

13. Looking out the window, we saw the visitors arriving.

13. _____

14. By his side stood the little girl.

14. _____

15. Have you finished the report yet?

15. _____

16. The company reached its campaign goal of $50,000.

16. _____

17. Bob and Lea arrived while we were gone.

17. _____

18. Please polish the brass fixtures in the lobby.

18. _____

19. They were watching the movie on television.

19. _____

20. The meeting had occurred several days ago.

20. _____

EXERCISE 4
Underline the *helping* verbs in the following sentences. Then write the *main* verbs in the spaces at the right.

1. Each concept will be highlighted in the visuals aids.

1. _____

2. The game has been played very well.

2. _____

3. Had you received my phone call?

3. _____

4. The cherry crop had been ruined by the late frost.

4. _____

5. It must have been raining when you left yesterday.

5. _____

6. Were you invited to the reception afterwards?

6. _____

7. He was merely asking for a raise.

7. _____

8. After three weeks, they were finally finished with the report.

8. _____

9. I would have gone with you to the open house.

9. _____

10. The new employees are being evaluated every three months.

10. _____

11. The plane must have been late.

11. _____

12. Norma was being interviewed for the position.

12. _____

13. Tim had studied very late last night.

13. _____

14. The managers were planning a meeting with the representatives from Globe Oil.

14. _____

15. The incidents were occurring as we watched from the second floor.

15. _____

16. The construction was completed last year.

16. _____

17. Did you receive your certificate in the mail?

17. _____

18. Our assignment had been given to us by the supervisor.

18. _____

19. We were supported by our friends in the Accounting Department.

19. _____

20. They were shown the evidence first.

20. _____

EXERCISE 5
Write two verb phrases for each of the following verbs.

1. employ _____ _____

2. start _____ _____

3. print _____ _____

4. collect _____ _____

5. be _____ _____

6. revise _____ _____

7. show _____ _____

8. work _____ _____

9. ask _____ _____

10. build _____ _____

More About Verbs

Sometimes the *helping verb* (or *auxiliary verb*) is separated from the main verb by an adverb. Do you remember from Lesson 2 what an adverb is? An *adverb* is a word that modifies a verb, an adjective, or another adverb. Adverbs tell "how," "when," and "where." Some common adverbs are:

always   soon   seldom   not   often   never   very

In the example below, you will see how adverbs sometimes separate the helping verb from the main verb. When an adverb does that, you'll always know that the main verb *follows* the adverb.

The company's annual report *is always released* in January. *Is released* is the verb phrase. *Is* is the helper; *released* is the main verb because it tells what has been done. *Remember:* The main verb is always the last word in the verb phrase. *Always* is an adverb that separates the helper *is* from the main verb *released*.

Have you *seen* our assistant? *Have seen* is the verb phrase. *Have* is the helper, *seen* is the main verb. *You* is the subject—a pronoun, not an adverb—that separates the helper from the main verb.

CHECKUP 1   Underline the verb phrases and any adverbs in the following sentences. Then write the main verbs and the adverbs in the spaces at the right.

1. Cynthia will soon become our manager.
2. The manager was seldom seen in his office.
3. Peter and I were finally given an appointment to see the doctor.
4. Mr. Grant had not been seen for several days.

1. **become, soon**
2. _____
3. _____
4. _____

PRINCIPAL PARTS OF VERBS   Verbs have four principal parts. They are the *present*, the *past*, the *past participle*, and the *present participle*. Here are the principal parts of the verb *to walk:*

Present:	walk (*to walk* is called *the infinitive*)
Past:	walked
Past participle:	walked (must always be used with a helping verb)
Present participle:	walking (must always be used with a helping verb)

These are called the *principal* parts of a verb because all other forms of the verb are determined from them. If you look in your dictionary, you'll find that it lists the principal parts for irregular verbs. An easy way to form the principal parts of verbs is to use the information you just learned. You saw that the main verb in a verb phrase is *always* the last word. For example, in the verb phrase *were typed* and *were typing*, the main verbs are *typed* and *typing* (*were* is the helper in both cases). *Typed* is the past participle of the verb *to type*, and *typing* is the present participle of the verb *to type*. Past participles are formed by adding *d* or *ed* to the verb. Present participles are formed by adding *ing* to the verb. If the verb ends in *e*, drop the *e* first and add *ing* as in *typing*.

CHECKUP 2   Underline the verb phrases in the following sentences. Then write the main verbs in the spaces at the right. Also, indicate whether the main verbs are present or past participles.

1. Samantha had responded to the call from her uncle.
2. Perry was enjoying the 90-degree weather.
3. Several of our clients were prepared to be witnesses.
4. They had been tracking the shipment for several days.
5. The employees had been discussing the state of the economy.

1. **responded, past participle**
2. _____
3. _____
4. _____
5. _____

LINKING VERBS

Some verbs join, or "link," the subject to a noun, pronoun, or adjective that follows the verb. These verbs are called *linking verbs.* Here are some common linking verbs:

1. *To be* (be, am, are, is, was, were, been, being):

> I am the general manager. (*Am* links *I* to *general manager.*)

2. *To appear:*

> He appeared tired after the long trip.

3. *To seem:*

> Thelma seems unhappy about the new policy.

4. Verbs of the senses, such as *to feel, to look, to smell, to taste, to hear:*

> It tasted too salty.

The word used to complete the meaning of the verb is a predicate noun, a predicate pronoun, or a predicate adjective. The noun or pronoun completes the meaning of a linking verb. The noun or pronoun is in the nominative case because it refers to the subject of the sentence. The predicate noun or pronoun means the same as the subject.

Sue is the secretary.   The secretary is Sue.

The secretary is she.   She is the secretary.

The adjective used after the linking verb is the predicate adjective because it completes the meaning of a linking verb. It describes the subject of the sentence.

Notice that the linking verb is never followed by an object. The linking verb does not show action. The function of the linking verb is to "link" the subject with the noun, pronoun, or adjective that follows the verb.

	SUBJECT	LINKING VERB	COMPLETER
Predicate nouns:	Mr. Hamilton	is	president.
	Ms. Armstrong	was	the director.
Predicate pronouns:	It	is	I.
	The announcers	are	they.
Predicate adjectives:	Iris	looks	beautiful.
	I	feel	bad.*

*It is incorrect to say "I feel badly"—unless your sense of touch is poor.

CHECKUP 3   Underline the predicate nouns, pronouns, or adjectives in the following sentences. Then state whether the underlined words are predicate nouns, pronouns, or adjectives in the spaces to the right.

1. Georgia's car was <u>green</u>.
2. The Browns were thrilled with their lottery winnings.
3. It was she at the door.
4. Our visitors were clients from Seattle.
5. Kathy is the new manager.
6. They seemed happy about the merger.
7. The chef's chili is spicy.
8. My law clerk is she.

1. <u>predicate adjective</u>
2. _____
3. _____
4. _____
5. _____
6. _____
7. _____
8. _____

EXERCISES

NAME _____ DATE _____ SCORE _____

EXERCISE 1   Underline the verb phrases and any adverbs in the following sentences. Then write the main verbs and the adverbs in the spaces at the right.

1. Rosa was finally determined to earn her bachelor's degree in economics.   1. _____
2. Did you really understand what he meant by that remark?   2. _____
3. The presentation was well received by the audience.   3. _____
4. The lawyers had evidently won their case.   4. _____
5. The delivery was not delayed because of traffic.   5. _____
6. The investigator had easily solved the case.   6. _____
7. We were seriously hoping that our bid would be accepted.   7. _____
8. Are you not receiving the money from the tenants?   8. _____
9. Ben and Peter will soon be graduating with honors from college.   9. _____
10. I have eagerly responded to the suggestion several times.   10. _____
11. The salesperson had quietly remarked that his commission would be $500.   11. _____
12. The manager was quickly explaining our duties before leaving the office.   12. _____
13. They were currently looking for a replacement for Mr. Sills.   13. _____
14. I had never intended to stay that long at your place.   14. _____
15. Were you often seen at the office after hours?   15. _____

EXERCISE 2   Write the principal parts of the following regular verbs in the spaces provided. You may use the dictionary to check for the correct spelling.

PRESENT (infinitive)	PAST (-d or -ed ending)	PAST PARTICIPLE (requires helper)	PRESENT PARTICIPLE (requires helper) (-ing ending)
1. create	_____	_____	_____
2. deliver	_____	_____	_____
3. install	_____	_____	_____
4. record	_____	_____	_____
5. learn	_____	_____	_____
6. accomplish	_____	_____	_____
7. examine	_____	_____	_____
8. supervise	_____	_____	_____
9. obtain	_____	_____	_____
10. train	_____	_____	_____

EXERCISE 3   Write the correct verb form for each of the verbs in parentheses. Then indicate whether the verb is a present or past participle.

1. Two of our reporters are *(cover)* the story.   1. _____
2. The computer people had *(develop)* a program for our use.   2. _____
3. The decorators had *(design)* our office for a showcase.   3. _____

4. Are you *(assemble)* the machine in the shop? 4. _____

5. The trustees are *(eliminate)* several staff positions. 5. _____

6. The investigators had *(solve)* the problem but were not reporting it. 6. _____

7. Humphrey Hardware had *(supply)* us in the past with nuts and bolts. 7. _____

8. Had the newly hired people *(perform)* well? 8. _____

9. Have you been *(consult)* very long for the American Bank? 9. _____

10. Will you be *(hire)* anyone in the next few months? 10. _____

11. Several of the employees had *(examine)* the cartons before delivering them to our office. 11. _____

12. John Sowa, our president, was *(talk)* to the auditors. 12. _____

13. The budget director had *(predict)* this successful quarter for our firm. 13. _____

14. Mr. Bandelli had *(promote)* three of his new employees. 14. _____

15. Sheila was *(direct)* the project. 15. _____

EXERCISE 4

Underline the verb phrases in the following sentences. Then write the main verbs in the spaces at the right. Also, indicate whether the main verbs are present or past participles.

1. Joanne's father was establishing a scholarship fund in honor of her mother. 1. _____

2. The store had expanded several times already. 2. _____

3. The antique furniture had been restored last year. 3. _____

4. The director was conducting a seminar on positive thinking. 4. _____

5. Members of the Garden Club were arranging the flowers for the grand opening. 5. _____

6. Jack and John were both generating sales of over $5,000 a month. 6. _____

7. Randy had managed the service station for five years. 7. _____

8. As a member of the board of reviewers, Kristen had reviewed many manuscripts. 8. _____

9. Many of them had volunteered their services to the Red Cross. 9. _____

10. We were very much interested in the voting results. 10. _____

EXERCISE 5

Underline the predicate nouns, pronouns, or adjectives in the following sentences. Then state whether the underlined words are predicate nouns, pronouns, or adjectives in the spaces to the right.

1. Robert is a master mechanic. 1. _____

2. It is he who called yesterday. 2. _____

3. She is extremely happy about the promotion. 3. _____

4. My mom was compassionate. 4. _____

5. It is they who wish to be nominated for positions on the Board of Directors. 5. _____

6. Adrienne is the chairperson of the research committee. 6. _____

7. Terry is vice president in charge of sales. 7. _____

8. Beulah was an expert seamstress. 8. _____

9. Joseph will be 25 years old this September. 9. _____

10. Howard is president of the company. 10. _____

11. Our receptionist became ill. 11. _____

12. Her dog is a Welsh corgi. 12. _____

13. The new employee seemed enthusiastic. 13. _____

14. The new research assistant was he. 14. _____

15. My neighbor is enthusiastic about team sports. 15. _____

Verb Tenses—Yesterday, Today, and Tomorrow

Verbs change their forms to show the time that something is happening, will happen, or has already happened. The time indicated is called the *tense* of a verb. Let's see how three of the tenses—*present, past,* and *future*—are formed.

TODAY—PRESENT TENSE   We use the *present* tense to show that something is happening *now*. We also use it to show that something is a habitual action, something that happens all the time.

Terry *accepts* your invitation. *Accepts* is a present tense form of the verb *to accept.* Here, the present tense indicates present action.

Kim *designs* clothes for Macy's. *Designs* is a present tense form. Here, it shows habitual action; in other words, Kim designs clothes for Macy's all the time.

Let's see the present tense forms of the verb *to move.*

I move	we move
you move	you move
he moves	they move
she moves	
it moves	

As you see, in the present tense we add an *s* when we say *he, she,* or *it moves.* Otherwise, the verb does not change.

CHECKUP 1   After each pronoun, write the correct present tense form of the given verb.

1. to play __it plays__   3. to sketch __they__
2. to teach __she__   4. to manage __he__

Beware!   Not all verbs that end in *y* will simply add an *s* in the present tense. Look at these examples:

VERB	PRESENT TENSE FORMS
to enjoy	he enjoys, she enjoys
to reply	he replies, she replies

See the vowel *o* before the *y* in *enjoy*? Since there is a vowel, just add *s.* See the consonant *l* before the *y* in *reply*? Since there is a consonant, change the *y* to *i* and then add *es.*

ACTION IN PROGRESS!   Verb phrases such as *is going* and *am typing* show present action that is *in progress.* We call these forms *present progressive tense.* The present progressive tense is always formed with a present tense helper—*am, is,* or *are* plus the present participle.

I *am being* careful. *Am being* is present progressive tense.

You *are going,* aren't you? *Are going* is present progressive tense.

She *is working* on her status report. *Is working* is present progressive tense.

They *are moving* to new quarters. *Are moving* is present progressive tense.

CHECKUP 2

After each pronoun, write the correct present progressive tense form of the given verb.

1. to print   she is printing
2. to walk   he
3. to order   they

4. to take   it
5. to analyze   you
6. to check   I

YESTERDAY—PAST TENSE

We use the *past* tense to show that something happened in the past.

They *acknowledged* our letter very promptly. *Acknowledged* is the past tense of the verb *to acknowledge*.

As you see, the past tense is formed by adding *d* or *ed* to the regular form. For verbs that end in *y*, change the *y* to *i* before you add *ed*, as in *replied, tried*, and so on.

CHECKUP 3

After each pronoun, write the past tense form of the given verb. (*Hint:* For one of the verbs, you must double the final letter before you add *ed*. Check your dictionary if you do not know for sure!)

1. to sign   he signed
2. to help   it
3. to report   we

4. to acknowledge   they
5. to transfer   she
6. to move   you

PAST ACTION IN PROGRESS!

By using the past tense helpers *was* and *were*, we can form past progressive tense forms, which show action that *was* in progress in the past. The past progressive tense is formed with a past tense helper (was or were) plus the present participle.

She *was playing* the piano while they *were reading*. *Was playing* and *were reading* show action in progress in the past; they are past progressive forms.

CHECKUP 4

After each pronoun, write the past progressive tense form of the given verb.

1. to revise   he was revising
2. to decline   it
3. to write   she

4. to review   they
5. to quote   you
6. to carry   I

TOMORROW—FUTURE TENSE

To show that something will happen in the future, we use the *future* tense. The helper *will* is used with the future tense.

They *will issue* the football tickets tomorrow at the stadium box office. *Will issue* is future tense.

CHECKUP 5

After each pronoun, write the future tense form of the given verb.

1. to print   it will print
2. to call   she
3. to edit   we

4. to announce   they
5. to visit   he
6. to work   you

FUTURE ACTION IN PROGRESS!

Yes, there is another progressive tense—future progressive tense. We use it to show action that *will be* in progress in the future. The future progressive tense is formed by using *will be* plus the present participle.

Tomorrow he *will be demonstrating* the new computer at the exhibit. *Will be demonstrating* shows action that will be in progress tomorrow; it is future progressive tense.

CHECKUP 6

After each pronoun, write the future progressive tense form of the given verb.

1. to confirm   you will be confirming
2. to clean   he
3. to speak   I

4. to taste   we
5. to hire   she
6. to cut   they

EXERCISES

EXERCISE 1   Underline the verb in each of the following sentences. Then in the space at the right, write *past, present,* or *future* for each verb. (*Hint:* A sentence may have more than one verb.)

1. Long reports usually begin with conclusions and recommendations.   1. _____
2. The letter focused on the progress of the new building.   2. _____
3. Will he go to the Career Fair at the Student Center?   3. _____
4. They will present him with a gift at his retirement party next week.   4. _____
5. Edward remembered the talk show host from his high school days.   5. _____
6. I hear congratulations are in order for Tim Saunders.   6. _____
7. They are two people who really listen to you.   7. _____
8. The speaker posed a hypothetical question to the audience.   8. _____
9. I will call the office every other day.   9. _____
10. I assured him that the address was correct.   10. _____

EXERCISE 2   For each verb in parentheses, write the form that shows *present* time.

1. The commission *(decide)* the issue today.   1. _____
2. You can *(sail)* away on the ship of your choice.   2. _____
3. He *(call)* the office every day when he is out of town.   3. _____
4. The FDA *(advise)* patients not to use that particular drug.   4. _____
5. He *(respond)* to his official mail promptly.   5. _____
6. She *(recommend)* that we have a one-page résumé.   6. _____
7. Ms. Tooley *(listen)* to what we have to say.   7. _____
8. Dad *(understand)* the meaning of the word *work*.   8. _____
9. Edward Brothers *(own)* several stores in Boston.   9. _____
10. That particular account *(earn)* 12 percent interest.   10. _____

EXERCISE 3   For each verb in parentheses, write the form that shows *present progressive* time.

1. James *(consult)* for a high-tech company in Riverdale.   1. _____
2. Gerald *(inspect)* the meat at the food supply warehouse.   2. _____
3. They *(take)* a long time to process my application.   3. _____
4. Her staff calls in from all parts of the country when they *(work)* in the field.   4. _____
5. The engineer *(write)* her report concerning the construction delays.   5. _____

EXERCISE 4   For each verb in parentheses, write the form that shows *past* time.

1. They immediately *(jump)* into the Pacific Ocean to swim.   1. _____
2. The Harrisons *(move)* to California about three years ago.   2. _____
3. I *(close)* the front door because of the draft.   3. _____
4. Several of them *(suggest)* going out for a sandwich.   4. _____
5. The attorney had *(conduct)* a jury selection for the case.   5. _____

6. Verna had *(complete)* the work in record time.   6. _____

7. The classrooms *(describe)* in the report are well-furnished.   7. _____

8. The opponents of the free-trade pact have *(embrace)* the concerns of environmental groups.   8. _____

9. A team of architects and planners have *(reinvent)* the suburb.   9. _____

10. One of his guests *(question)* him about his politics.   10. _____

EXERCISE 5   For each verb in parentheses, write the form that shows *past progressive* time.

1. The author *(direct)* most of his compliments to his colleagues.   1. _____

2. They *(talk)* about the conditions of the plant.   2. _____

3. He *(suggest)* that you take the week off for a well-deserved vacation.   3. _____

4. The participants *(note)* the irony in his talk.   4. _____

5. The meteorologist *(predict)* a mild winter.   5. _____

6. They *(plan)* their vacation carefully since they had limited funds.   6. _____

7. Jerry *(design)* the sets for the Drama Club's production.   7. _____

8. Roger *(order)* dinner when the last guests arrived.   8. _____

9. A group of volunteers *(form)* to organize the food drive.   9. _____

10. The argument *(happen)* in the next room.   10. _____

EXERCISE 6   For each verb in parentheses, write the form that shows *future* time.

1. I *(give)* the directions to the cabdriver.   1. _____

2. Genetics *(play)* a strong role in your future.   2. _____

3. He *(drink)* about eight glasses of water a day on his new diet.   3. _____

4. None of us *(go)* to the concert tonight because of exams.   4. _____

5. Before the end of the day, we *(collect)* enough samples for our survey.   5. _____

6. Ms. Tillman, the head accountant, *(visit)* us this afternoon.   6. _____

7. To prepare the report, you *(need)* last month's sales figures.   7. _____

8. Next Friday we *(meet)* to discuss our plans for the move to Chicago.   8. _____

9. Tomorrow we *(propose)* another solution.   9. _____

10. Mr. Quittle *(help)* you write the proposal.   10. _____

11. They *(prepare)* another version of the product.   11. _____

12. George and I *(offer)* several alternatives.   12. _____

EXERCISE 7   For each verb in parentheses, write the form that shows *future progressive* time.

1. Several of the students *(apply)* for the one position.   1. _____

2. We *(outline)* several chapters for the new book on leadership.   2. _____

3. I hope the managers *(approve)* our plans at the meeting so that we can move ahead.   3. _____

4. We *(reply)* to your letter within the week.   4. _____

5. The real estate agent *(show)* the house this afternoon.   5. _____

6. The product manager *(speak)* at the stockholders' meeting next week.   6. _____

7. Jennifer Nunoz *(delay)* her trip if the storm continues.   7. _____

8. Bob and Tom *(organize)* the tailgate picnic on Saturday.   8. _____

9. We *(review)* the applications next week.   9. _____

10. They *(plan)* the banquet for the first week in December.   10. _____

11. Our supervisor *(move)* to the Detroit office.   11. _____

12. Clara *(travel)* to Spain next year.   12. _____

The Regulars and the Irregulars

Some verbs are called "irregular" because they do not form their tenses in a "regular" way. Since these are the verbs that will cause you the most trouble, take the time now to carefully study the chart on this page—then study it again! As you will see, the verbs in this chart are indeed "irregular."

Say each set of verbs to yourself: for example, "begin, began, begun." Then use each with the proper pronouns. Say the present tense forms: "I begin, you begin, he begins, we begin, you begin, they begin." Say the past tense forms: "I began, you began, she began," and so on. Then use the past participle: "I have begun, you have begun, she has begun," and so on. *Remember:* The past tense *never* has a helper. The past participle *always* has a helper (have, has, had).

PRINCIPAL PARTS OF VERBS

PRESENT	PAST	PAST PARTICIPLE	PRESENT	PAST	PAST PARTICIPLE
am	was	been	fight	fought	fought
arise	arose	arisen	fit	fitted, fit	fitted, fit
awake	awoke, awaked	awaked, awoken	flee	fled	fled
beat	beat	beat, beaten	fling	flung	flung
begin	began	begun	fly	flew	flown
bend	bent	bent	forget	forgot	forgotten
bid (to offer)	bid	bid	freeze	froze	frozen
bind	bound	bound	get	got	gotten
bite	bit	bitten	give	gave	given
blow	blew	blown	go	went	gone
break	broke	broken	grow	grew	grown
bring	brought	brought	hang	hung	hung
burst	burst	burst	hang (to put to death)	hanged	hanged
buy	bought	bought	hear	heard	heard
catch	caught	caught	hide	hid	hidden
choose	chose	chosen	hold	held	held
climb*	climbed	climbed	keep	kept	kept
cling	clung	clung	know	knew	known
come	came	come	lay	laid	laid
deal	dealt	dealt	leave	left	left
dive	dived, dove	dived	lend	lent	lent
do	did	done	lie	lay	lain
drag*	dragged	dragged	lose	lost	lost
draw	drew	drawn	meet	met	met
dream	dreamed, dreamt	dreamed, dreamt	pay	paid	paid
drink	drank	drunk	read	read	read
drive	drove	driven	ride	rode	ridden
drown*	drowned	drowned	ring	rang	rung
eat	ate	eaten	rise	rose	risen
fall	fell	fallen	run	ran	run

PRESENT	PAST	PAST PARTICIPLE	PRESENT	PAST	PAST PARTICIPLE
say	said	said	strike	struck	struck
see	saw	seen	swear	swore	sworn
set	set	set	swim	swam	swum
shake	shook	shaken	swing	swung	swung
shine†	shone	shone	take	took	taken
show	showed	showed, shown	teach	taught	taught
shrink	shrank	shrunk	tear	tore	torn
sing	sang	sung	tell	told	told
sink	sank, sunk	sunk	think	thought	thought
sit	sat	sat	throw	threw	thrown
speak	spoke	spoken	wake	waked, woke	waked, woken, woke
spring	sprang	sprung	wear	wore	worn
stand	stood	stood	wring	wrung	wrung
steal	stole	stolen	write	wrote	written

*These are regular verbs, but wrong forms are often used in the past tense and the past participle.

†When *shine* means "to polish," the parts are *shine, shined, shined.*

CHECKUP 1

How well do you know the irregulars? In the space at the right, write the past tense of each verb given in parentheses. Check your answers to make sure they are correct.

1. We *(begin)* the meeting nearly two hours late.
2. The doorknob *(break)* when I touched it.
3. The wildflowers *(blow)* in the breeze.
4. They *(hide)* the Easter eggs in the bushes.
5. The witness *(think)* about his testimony before he answered the judge's question.
6. Are you sure you *(meet)* them before today?

1. **began**
2. _____
3. _____
4. _____
5. _____
6. _____

CHECKUP 2

Now write the past participle of each verb given in parentheses. Note that there is a helper before each past participle.

1. We had *(write)* several times before we received an answer to our letter.
2. I had *(teach)* high school English for several years.
3. He had *(pay)* for his purchases with cash.
4. Arlene had *(say)* earlier that she wanted to go to the fair.
5. The car had *(run)* out of gas before we reached the service station.
6. The little boys had *(sit)* patiently waiting for their mother.

1. **written**
2. _____
3. _____
4. _____
5. _____
6. _____

CHECKUP 3

Underline any incorrect use of verbs in the following sentences. Then write your corrections in the spaces at the right.

1. The children <u>sing</u> in the church choir yesterday.
2. Mark <u>ride</u> his bike to the ballpark.
3. To everyone's surprise, that small child <u>swim</u> the entire length of the pool.
4. Fortunately, no exchange <u>take</u> place in the market.
5. Jeffrey <u>ring</u> the doorbell at his aunt's house.
6. Jayne <u>choose</u> a biography for her report.

1. **sang or had sung**
2. _____
3. _____
4. _____
5. _____
6. _____

EXERCISES

NAME _____ DATE _____ SCORE _____

EXERCISE 1   In the spaces at the right, write the past tense of each verb given in parentheses.

1. I *(drive)* to Colorado last weekend for a ski trip.   1. _____
2. *(Do)* you see any famous movie stars when you were in Hollywood?   2. _____
3. As Wanda was running down the hall, she *(fall)*.   3. _____
4. The audience *(give)* her a standing ovation.   4. _____
5. We *(flee)* indoors when we heard the thunder.   5. _____
6. He swore that he *(keep)* it a secret from the others.   6. _____
7. After the washer broke, she *(wring)* the clothes by hand.   7. _____
8. Dad said he *(pay)* the ticket agent.   8. _____
9. The picture was so great that I *(show)* it to my friends.   9. _____
10. His performance *(steal)* the show.   10. _____
11. I just *(see)* her yesterday at the theater.   11. _____
12. As soon as Burt was called, he *(come)* to the office.   12. _____
13. Marie's mother never *(think)* her daughter would become a doctor. 13. _____
14. After months of not receiving payment, we *(hire)* a lawyer.   14. _____
15. They *(forget)* to set their clocks ahead and were late for class. 15. _____
16. The children *(draw)* pictures of their favorite animals.   16. _____
17. Marcy believed she *(lose)* her wallet in the parking garage.   17. _____
18. After working 12 hours, he *(leave)* for home.   18. _____
19. Hank *(lay)* the book on the counter.   19. _____
20. We all *(rise)* when the faculty members entered the room.   20. _____

EXERCISE 2   In the spaces at the right, write the past participle of each verb given in parentheses. **Note that** there is a helper for each past participle.

1. The work was *(do)* by noon.   1. _____
2. The trees had *(grow)* tall in the five years since they had planted them. 2. _____
3. Our parents had *(eat)* dinner by the time we arrived home.   3. _____
4. They had *(give)* away their outgrown clothes.   4. _____
5. The play had *(begin)* about an hour ago.   5. _____
6. I think she had *(bite)* off more than she could chew.   6. _____
7. The couple had *(met)* several years earlier.   7. _____
8. The men had *(fight)* against the ruling.   8. _____
9. The student had *(see)* her grades before the teacher posted them. 9. _____
10. Are you sure you have *(wear)* this dress before?   10. _____
11. I have *(stand)* in that spot before.   11. _____
12. Jessica did not remember how she had *(tear)* the fabric.   12. _____
13. Brenda had *(take)* the contracts to the lawyer herself.   13. _____
14. My mother had *(teach)* me how to spell before I entered school. 14. _____
15. We had *(say)* before that they could do it.   15. _____
16. Had you *(know)* about the staff changes?   16. _____
17. Sam had *(keep)* a complete record of his time and expenses.   17. _____
18. The temperature had *(fall)* drastically before the storm.   18. _____

EXERCISE 3   Underline any incorrect use of irregular verbs in the following sentences. Then write your corrections in the spaces at the right.

1. Several people have fell on the wet cement.
2. Has Jamie already went to the airport?
3. The professor has gave me all the assignments I care to do.
4. The meeting had began by the time we arrived.
5. Yes, we had came earlier, but no one was here yet.
6. The furniture that he has chose will be just fine for the living room.
7. Didn't you knew about the meeting this afternoon?
8. I think we should have wrote to our cousins saying we would be arriving at noon.
9. Most of us had keep the ticket stubs as souvenirs.
10. After working late, Todd had went to sleep.
11. Richard leave the garage door open all night.
12. No, I had not see that article in the journal.
13. The carpenters had took the tools from the van.
14. Our stockbroker buy 200 shares of Anytime Telephone stock for us.
15. The supervisors flied first class when they traveled to Europe.
16. Dave drive to the airport to meet the clients.
17. Did Mrs. Harrison knew about the promotions?
18. I wake several minutes before the alarm.
19. She draw a sketch of the lake.
20. Our parents had bring us souvenirs.

1. _____
2. _____
3. _____
4. _____
5. _____
6. _____
7. _____

8. _____
9. _____
10. _____
11. _____
12. _____
13. _____
14. _____
15. _____
16. _____
17. _____
18. _____
19. _____
20. _____

EXERCISE 4   Underline any incorrect use of irregular verbs in the following sentences. Then write your corrections in the spaces at the right. If a sentence is correct, write OK.

1. The toy boats were sink by the children.
2. The books will be purchased when the library is complete.
3. Have you not wrote to your brother yet?
4. Fortunately I had pay most of my bills before running short of money.
5. I am in the store yesterday buying groceries.
6. Have you ate your vegetables?
7. Yes, I hanged the pictures in our den as you suggested.
8. Have you driven across the country yet?
9. Where have you hidden the chocolates?
10. We had forgot to lock the doors before we left.
11. I dream last night that I was the scholarship recipient.
12. The children were teach how to swim at an early age.
13. Were you tell how to work that machine?
14. Finally, our division took first place in the contest.
15. Both of the executives were flied to headquarters on the corporate jet.
16. Our department took first place in the public relations contest.
17. They taked extra food with them for the hike through Acadia National Park.
18. We had already see the movie.
19. After completing the essay, she leaved.
20. I seen the revised proposal.

1. _____
2. _____
3. _____
4. _____
5. _____
6. _____
7. _____
8. _____
9. _____
10. _____
11. _____
12. _____
13. _____
14. _____
15. _____
16. _____

17. _____
18. _____
19. _____
20. _____

To Be and To Have

To be and *to have* are two of the most used verbs in the English language. Since you will be using *to be* and *to have* so much, you should make sure you know their tenses.

TODAY—PRESENT TENSE   Remember that we use the *present* tense to show that something is happening *now*. We also use it to show a habitual action, an action that happens all the time.

The present tenses of the verbs *to be* and *to have* are unique—they are both irregular. The present tense of *to be* has three forms: *am, are,* and *is*. The present tense of *to have* has two forms: *has* and *have*.

(TO BE) PRESENT TENSE		(TO HAVE) PRESENT TENSE	
I *am*	we *are*	I *have*	we *have*
you *are*	you *are*	you *have*	you *have*
he, she, it *is*	they *are*	he, she, it *has*	they *have*

I *am* on my way to the store.

Sue *is* a good worker.

He *has* many books.

I *have* the survey results.

Action in Progress!   Sometimes the verbs *to be* and *to have* can be used to show action *in progress*. As you learned in Lesson 17, verbs showing action in progress are in the *present progressive tense*. The present progressive tense is always formed with a present tense helper—*am, is,* or *are*. Here's how the verbs *to be* and *to have* are used in the present progressive tense.

(TO BE) PRESENT PROGRESSIVE TENSE		(TO HAVE) PRESENT PROGRESSIVE TENSE	
I *am being*	we *are being*	I *am having*	we *are having*
you *are being*	you *are being*	you *are having*	you *are having*
he, she, it *is being*	they *are being*	he, she, it *is having*	they *are having*

Each payment *is being* verified.

Carrie *is having* a good time.

CHECKUP 1   For each item below, write the correct present progressive tense of the verb in parentheses.

1. this child (to be)   **is being** _____
2. Dr. Huff's helper (to be) _____
3. they (to be)   _____
4. the brokers (to have) _____
5. I (to have) _____
6. your assistant (to have) _____

YESTERDAY—PAST TENSE   You probably remember that the *past tense* of a verb shows that something has happened in the past. Here's how to form the past tense of the verbs *to be* and *to have*.

(TO BE) PAST TENSE		(TO HAVE) PAST TENSE	
I *was*	we *were*	I *had*	we *had*
you *were*	you *were*	you *had*	you *had*
he, she, it *was*	they *were*	he, she, it *had*	they *had*

I *was* on my way home when you called.

The project director *had* nothing but praise for the design.

Notice that the verb *to be* has only two forms in the past tense: *was* and *were.* The verb *to have* has only one form in the past tense: *had.* See how easy it is to use *to be* and *to have* in the past tense!

Past Action in Progress!   By using the past tense helpers *was* and *were,* we can form past progressive tense forms. *Past progressive tense* forms show action that *was* in progress in the past. Here's how the verbs *to be* and *to have* are used in the past progressive tense.

(TO BE) PAST PROGRESSIVE TENSE		(TO HAVE) PAST PROGRESSIVE TENSE	
I *was being*	we *were being*	I *was having*	we *were having*
you *were being*	you *were being*	you *were having*	you *were having*
he, she, it *was being*	they *were being*	he, she, it *was having*	they *were having*

My supervisor and I *were being* cautious in our optimism.

The committee *was having* a meeting this afternoon.

CHECKUP 2   After each of the following words, write the correct past progressive tense form of the verb in parentheses.

1. the woman (to be) __was being__

2. our carriers (to be) _____

3. I (to be) _____

4. the group (to have) _____

5. the members (to have) _____

6. you (to have) _____

TOMORROW—FUTURE TENSE   To show that something will happen in the future, we use the *future tense.* The helper *will* is used with the future tense. Here's how the verbs *to be* and *to have* are used in the future tense.

(TO BE) FUTURE TENSE		(TO HAVE) FUTURE TENSE	
I *will be*	we *will be*	I *will have*	we *will have*
you *will be*	you *will be*	you *will have*	you *will have*
he, she, it *will be*	they *will be*	he, she, it *will have*	they *will have*

She and he *will be* delighted to meet with you next week.

I *will have* to make arrangements for the presentation.

What do you notice about the future tense of the verbs *to be* and *to have? Each verb has only one form!* Thus it is easy to form the future tense of the verbs *to be* and *to have.*

Future Action in Progress!   Remember one more thing about tenses from your study of Lesson 17. There is another progressive tense—the *future progressive tense.* We use it to show action that *will be* in progress in the future. We use the helper *will be* to form the future progressive tense. Here's the future progressive tense of the verb *to have.*

(TO HAVE) FUTURE PROGRESSIVE TENSE	
I *will be having*	we *will be having*
you *will be having*	you *will be having*
he, she, it *will be having*	they *will be having*

The plumbers *will be having* to work late tonight.

You *will be having* a review after three months.

We *will be having* a discussion about the new policy.

EXERCISES

NAME _____ DATE _____ SCORE _____

EXERCISE 1   Underline the entire form of the verb *to be* in each of the following sentences. Then write the entire form of the verb *to be* in the space at the right. (*Hint:* A sentence may have more than one verb.)

1. Andrew is the best one for the job.   1. _____ 6 _____
2. Many of your suggestions were helpful to me.   2. _____ 142 _____
3. All the posted grades were fair.   3. _____ 899 _____
4. You are sure that the light was on when you left.   4. _____
5. Charlie was being optimistic about the award.   5. _____
6. The guests will be here any minute.   6. _____
7. The designers were hopeful about winning the contract.   7. _____
8. Our clients were being enthusiastic about the changes.   8. _____
9. All of us will be happy with the new contract.   9. _____
10. I am pleased with the results.   10. _____

EXERCISE 2   Select and underline the correct form of the verb *to be* in parentheses. Then write it in the space at the right.

1. I *(am, are)* most happy with the color you chose.   1. _Photocopy all_
2. Our renters *(is being, are being)* quiet this evening.   2. _then._
3. We *(was, were)* thrilled with the results of the voting.   3. _think_
4. The election returns *(was, will be)* announced before 11 p.m.   4. _know_
5. Willie *(is, are)* sure that he'll be elected president.   5. _them._
6. The technicians *(were, will be)* pleased about the proposal.   6. _____
7. He *(was, were)* grateful for all the attention he received.   7. _____
8. Applications *(is being, are being)* accepted this week.   8. _____
9. The artist *(was, will be)* here sometime this afternoon.   9. _____
10. The employees *(is, are)* ready to sign the contract.   10. _____

EXERCISE 3   Replace the question mark in each sentence with the correct present tense form of the verb *to be*. Write your answer in the space at the right.

1. I (?) surprised to hear you say that.   1. _____
2. You (?) ready to assume responsibility as chairperson.   2. _____
3. Seth (?) eager to learn how to use the computer.   3. _____

Now replace the question mark in each sentence with the correct past tense form of the verb *to be*.

4. You and he (?) adamant about the changes, weren't you?   4. _____
5. Denise (?) concerned about the move to Delaware.   5. _____
6. We (?) sure you would agree with us.   6. _____

Now replace the question mark in each sentence with the correct future tense form of the verb *to be*.

7. Donna and Jim (?) happy with their new addition to the house.   7. _____
8. Are you sure we (?) out of town when you return?   8. _____
9. The manager (?) available for conferences after 2 p.m.   9. _____

EXERCISE 4   Underline the entire form of the verb *to have* in each of the following sentences. Then write the entire form of the verb *to have* in the space at the right. (*Hint:* A sentence may have more than one verb.)

1. She has several autographed copies of the star's picture.   1. _____
2. The classes of 1980 and 1985 were having high school reunions.   2. _____
3. The balcony will have garlands of flowers around it.   3. _____
4. The Klammers are having a fiftieth anniversary celebration on June 16.   4. _____
5. We will be having our open house during the summer.   5. _____
6. Do you have a copy of the brochure that I had yesterday?   6. _____
7. I certainly had time to review the materials.   7. _____
8. Each of the employees was having a good time at the party.   8. _____
9. Chris is having to move to a two-bedroom apartment.   9. _____
10. She will have a new neighbor in about two weeks.   10. _____

EXERCISE 5   Select and underline the correct form of the verb *to have* in parentheses. Then write it in the space at the right.

1. Many of us *(is having, are having)* to change our vacation plans.   1. _____
2. It *(has, have)* rained for five days now.   2. _____
3. I *(has, had)* a hat the same color as that one.   3. _____
4. Meredith *(is having, are having)* fun playing with the new puppy.   4. _____
5. Our parents *(will has, will have)* an anniversary to celebrate on Sunday.   5. _____
6. I *(am having, are having)* an open house for the Wilsons next month.   6. _____
7. She *(was having, were having)* to work nights to pay for her tuition.   7. _____
8. I *(has, have)* several phone calls to make before leaving the office.   8. _____
9. My friends and I *(am having, are having)* to reschedule the bowling tournament.   9. _____
10. We *(has, had)* several people inquire about the property.   10. _____

EXERCISE 6   Replace the question mark in each sentence with the correct present tense form of the verb *to have*. Write your answer in the space at the right.

1. Our department head (?) several interviews this afternoon.   1. _____
2. I (?) many requests for a tour of the Fetzer Development Center.   2. _____
3. Doralee (?) several assistants to help her.   3. _____

Now replace the question mark in each sentence with the correct past tense form of the verb *to have*.

4. Where (?) all the markers gone?   4. _____
5. The host family (?) two French students staying at their home.   5. _____
6. Because of the election, we (?) to postpone our trip.   6. _____

Now replace the question mark in each sentence with the correct future tense form of the verb *to have*.

7. Members of the family (?) to share rooms when the relatives arrive.   7. _____
8. My assistants and I (?) new offices next fall.   8. _____
9. The auditor's report (?) to be duplicated for the partners.   9. _____
10. Our vacation plans (?) to be changed because of the weather.   10. _____
11. They (?) to report the problems to the supervisor.   11. _____
12. Sharon and her cousins (?) a good time at the reunion.   12. _____

To Do and To Go

To do and *to go*—like *to be* and *to have*—are troublesome but commonly used irregular verbs. The best way to familiarize yourself with *to do* and *to go* is to look at their tenses.

TODAY—PRESENT TENSE   Remember from Lesson 17 that we use the *present tense* to show that something is happening *now*. We also use it to show that something is a habitual action, something that happens all the time.

The present tense of *to do* has two forms: *do* and *does*. The present tense of *to go* has two forms: *go* and *goes*.

(TO DO) PRESENT TENSE		(TO GO) PRESENT TENSE	
I *do*	we *do*	I *go*	we *go*
you *do*	you *do*	you *go*	you *go*
he, she, it *does*	they *do*	he, she, it *goes*	they *go*

He *goes* to the bank early.   I *do* all my sewing by hand.

Action in Progress!   Sometimes the verbs *to do* and *to go* can be used to show *action in progress*. Verbs showing action in progress are in the *present progressive tense*. The present progressive is always formed with a present tense helper—*am, is,* or *are*.

(TO DO) PRESENT PROGRESSIVE TENSE		(TO GO) PRESENT PROGRESSIVE TENSE	
I *am doing*	we *are doing*	I *am going*	we *are going*
you *are doing*	you *are doing*	you *are going*	you *are going*
he, she, it *is doing*	they *are doing*	he, she, it *is going*	they *are going*

I *am doing* the best job I can.   They *are going* to the convention in Seattle.

CHECKUP 1   After each of the following words, write the correct present progressive tense of the verb in parentheses.

1. employee (to do) __is doing_____
2. I (to do) _____
3. assistants (to do) _____

4. this project (to go) _____
5. neighbors (to go) _____
6. friends (to go) _____

YESTERDAY—PAST TENSE   You probably remember that the past tense of a verb shows that something has happened in the past. Here's how to form the past tense of the verbs *to do* and *to go*. Notice that the verbs *to do* and *to go* have only one form in the past tense.

(TO DO) PAST TENSE		(TO GO) PAST TENSE	
I *did*	we *did*	I *went*	we *went*
you *did*	you *did*	you *went*	you *went*
he, she, it *did*	they *did*	he, she, it *went*	they *went*

Her group *did* an excellent job.   Ann *went* for a consultation.

Past Action in Progress!   By using the past tense helpers *was* and *were*, we can form past progressive tense forms. *Past progressive tense* forms show action that *was* in progress in the past. Here's how the verbs *to do* and *to go* are used in the past progressive tense.

(TO DO) PAST PROGRESSIVE TENSE		(TO GO) PAST PROGRESSIVE TENSE	
I *was doing*	we *were doing*	I *was going*	we *were going*
you *were doing*	you *were doing*	you *were going*	you *were going*
he, she, it *was doing*	they *were doing*	he, she, it *was going*	they *were going*

Barbara *was doing* her exercises at 9 o'clock last night.

Four of them *were going* to the training session.

CHECKUP 2   After each of the following words, write the correct past progressive tense form of the verb in parentheses.

1. our client (to do)   **was doing**
2. the students (to do) _____
3. workers (to do) _____
4. Bill and I (to do) _____
5. they (to do) _____

6. both of them (to go) _____
7. one of them (to go) _____
8. Mark (to go) _____
9. the team (to go) _____
10. your son (to go) _____

TOMORROW—FUTURE TENSE   To show that something will happen in the future, we use the *future tense*. The helper *will* is used with the future tense. Here's how to form the future tense of the verbs *to do* and *to go*. Notice that the future tense of the verbs *to do* and *to go* has only one form!

(TO DO) FUTURE TENSE		(TO GO) FUTURE TENSE	
I *will do*	we *will do*	I *will go*	we *will go*
you *will do*	you *will do*	you *will go*	you *will go*
he, she, it *will do*	they *will do*	he, she, it *will go*	they *will go*

Our nontechnical employees *will do* the preliminary checking.

The proposal *will go* to all our managers for review.

Future Action in Progress!   The *future progressive tense* is used to show action that *will be* in progress in the future. Here's how to form the future progressive tense of the verbs *to do* and *to go*.

(TO DO) FUTURE PROGRESSIVE TENSE		(TO GO) FUTURE PROGRESSIVE TENSE	
I *will be doing*	we *will be doing*	I *will be going*	we *will be going*
you *will be doing*	you *will be doing*	you *will be going*	you *will be going*
he, she, it *will be doing*	they *will be doing*	he, she, it *will be going*	they *will be going*

Martha's staff *will be doing* the original analysis this November.

The dispatchers *will be going* to their stations early for the next few weeks.

CHECKUP 3   After each of the following words, write the correct future progressive tense of the verb in parentheses.

1. the doctor (to do)   **will be doing**
2. the committee (to do) _____
3. you and she (to do) _____
4. he and Janet (to do) _____
5. our company (to do) _____

6. Alice (to go) _____
7. managers (to go) _____
8. they (to go) _____
9. our family (to go) _____
10. our officer (to go) _____

EXERCISE 1   Underline the entire form of the verb *to do* in each of the following sentences. Then write the entire form of the verb *to do* in the space at the right.

1. What is he doing in the lab?   1. _____
2. The clerks are doing work on the computers.   2. _____
3. I was doing all the work by hand.   3. _____
4. What were you doing when we interrupted you?   4. _____
5. Dad will be doing the laundry when he returns.   5. _____
6. They did the screening after hours.   6. _____
7. The assistants do most of the library research.   7. _____
8. Cybil does the reconciling of the bank statements.   8. _____
9. I will do the work if you want me to.   9. _____
10. They did most of the mowing with the electric mower. 10. _____

EXERCISE 2   Select and underline the correct form of the verb *to do* in parentheses, and write it in the space at the right.

1. The assistant manager *(am doing, is doing)* the preliminary screening of applicants.   1. _____
2. The research team *(was doing, were doing)* the experiments in the lab.   2. _____
3. They *(do, does)* that kind of training in the Learning Center.   3. _____
4. Several of them *(did, had did)* their graduate work at Notre Dame.   4. _____
5. You representatives *(will do, will had do)* a lot for the image of the company.   5. _____
6. The editing department *(will being doing, will be doing)* all the corrections for us.   6. _____
7. The new recruits *(is doing, are doing)* a wonderful job.   7. _____
8. Rita *(do, does)* most of her calling in the mornings when people are likely to be in.   8. _____
9. He *(did, had did)* the work quickly and correctly.   9. _____
10. What you *(was doing, were doing)* was right.   10. _____

EXERCISE 3   Replace the question mark in each sentence with the correct present tense form of the verb *to do*. Write your answer in the space at the right.

1. Marcella (?) work very hard.   1. _____
2. You always (?) the best job for us.   2. _____

Now replace the question mark with the correct past tense form of the verb *to do*.

3. We (?) the printing on colored paper.   3. _____
4. The professor (?) a thorough job of teaching a complex subject.   4. _____

Now replace the question mark with the correct future tense form of the verb *to do*.

5. That room (?) nicely for our meeting.   5. _____
6. We (?) the next survey sometime this spring.   6. _____

EXERCISE 4

Underline the entire form of the verb *to go* in each of the following sentences. Then write the entire form of the verb *to go* in the space at the right.

1. The first-year residents are going through some tough times right now.   1. _____
2. Jack is going on an expedition to Antarctica this December.   2. _____
3. She was going to the library that evening.   3. _____
4. Many of us were going to see the new film at the Prince Theater.   4. _____
5. Will you be going to town this afternoon?   5. _____
6. I am going to hear Dr. Segal's talk on stress management.   6. _____
7. Please go to the research lab to pick up the samples.   7. _____
8. She goes to the office every other day now.   8. _____
9. I will go there after the meeting.   9. _____
10. Nancy did go to see the doctor about her arm.   10. _____

EXERCISE 5

Underline the correct form of the verb *to go* from each pair in parentheses, and write it in the space at the right.

1. Rita *(am going, is going)* to Antioch College in Yellow Springs.   1. _____
2. Raymond *(was going, were going)* to post the notices on the telephone poles.   2. _____
3. They *(go, goes)* every Saturday to see her family.   3. _____
4. The coordinator *(gone, went)* to supervise the student teachers.   4. _____
5. We *(will go, will had go)* to the plant tomorrow morning.   5. _____
6. They *(will being going, will be going)* on the next plane.   6. _____
7. Paul *(is going, are going)* to visit our office in the South.   7. _____
8. If she *(go, goes)*, will you go also?   8. _____
9. Many of us *(went, had go)* to the open house.   9. _____
10. All of us *(was going, were going)* on the retreat in South Haven.   10. _____

EXERCISE 6

Replace the question mark in each sentence with the correct present tense form of the verb *to go*. Write your answer in the space at the right.

1. Every Friday we (?) to the supermarket to stock up for the weekend.   1. _____
2. That letter (?) on Mr. Haden's desk.   2. _____
3. We (?) to the post office every morning to pick up the mail.   3. _____

Now replace the question mark with the correct past tense form of the verb *to go*.

4. Walter (?) to Springfield to visit his cousin.   4. _____
5. Many of us (?) to the program out of curiosity.   5. _____
6. We (?) over the totals a second time to search for the error.   6. _____

Now replace the question mark with the correct future tense form of the verb *to go*.

7. We (?) if you think it would be best for us to do so.   7. _____
8. Betty (?) to Adams Manufacturing for an interview.   8. _____
9. Surely you (?) to Hong Kong to attend the conference, won't you?   9. _____
10. They (?) to the sales conference in October.   10. _____

Just *Perfect!*
The Perfect Tenses

THE PRESENT PERFECT TENSE   Notice how the following sentences show action that began in the past but continues into the present:

He *has estimated* sales figures for several years. And he *still* estimates sales figures! This action—estimating sales figures—began quite a while ago, but it isn't over yet. *Has estimated* is present perfect tense.

We *have received* requests for additional copies of our poster. Here is another action that began in the past and continues into the present. *Have received* is present perfect tense.

Have you noticed that the helper *has* or *have* is always used with the past participle of the main verb? Be sure that you use *has* and *have* correctly. *Remember:*

I *have*	we *have*
you *have*	you *have*
he, she, or it *has*	they *have*

CHECKUP 1   After each pronoun, write the present perfect tense of the given verb.

1. to design   **we have designed**
2. to supervise   **he** _____
3. to agree   **I** _____
4. to increase   **you** _____
5. to print   **she** _____
6. to request   **they** _____

Now underline the present perfect tense verb in each of the following sentences. Then write each verb phrase in the space at the right.

7. Jackie has provided nutritious meals for the camping trip this weekend.   7. _____
8. They have recommended five of us for the outstanding teaching award.   8. _____
9. The group has prepared its final report.   9. _____
10. The creative engineer has designed a tool that we can use.   10. _____
11. Management has agreed to all the terms in the new contract.   11. _____
12. The caterer has requested the final guest list.   12. _____

THE PAST PERFECT TENSE   In the following sentence, is it clear which action occurred first?

Kathleen *wanted to speak* to Ms. Jaeger, but Ms. Jaeger *had* already *left* for the day. Yes, it is clear: Ms. Jaeger left for the day *before* Kathleen wanted to speak to her. Both actions occurred in the past, but the phrase *had left* shows which happened first. *Had left* is an example of past perfect tense.

Ed *stopped* by for the contract, but Carol *had mailed* it to him already. *Had mailed* is past perfect tense; it shows what happened before Ed stopped by. *Stopped* is simply past tense, of course.

As you see, past perfect tense is always formed with the helper *had* and the past participle of the main verb: he *had explained,* she *had demanded,* we *had examined,* and so on.

CHECKUP 2 — After each pronoun, write the past perfect tense of the given verb.

1. to build **she had built** _____
2. to audit **he** _____

3. to suggest **they** _____
4. to identify **we** _____

Now underline the past perfect tense verb in each of the following sentences. Then write each verb phrase in the space at the right.

5. Sylvia and Kyle had completed the manuscript before their deadline. 5. _____
6. Before he left for Asia, Ed had reviewed several books for publishers. 6. _____
7. We had notified them of the changes several weeks in advance. 7. _____
8. The actors had performed very well that afternoon. 8. _____

THE FUTURE PERFECT TENSE

The future perfect tense shows that an action will be completed at a particular time in the future. To form the future perfect tense, use the helpers *will have* plus the past participle of the main verb.

By noon, I will have seen Ms. Morvay. *Will have seen* is future perfect tense; it shows action that will be completed at a particular future time—*by noon*.

CHECKUP 3 — After each pronoun, write the future perfect tense of the given verb.

1. to study
2. to serve
3. to operate
4. to detect

1. **you will have studied** _____
2. **he** _____
3. **she** _____
4. **we** _____

Now underline the future perfect tense verb in each of the following sentences. Then write each verb phrase in the space at the right.

5. Before the end of the year, Andreas Brothers will have closed its main store in Boston. 5. _____
6. By noon, the race walkers will have walked over five miles. 6. _____
7. By the end of the class period, the teacher will have listened to over ten oral presentations. 7. _____
8. Martin and Jamal will have gone to Alaska by July 1. 8. _____

CHECKUP 4 — In the space provided, indicate the tense (present perfect, past perfect, or future perfect) of each of the italicized verbs in the following sentences.

1. The plumbers *will have fixed* the leaky faucet under the sink by this afternoon. 1. **future perfect** _____
2. Many of the travelers *had brought* back artifacts from the countries they visited. 2. _____
3. By the time the case comes to trial, the defendants *will have proved* their innocence. 3. _____
4. Bob Hawley's sales group *had exceeded* our expectations for the last quarter. 4. _____
5. The students *have taken* part in many of the school's activities. 5. _____
6. The rock group *will have performed* in six countries by the end of the tour. 6. _____
7. For the past two months they *have participated* in an exchange program. 7. _____
8. She *had chosen* to stay at home. 8. _____
9. Our supervisor *had recommended* a change in policy. 9. _____
10. Alice *will have completed* the appraisals by tomorrow. 10. _____

EXERCISES

NAME _____ DATE _____ SCORE _____

EXERCISE 1   After each pronoun, write the present perfect tense of the given verb.

1. to resolve	1. he _____	6. to conduct	6. they _____
2. to improve	2. she _____	7. to collect	7. he _____
3. to distribute	3. we _____	8. to advise	8. she _____
4. to achieve	4. you _____	9. to maintain	9. he _____
5. to assist	5. she _____	10. to generate	10. they _____

Now underline the present perfect tense verb in each of the following sentences. Then write each verb phrase in the space at the right.

11. Eleanor has seen the movie several times.   11. _____

12. José has expressed a desire to go to law school.   12. _____

13. Each of them has worked long hours in the factory.   13. _____

14. Chris has exceeded his own expectations.   14. _____

15. Every participant has merited recognition for his or her contributions to the
    drive.   15. _____

EXERCISE 2   After each pronoun, write the past perfect tense of the verb indicated.

1. to add	1. he _____	6. to equip	6. she _____
2. to close	2. she _____	7. to arrange	7. we _____
3. to expand	3. it _____	8. to eat	8. he _____
4. to play	4. you _____	9. to decide	9. you _____
5. to insist	5. they _____	10. to approve	10. they _____

Now underline the past perfect tense verb in each of the following sentences. Then write each verb phrase in the space at the right.

11. The manager had received an announcement from the director.   11. _____

12. Several of the drivers had counted their tips before leaving the garage. 12. _____

13. Because of her concern, Dan had gone to the doctor.   13. _____

14. The controller had audited all departmental expense accounts.   14. _____

15. Several of the accounting students had interviewed with the local firms. 15. _____

16. Because of the newspaper advertisement, sales had increased tremendously. 16. _____

EXERCISE 3   After each pronoun, write the future perfect tense of the given verb.

1. to break	1. they _____	6. to promise	6. he _____
2. to notify	2. she _____	7. to attend	7. she _____
3. to plan	3. he _____	8. to write	8. they _____
4. to do	4. we _____	9. to provide	9. we _____
5. to go	5. you _____	10. to evaluate	10. he _____

Now underline the future perfect tense verb in each of the following sentences. Then write each verb phrase in the space at the right.

11. Pete will have played the guitar all day. 11. _____
12. The fruit will have ripened by this time tomorrow. 12. _____
13. The officials will have notified us of any emergency. 13. _____
14. The principal will have approved the students' plans for an assembly. 14. _____
15. Mother and Dad will have discussed their plans for a family vacation. 15. _____

EXERCISE 4

In the space provided, indicate the tense (present, past, or future perfect) of each of the verbs.

1. had begun 1. _____
2. has ordered 2. _____
3. will have seen 3. _____
4. had advised 4. _____
5. have returned 5. _____
6. will have reviewed 6. _____
7. has sold 7. _____
8. will have insisted 8. _____
9. had started 9. _____
10. have borrowed 10. _____

11. had called 11. _____
12. will have begun 12. _____
13. had reached 13. _____
14. had recorded 14. _____
15. will have seen 15. _____
16. had asked 16. _____
17. had written 17. _____
18. have discussed 18. _____
19. will have arrived 19. _____
20. had registered 20. _____

EXERCISE 5

In the space provided, indicate the tense (present; past; future; present, past, or future progressive; or present, past, or future perfect) of each of the italicized verbs.

1. Carol *had promised* us that we would receive recognition for our efforts. 1. _____
2. You *have received* all the information you need to conduct your research. 2. _____
3. By this time next week we *will have answered* most of the inquiries. 3. _____
4. The vice president *notified* us of the delay. 4. _____
5. The actor *performs* very well on stage. 5. _____
6. Few of us *will win* the million-dollar lottery. 6. _____
7. The chief executive officer *is convincing* us that the company will remain independent. 7. _____
8. The Humphrey Products Corporation announced that it *will be increasing* its prices on July 1. 8. _____
9. Brett *was jumping* for joy when he heard the good news. 9. _____
10. The lumber company *had supplied* us with scraps to build our stage props. 10. _____
11. David really *wants* a new car when he graduates from college. 11. _____
12. The checks *have cleared* the bank. 12. _____
13. We *will have received* our notice to transfer the funds to the bank in Columbus, Ohio. 13. _____
14. The tests results *showed* that the students had studied hard. 14. _____
15. Her history teacher *corrects* about 200 papers a week. 15. _____
16. Many people *visited* our booth at the trade show in New York. 16. _____
17. The MacKay Corporation *will celebrate* its tenth year in business. 17. _____
18. We *will have paid* our mortgage in four years. 18. _____
19. Miles *had approved* all the charts for the brochure. 19. _____
20. We *will be visiting* six European countries. 20. _____

Subjects and Verbs
Must Agree!

FOLLOW THE LEADER AGAIN!   When we discussed pronouns in Lesson 10, you saw that pronouns must agree with their leaders (their antecedents):

I **prefer paying** *my* **bills by check.** The pronoun *my* follows another pronoun, *I*. Since the leader *I* is singular, the singular *my* must follow the leader.

Well, verbs must also agree with their leaders—the nouns or pronouns to which they refer. In the sentence above, the verb *prefer* agrees with *I*. Let's see why.

	SINGULAR	PLURAL
First person:	I prefer	we prefer
Second person:	you prefer	you prefer
Third person:	he prefers	they prefer
	she prefers	
	it prefers	

Since *I* is first person singular, we must use *prefer*, also first person singular.

The general rule is this: *A verb must agree with its subject in person* (first, second, or third?) *and in number* (singular or plural?). Thus *I* and *prefer* agree. Let's look at a few more examples:

Mark **is** **our manager.** *Is* agrees with *Mark* (I am, you are, he is).

The *directors* *are* **having a meeting.** *Are* agrees with *directors* because nouns are always third person, and *directors* is plural, of course.

CHECKUP 1   Select the correct verb in parentheses, and write it in the space at the right. Make sure your choice agrees with its subject!

1. Edmond *(celebrate, celebrates)* his birthday on May 23.
2. Janice and Johanna *(was, were)* visiting our office.
3. Carl *(move, moves)* into his new apartment the first of the month.
4. The new book *(has, have)* over 500 pages.

1. **celebrates** _____
2. _____
3. _____
4. _____

COLLECTIVE NOUNS AND COMPOUND SUBJECTS   Do you remember collective nouns from Lesson 7? They usually take singular verbs when the group acts as *one*. Collective nouns take plural verbs when the members of the group act as individuals.

The *jury* *plans* **to reconvene at 1 p.m.** *Plans* agrees with *jury*, a collective noun (the jury is acting as a group).

The *jury* *were* *divided* **in their opinions.** Because *jury* refers to the jury members acting as individuals, the plural verb *were* is used.

Compound subjects, as you know, have two or more nouns or pronouns. If the parts of the compound subject are joined by *or* (or *nor*), the verb must agree with the subject that *follows* the word *or* (or *nor*).

Neither the supervisors nor the *assistant* *has* **the authority to approve the change.** *Has*, singular, agrees with *assistant*, a singular noun.

But watch what happens when the sentence is changed:

Neither the assistant nor the *supervisors have* the authority to approve the change. *Have,* plural, agrees with *supervisors,* a plural noun.

If the parts of the compound subject are joined by *and,* the subject is plural and requires a plural verb:

Pat, Mike, and Tim *were* transferred to Oregon. The plural verb *were* agrees with the compound subject *Pat, Mike, and Tim.*

Exception! Two subjects joined by *and* are still considered singular if they are modified by the indefinite pronoun *each* or *every.*

Every woman and child *was* given preference. *Was* is correct because *every* means every single one.

Each man and woman *was* identified with a name tag. *Was* is correct because *each* means each one person.

CHECKUP 2   Select the correct verb from each pair in parentheses, and write it in the space at the right.

1. Neither the pen nor the papers *(was, were)* on the desk.
2. A few of the people *(is, are)* here already.
3. Most of the work *(was, were)* finished by noon.
4. Each of the students *(has, have)* an assignment to complete.
5. Jeff and Brad *(is, are)* analyzing the data.
6. Several of their furnishings *(was, were)* antiques.
7. The jury *(has, have)* reached a decision.
8. Each of the candidates *(was, were)* present at the rally.

1. **were** _____
2. _____
3. _____
4. _____
5. _____
6. _____
7. _____
8. _____

OTHER PROBLEMS   When a sentence is not in normal order, the correct verb may not be clear. Change the sentence to normal order: subject first, then verb.

Where *(is, are)* the "rush" cartons? Normal order: The "rush" cartons *are* where? *Are,* plural, is correct; it agrees with the plural *cartons.*

Somewhere in that pile of papers *(is, are)* the missing contract. Normal order: The missing contract *is* somewhere in that pile of papers. *Is* agrees with the singular *contract.*

A sentence that begins with *there* may also cause problems because its subject follows the verb. *There* is an expletive, a word that fills the position of another word. *There* is never used as a subject of a sentence.

There *(is, are)* several candidates. The subject is *candidates,* a plural noun. Thus: There *are* several candidates.

***(Is, Are)* there a doctor in the house?** The subject is *doctor,* a singular noun. Thus: *Is* there a doctor in the house?

Indefinite pronouns also cause trouble. Recall from Lesson 14 that some indefinite pronouns are always singular, some are always plural, and some others may be singular or plural, depending on the meaning of the sentence.

Either of the two employees *is* welcome to attend the reception. (*Either* is always singular.)

Both of the secretaries *are* here today. (*Both* is always plural.)

Most of the printing *is* finished. (*Most* is singular here; it refers to the singular noun *printing.*)

Most of the terminals *are* down. (*Most* is plural here; it refers to the plural noun *terminals.*)

EXERCISES

NAME _____ DATE _____ SCORE _____

EXERCISE 1
Select the correct verb from each pair in parentheses, and write it in the space at the right. Make sure your choice agrees with its subject!

1. Where *(is, are)* the letter from Cooper Trust Bank?　　　　1. _____

2. *(Does, Do)* Rob and Ethel need a ride to the office?　　　　2. _____

3. There *(is, are)* some secretaries who always do well.　　　　3. _____

4. None of the committee members *(was, were)* agreeing on the budget.　　　　4. _____

5. Many on the commission *(wants, want)* more time to read the report.　　　　5. _____

6. There *(is, are)* only two weeks left before the introductory offer ends.　　　　6. _____

7. The construction of several buildings *(was, were)* being supervised by Matt Pierson, a general contractor.　　　　7. _____

8. Here *(is, are)* the list of names that you requested.　　　　8. _____

9. Either Harry or his assistants *(is, are)* supervising the installation.　　　　9. _____

10. All of that work *(is, are)* ready for evaluation.　　　　10. _____

11. Each of the reports *(require, requires)* scrutiny.　　　　11. _____

12. A combination of these techniques *(is, are)* what we recommend for success.　　　　12. _____

13. Either the manufacturer or the dealers *(has, have)* the power to guarantee the product.　　　　13. _____

14. Terry and Linda *(is, are)* writing a play to be produced this fall.　　　　14. _____

15. You and he *(has, have)* been selected as contest judges.　　　　15. _____

16. Each of their sons *(referees, referee)* for a soccer team.　　　　16. _____

17. Calvin's answers to the questions on the questionnaire *(was, were)* complete.　　　　17. _____

18. Something about these forms *(seem, seems)* strange.　　　　18. _____

19. Much time and money *(was, were)* devoted to this project.　　　　19. _____

20. Rebecca, like many in her family, *(is, are)* an artist.　　　　20. _____

21. Only one of the offices *(is, are)* well-ventilated.　　　　21. _____

22. *(Is, Are)* there four or five departments in your college?　　　　22. _____

23. Grandmother's stories of fantasy and adventure *(appeals, appeal)* to the grandchildren.　　　　23. _____

24. The time for dedication and commitment *(is, are)* now.　　　　24. _____

25. *(Was, Were)* the students happy to be out of school?　　　　25. _____

26. The catalog of sports equipment and accessories *(is, are)* published every six months.　　　　26. _____

27. Neither of the books *(is, are)* available in the public library.　　　　27. _____

28. Everyone *(want, wants)* a nice place to live.　　　　28. _____

29. A few of the boxes *(was, were)* left on the platform.　　　　29. _____

30. The team *(need, needs)* more time to practice.　　　　30. _____

31. The statistics on this graph *(seem, seems)* incorrect.　　　　31. _____

32. Each of their children *(plays, play)* a musical instrument.　　　　32. _____

33. Both writers *(are, is)* available to start on Monday.　　　　33. _____

34. Robin and Doug *(need, needs)* a ride to the company picnic.　　　　34. _____

35. The evidence in the case *(was, were)* clear.　　　　35. _____

EXERCISE 2

Underline any error in subject-verb agreement in the following sentences. If there is an error, correct the verb, not the subject. Write your correction in the space at the right. If there is no error, write *OK*.

1. Do Pat or Maggie know the reason that Hank is leaving the firm?   1. _____
2. Not one of the applicants were recommended for the position.   2. _____
3. Has Philip and Linda reported for work yet?   3. _____
4. The committee members were evenly divided over the proposal.   4. _____
5. One of my best friends were leaving for a month's trip to Australia.   5. _____
6. Supervising students under these conditions are exhausting.   6. _____
7. Two members of the choral group has taken private lessons.   7. _____
8. Any one of the computers is available.   8. _____
9. Several people in our group was members of the Association for Business Communication.   9. _____
10. There were a list of items to be repaired on the bulletin board.   10. _____
11. The quest for health and wealth were her main concern.   11. _____
12. Some of the quarters were missing from the jar.   12. _____
13. The manuscript, with all its corrections and suggestions, were left at the print shop.   13. _____
14. Molly and her twin sister was writing articles for a national magazine.   14. _____
15. One-third of the athletes were on time for the track meet.   15. _____
16. Warm temperatures and plenty of rain produces lovely vegetables in our garden.   16. _____
17. John Earhart, our corporate lawyer, review about ten new cases a day.   17. _____
18. Market research surveys conducted in New York last year indicates that consumer buying has increased 5 percent.   18. _____
19. The poor-tasting and overpriced meal were not what we expected at the fine restaurant.   19. _____
20. Most of the people in the audience was pleased with the performance.   20. _____

EXERCISE 3

For each of the following phrases, identify whether the subject is singular or plural by writing *singular* or *plural* in the space provided.

1. a few members of the cast   1. _____
2. each member of the senator's staff   2. _____
3. all of the offices   3. _____
4. one of the women   4. _____
5. the group of men, women, and children   5. _____
6. something about these letters   6. _____
7. the mailing costs for the letters   7. _____
8. someone in the office   8. _____
9. every sophomore   9. _____
10. a number of women   10. _____
11. the dimensions of the box   11. _____
12. the president and vice president   12. _____
13. not one of the employees   13. _____
14. the number of people   14. _____
15. the result of the tests   15. _____
16. each player on the team   16. _____
17. both of the assistants   17. _____
18. most of our supplies   18. _____

Lie and Lay

Can you memorize a few words? Of course you can! Memorize the past tense and past participle of the following verbs, and you will avoid some of the most difficult verb problems in our language. Read them slowly, and look for easy ways to remember these few words.

PRESENT	PAST	PAST PARTICIPLE	PRESENT PARTICIPLE
lay	laid	laid	laying
lie	lay	lain	lying

Notice that *lay/laid/laid* is easy to remember because the past and the past participle are the same. Notice, too, that *lay always* takes a direct object. It is a transitive verb. *Lie* is an intransitive verb, so use the *i* in *intransitive* to remind you of the *i* in *lie.* Intransitive verbs do not take direct objects.

Please *lay* the *book* on the table. *Book* is the direct object of the verb *lay.* Lay what? The *book.*

The book has been laid on the table. *Book* is the subject of *has been laid* (a past participle with a *being* verb helper). What has been laid? *Book.* The subject, *book,* is the receiver of the action.

Now you will see that *lie* never has a direct object.

Our cat lies on the carpet. Lies what? No answer. There is no direct object to receive the action.

Since *lie* never has a direct object, its past participle cannot be used with *being* verb helpers.

CHECKUP 1   Underline the direct objects in the following sentences. Then write the direct objects in the spaces at the right. If a sentence has no direct object, write *have-not.*

1. Chris laid the library books on the table.
2. I was lying on the sofa for several hours.
3. The mail was lying on the receptionist's desk waiting to be distributed.
4. Would you please lay these keys on the counter for me.
5. The crates were lying on the floor.
6. Please lay the carpet in the den.
7. The keys were lying on the counter.
8. Lie down if you feel ill.
9. Whose clothes are lying on the floor?
10. Lay the reports on Mr. Harrison's desk.

1. **books** _____
2. _____
3. _____
4. _____
5. _____
6. _____
7. _____
8. _____
9. _____
10. _____

LIE and LAY   Read the following tenses of *lie* aloud—and pay special attention to them. As you know, *to lie* means "to recline."

TO LIE (NO DIRECT OBJECT)

PRESENT *(LIE)*		PRESENT PROGRESSIVE (PRESENT PARTICIPLE: *LYING*)	
I lie	we lie	I am lying	we are lying
you lie	you lie	you are lying	you are lying
he lies	they lie	he is lying	they are lying

PAST (LAY)		PRESENT PERFECT (PAST PARTICIPLE: LAIN)	
I lay	we lay	I have lain	we have lain
you lay	you lay	you have lain	you have lain
he lay	they lay	he has lain	they have lain

Now do the same for the tenses of *to lay*, which means "to place something."

TO LAY (ALWAYS HAS A DIRECT OBJECT)

PRESENT (LAY)		PRESENT PROGRESSIVE (PRESENT PARTICIPLE: LAYING)	
I lay	we lay	I am laying	we are laying
you lay	you lay	you are laying	you are laying
she lays	they lay	she is laying	they are laying

PAST (LAID)		PRESENT PERFECT (PAST PARTICIPLE: LAID)	
I laid	we laid	I have laid	we have laid
you laid	you laid	you have laid	you have laid
she laid	they laid	she has laid	they have laid

Let's start with the verb *lay*. As we said, it *always* takes a direct object.

I *lay* the newspaper on the table. The executive *laid* the newspaper on the desk. The librarian *had laid* the newspaper on the counter. *Lay, laid,* and *had laid* all have the same direct object—*newspaper*. Lay what? Laid what? Had laid what? Answer: the *newspaper*.

But *lie* never has a direct object:

The leaves *lie* on the ground. Kelly *lay* down for an hour. The exhausted children *have lain* on the bed for several hours. Lie what? Lay what? Have lain what? No answer to all these questions because the verb *lie* has no direct object.

Beware!   *Lay* is used as both the past tense of *lie* and the present tense of *lay*.

CHECKUP 2   Select the correct verb from each pair in parentheses, and write it in the space at the right.

1. She and her friends *(lie, lay)* on the beach any chance they get.
2. Do you want those letters *(lying, laying)* over there to be mailed this afternoon?
3. Will and Andy have *(lain, laid)* the new carpet.
4. He *(lies, lays)* about 50 miles of pipe each day.
5. The painter *(lies, lays)* his brushes on the palette when he's not using them.
6. Please *(lie, lay)* the portfolio on the counter in the lobby.
7. The cat just *(lies, lays)* there so peacefully all morning.
8. The mason is *(laying, lying)* the new foundation.
9. Bill said he *(laid, lied)* the letter on the desk.
10. Your hat is *(laying, lying)* on the table.
11. *(Lay, lie)* the cartons by the elevator.
12. She *(lied, laid)* the memo on Mr. Herbert's desk.
13. They *(lied, laid)* the reports on the cabinet.
14. Our house *(lies, lays)* on a steep hill.
15. I *(laid, lied)* the blanket on the shelf.
16. Gary is *(laying, lying)* under the tree.

1. **lie** _____
2. _____
3. _____
4. _____
5. _____
6. _____
7. _____
8. _____
9. _____
10. _____
11. _____
12. _____
13. _____
14. _____
15. _____
16. _____

EXERCISES

NAME _____ DATE _____ SCORE _____

EXERCISE 1 Select the correct verb from each pair in parentheses, and write it in the space at the right.

1. Are you sure you want your dog to *(lie, lay)* on your new sofa?   1. _____
2. Maria *(layed, laid)* the mail on the kitchen table.   2. _____
3. Each afternoon, Norman *(lies, lays)* down to take a nap.   3. _____
4. The tired camper was *(lying, laying)* on the blanket.   4. _____
5. The books had been *(lying, laying)* on the shelf for some time.   5. _____
6. The attorneys had *(lain, laid)* the contracts aside for the time being.   6. _____
7. Where had the manager *(lain, laid)* the annual report?   7. _____
8. The papers *(laid, lay)* untouched for several days.   8. _____
9. The fabric has *(laid, lain)* on the counter for quite some time.   9. _____
10. The papers had *(laid, lain)* here for about a week.   10. _____
11. The baby had *(lain, laid)* in the crib waiting for the nurse to bathe him.   11. _____
12. Who *(lay, laid)* their umbrellas on my car?   12. _____
13. All the cards were *(laying, lying)* face down on the card table.   13. _____
14. I was sure that I had *(lain, laid)* the earrings on the dresser.   14. _____
15. Please *(lay, lie)* those cartons by the door in the lobby.   15. _____
16. Last evening, as I *(lay, laid)* sleeping, I dreamt about you.   16. _____
17. The beautiful kittens were *(laying, lying)* in the box.   17. _____
18. Would you care to *(lie, lay)* down before leaving on your trip?   18. _____
19. His wallet was *(lying, laying)* on the dashboard of the car.   19. _____
20. Earlier this evening she *(lay, laid)* on the sofa and watched television.   20. _____

EXERCISE 2 Replace the question mark with the correct form of *lie* or *lay*. Write your answers in the spaces at the right.

1. After back surgery, Lyle (?) on his stomach for several weeks.   1. _____
2. The artist had (?) his paintbrushes on the easel.   2. _____
3. Please help me (?) this carpet down before dinner.   3. _____
4. Did you get that tan from (?) in the sun or from working in the garden?   4. _____
5. The men (?) their hats on the bench before entering the church.   5. _____
6. The new schedules were (?) on the supervisor's desk.   6. _____
7. The librarian said that she was (?) the books on the cart.   7. _____
8. This morning as I (?) in bed, I thought about all the things I had to do before work.   8. _____
9. Rick's sport jacket is (?) on the bed.   9. _____
10. Would you please (?) those file folders on the cabinet.   10. _____
11. The ball was (?) on the twenty-yard line.   11. _____
12. The jeweler had just (?) the necklace on the glass counter when Mike saw it.   12. _____
13. The subcontractor had been (?) tile for the new bathroom.   13. _____
14. Her note was (?) on the table near the door.   14. _____
15. Why not (?) down for a few minutes before dinner?   15. _____

EXERCISE 3

Correct any errors in the use of *lie* and *lay* in the following sentences. Underline each error. Then write your corrections in the spaces at the right. If a sentence is correct, write *OK*.

1. You certainly are able to laid carpet down easily.   1. _____
2. The strategists were busy lying plans for the campaign.   2. _____
3. They had been lying around all afternoon.   3. _____
4. You may lay down anytime you feel like doing so.   4. _____
5. Our manager just lies the schedules on our desks.   5. _____
6. The boy has layed there for several hours.   6. _____
7. Irene thought that she had layed them there several hours ago.   7. _____
8. Are you still lying in the sun?   8. _____
9. The prints you had ordered from Frames Unlimited are laying on the
   table.   9. _____
10. After you price the dresses, please lie them across the table.   10. _____
11. How long has he been lying on the couch?   11. _____
12. He layed the materials on your desk an hour ago.   12. _____
13. After picking up the folders from the auditors, he lain them on his desk.   13. _____
14. The truck had been laying in the ditch for several days.   14. _____
15. Jo had lain in the tub for hours.   15. _____

EXERCISE 4

In each space below write a sentence using each of the following verbs correctly.

1. lay _____
2. lays _____
3. have lain _____
4. laid _____
5. have lain _____
6. lays _____
7. is laying _____
8. lies _____
9. have laid _____
10. laid _____
11. has lain _____
12. lays _____
13. lies _____
14. lie _____
15. have laid _____
16. has laid _____
17. has lain _____
18. laid _____
19. lie _____
20. lays _____
21. laying _____
22. lying _____
23. lie _____
24. laid _____
25. lay _____

Sit and Set; Rise and Raise

SIT AND SET   *Sit* means "to rest, recline, or take a seat"; it never has an object. *Set* means "to place or put something somewhere." *Set* always has an object—the thing that is being put somewhere.

Please *sit* near the window. (No direct object.) Sit is an intransitive verb.

They *were sitting* in the last row of the theater. (No direct object.)

Al *set* the portable copier on the cabinet. Al *placed* the copier on the cabinet. (Direct object: *copier.*)

Let's take a look at the commonly used tenses of the verb *to sit:*

TO SIT (*NO* DIRECT OBJECT)

PRESENT *(SIT)*		PRESENT PROGRESSIVE (PRESENT PARTICIPLE: *SITTING*)	
I sit	we sit	I am sitting	we are sitting
you sit	you sit	you are sitting	you are sitting
he sits	they sit	he is sitting	they are sitting

PAST *(SAT)*		PRESENT PERFECT (PAST PARTICIPLE: *SAT*)	
I sat	we sat	I have sat	we have sat
you sat	you sat	you have sat	you have sat
he sat	they sat	he has sat	they have sat

Now also make sure that you know the forms of the verb *to set:*

TO SET (*ALWAYS HAS* A DIRECT OBJECT)

PRESENT *(SET)*		PRESENT PROGRESSIVE (PRESENT PARTICIPLE: *SETTING*)	
I set	we set	I am setting	we are setting
you set	you set	you are setting	you are setting
she sets	they set	she is setting	they are setting

PAST *(SET)*		PRESENT PERFECT (PAST PARTICIPLE: *SET*)	
I set	we set	I have set	we have set
you set	you set	you have set	you have set
she set	they set	she has set	they have set

CHECKUP 1   Select the correct verb from each pair in parentheses, and write it in the space at the right.

1. I want to *(sit, set)* in the front row of the balcony.
2. The caterer has *(sat, set)* ten extra tables for our banquet.
3. From where we *(sat, set)* in the auditorium, we could see everything.
4. As we walked into the room, the waiters were *(sitting, setting)* the tables.
5. Why are you *(sitting, setting)* in the rain?
6. Have Tom and Diane *(sit, set)* their wedding date yet?
7. At Brookfield Zoo we saw many animals just *(sitting, setting)* in the warm sun.

1. <u>sit</u>
2. _____
3. _____
4. _____
5. _____
6. _____
7. _____

RISE AND RAISE   *Raise,* like *set,* always has a direct object; *rise,* like *sit,* never has a direct object. *Rise* means "to get up." *Raise* means "to lift something higher, to increase, or to bring up."

Did you *rise* when you were introduced to his grandmother? Did you *get up* when you were introduced? (No object.)

When the judge entered the courtroom, we *rose.* We *got up.* (No object.)

Rita *raised* her hand to ask a question. She *lifted* her hand. (Direct object: *hand.*)

Hands *were raised* by the inquiring students. (*Hands* is the subject of the verb *were raised.*)

Here are the most frequently used forms of *to rise:*

TO RISE (NO DIRECT OBJECT)

PRESENT *(RISE)*		PRESENT PROGRESSIVE (PRESENT PARTICIPLE: *RISING*)	
I rise	we rise	I am rising	we are rising
you rise	you rise	you are rising	you are rising
she rises	they rise	she is rising	they are rising

PAST *(ROSE)*		PRESENT PERFECT (PAST PARTICIPLE: *RISEN*)	
I rose	we rose	I have risen	we have risen
you rose	you rose	you have risen	you have risen
she rose	they rose	she has risen	they have risen

Now here are the most frequently used forms of *to raise:*

TO RAISE (ALWAYS HAS A DIRECT OBJECT)

PRESENT *(RAISE)*		PRESENT PROGRESSIVE (PRESENT PARTICIPLE: *RAISING*)	
I raise	we raise	I am raising	we are raising
you raise	you raise	you are raising	you are raising
it raises	they raise	it is raising	they are raising

PAST *(RAISED)*		PRESENT PERFECT (PAST PARTICIPLE: *RAISED*)	
I raised	we raised	I have raised	we have raised
you raised	you raised	you have raised	you have raised
it raised	they raised	it has raised	they have raised

CHECKUP 2   Select the correct verb from each pair in parentheses, and write it in the space at the right.

1. The sun *(rises, raises)* in the east and sets in the west.   1. __rises__
2. The boys will be *(rising, raising)* in about an hour.   2. _____
3. Please *(rise, raise)* your hand if you wish to be acknowledged.   3. _____
4. Grandmother's bread dough *(rose, rised)* over the top of the bowl.   4. _____
5. The Boy Scouts had the honor of *(raising, rising)* the flag before the game.   5. _____

Now correct any errors in the use of *rise* or *raise* in the following sentences. Underline each error. Then write your corrections in the spaces at the right.

6. Our teacher encouraged us to rise questions when we didn't understand the material.   6. _____
7. Will you be raising before 8 o'clock tomorrow?   7. _____
8. I can't believe that their prices have raised so much this past year.   8. _____

EXERCISES

NAME _____ DATE _____ SCORE _____

EXERCISE 1   Select the correct verb from each pair in parentheses, and write it in the space at the right.

1. The full moon *(rised, rose)* in the sky.   1. _____
2. They *(sat, set)* there waiting for their names to be called.   2. _____
3. Can we *(sit, set)* someplace and talk?   3. _____
4. When Jessie is troubled about something, she just *(sits, sets)* and thinks the problem through.   4. _____
5. He *(sits, sets)* the table every evening for his parents.   5. _____
6. Please don't *(sit, set)* those boxes on that table.   6. _____
7. *(Sit, Set)* the packages over here.   7. _____
8. Where would you like the president to *(sit, set)*?   8. _____
9. Janice was thrilled because she *(sat, set)* next to a celebrity at lunch.   9. _____
10. Are you going to be *(sitting, setting)* new prices soon?   10. _____
11. The objection he *(raised, risen)* concerned flextime.   11. _____
12. The speaker *(rise, rose)* from his chair and answered the question.   12. _____
13. Mother wants to *(raise, rise)* some vegetables in her garden this summer.   13. _____
14. The dough had *(raised, risen)* so we were able to roll it out and make dinner rolls.   14. _____
15. Are you still *(raising, rising)* each morning before 6 o'clock?   15. _____
16. Have you been able to *(raise, rise)* enough money for a scholarship?   16. _____
17. The bear *(raised, rose)* to its full height.   17. _____
18. The participants *(raised, risen)* several good questions after the speaker's talk.   18. _____
19. *(Raising, Rising)* early to jog each morning takes a lot of discipline.   19. _____
20. Please *(raise, rise)* when the judge enters the room.   20. _____
21. They will be *(raising, rising)* funds for the Special Olympics.   21. _____
22. The sun *(raised, rose)* and heated the ground quickly.   22. _____
23. He *(raises, roses)* beautiful flowers each year in his garden.   23. _____
24. The price of that fabric has *(raised, risen)* tremendously over the past several months.   24. _____
25. Will you be *(raising, rising)* at your usual time tomorrow?   25. _____
26. Our Himalayan cat always *(sets, sits)* on the sill of our bay window.   26. _____
27. After the meeting, our boss told us about the sales quotas that were *(set, sat)*.   27. _____
28. That particular manager *(sits, sets)* appointments but doesn't always keep them.   28. _____
29. The hecklers were *(raising, rising)* a commotion at the political rally.   29. _____
30. While camping in Colorado, Lowell *(rised, rose)* at 6 a.m. each day.   30. _____
31. People in the courtroom *(raise, rise)* when the judge enters.   31. _____
32. Meg was asked to *(raise, rise)* the flag at the start of the ceremony.   32. _____
33. *(Sit, Set)* the water glasses on the table before the meeting begins.   33. _____
34. Please *(raise, rise)* your hand if you wish to be on the committee.   34. _____
35. We saluted while the flag was being *(raised, rised)*.   35. _____

EXERCISE 2

In the sentences below, underline each incorrectly used verb. Then write your corrections in the spaces at the right. If a sentence is correct, write *OK*.

1. Perhaps she would like to set over here.
2. Are you sure you want to sit those boxes so close to the heater?
3. With your German shepherd setting in the house, you won't need an alarm system.
4. The waiters were sitting the tables for 500 guests.
5. Tell the messenger to set the packages by the door.
6. The cat just set there and watched us as we worked.
7. The baby sets quietly and plays with his toys.
8. Do sit back in your chair and relax for a few minutes.
9. The boys set in the front row so they could see the performers up close.
10. Have you sit the prices for the new fall dresses?
11. We were all setting in the park enjoying the free concert by the symphony orchestra.
12. Do you prefer to set in the smoking or nonsmoking section?
13. Please raise and sing our national anthem.
14. He always rise when his great-grandmother enters the room.
15. The cost of publishing a company newsletter is rising.
16. Unfortunately, the prices have been raising ever since we started looking for a computer.
17. Will you be rising any cattle on your farm?
18. She was too shocked to rise any questions.
19. The fish raised to the surface when we gave them some food.
20. Daniel is a good fund-raiser; last year he rose $1,000 just from his neighborhood.
21. An early morning haze had raised over the lake.
22. The students rose over $500 for their trip to Washington, D.C.
23. We'll be raising at 4 a.m. tomorrow to get an early start.
24. May I please set here.
25. Because she was recording his speech, she tried to set as close to the stage as possible.

1. _____
2. _____
3. _____
4. _____
5. _____
6. _____
7. _____
8. _____
9. _____
10. _____
11. _____
12. _____
13. _____
14. _____
15. _____
16. _____
17. _____
18. _____
19. _____
20. _____
21. _____
22. _____
23. _____
24. _____
25. _____

EXERCISE 3

Write a sentence using each of the following verbs correctly.

1. sit _____
2. sitting _____
3. sat _____
4. set _____
5. setting _____
6. sets _____
7. rise _____
8. raise _____
9. raising _____
10. rose _____
11. rise _____
12. set _____
13. raised _____
14. sat _____

More Troublesome Verbs

LEARN AND *TEACH*   Simply put, *learn* means "to acquire knowledge." *Teach* means "to instruct." Never say, "He *learned* me." Say instead, "He taught me."

Ms. Cartwright *taught* us European history. We *learned* European history from Ms. Cartwright. She taught; we learned. (Never say, "Ms. Cartwright *learned* us"—no one can *learn* you!)

Mr. Carrone *taught* me how to write computer programs. I *learned* how to write computer programs from Mr. Carrone. He taught; I learned. (Never say, "*learned* me how to write computer programs.")

LEAVE AND *LET*   If you ever confuse *leave* and *let*, just remember that *leave* means "to depart or go away" and that *let* means "to permit or allow."

Please *let* me see Mr. Jackson. *Let* means "allow"—please allow me to see Mr. Jackson.

I *am leaving* the office now. *Leaving* means "departing"—I am departing from the office now.

Let Mark help you. *Let* means "allow"—please allow Mark to help you.

The skiers did not want to *leave* the warm lodge. *Leave* means "depart"—the skiers did not want to depart from the warm lodge.

Leave sometimes can also mean "to deliver or place," as in the sentence below:

If I were you, I would *leave* a note saying where I was going.

CHECKUP 1   Select the correct verb from each pair in parentheses, and write it in the space at the right.

1. When you *(let, leave)*, please turn out the lights.
2. I was sure that I did not *(let, leave)* him borrow that book.
3. Tracy *(let, leave)* her use the computer that was in the workroom.
4. We were *(taught, learned)* how to use the computer only last week.
5. I *(taught, learned)* much from past experience.
6. The teacher told us what we were going to *(teach, learn)* that day.
7. Will you be *(teaching, learning)* the stress management course this semester?

1. **leave** _____
2. _____
3. _____
4. _____
5. _____
6. _____
7. _____

BRING TO AND *TAKE* AWAY   *Bring* means "to carry something to someone." *Take* means "to carry something away from someone."

When Calvin returns, please have him *bring* me his report. Have Calvin carry his report to me.

When Denise leaves the office, please have her *take* the books to the library. Have Denise carry the books away from the office.

CHECKUP 2   Select the correct verb from each pair in parentheses, and write it in the space at the right.

1. On your way home from work, please stop at the store and *(bring, take)* home some milk.

    1. **bring** _____

2. Do you want to *(bring, take)* your lunch to work today?

    2. _____

3. They'll *(bring, take)* whatever size boxes we want when they come to the office.

    3. _____

4. It *(brings, takes)* about 30 minutes to walk the two miles.

    4. _____

5. You'll need to *(bring, take)* two photographs of yourself to this office to get a passport.

    5. _____

6. Dad always *(brings, takes)* some candy home for the children.

    6. _____

7. Yes, I did *(bring, take)* the copy of the letter with me to the attorney's office.

    7. _____

AFFECT **AND** *EFFECT*   *Affect* is a verb that means "to influence or to change." *Effect* is a verb that means "to bring about, to accomplish, or to do something." *Effect* can also be used as a noun meaning "a result or a consequence."

Increased prices will *affect* sales. Increased prices will influence sales.

Our personnel director plans to *effect* a change in hiring practices. The director plans to bring about a change in hiring practices.

The revised schedule had a positive *effect* on the employees. The schedule had a positive result on the employees.

CHECKUP 3   Select the correct verb from each pair in parentheses, and write it in the space at the right.

1. Our office will be *(affected, effected)* by the schedule changes.

    1. **affected** _____

2. A number of improvements were *(affected, effected)* by the company executives.

    2. _____

3. Will working late *(affect, effect)* your grades?

    3. _____

4. We were all *(affected, effected)* by the team's loss.

    4. _____

5. *(Affects, Effects)* of the storm were felt by everyone.

    5. _____

6. Were you *(affected, effected)* by the railroad strike?

    6. _____

7. An increase in state taxes will *(affect, effect)* our company.

    7. _____

BORROW **AND** *LEND*   *Borrow* means "to obtain, to take, or to receive something on loan." *Lend* means "to give out or to allow the use of something for a period of time."

May I please *borrow* your pen. May I please take your pen.

Dad promised to *lend* me his car until mine is back from the garage. Dad promised to allow me the use of his car until mine was back from the garage.

CHECKUP 4   Select the correct verb from each pair in parentheses, and write it in the space at the right.

1. I would like to *(borrow, lend)* $5 from you.

    1. **borrow** _____

2. Would you please *(borrow, lend)* me $5.

    2. _____

3. Sally needed to *(borrow, lend)* a book from the public library.

    3. _____

4. Dad didn't want to *(borrow, lend)* him the car for the evening.

    4. _____

5. You're welcome to *(borrow, lend)* my book on Alaska.

    5. _____

6. Would you *(borrow, lend)* me your magazines on world news.

    6. _____

7. She needs to *(borrow, lend)* your pen to sign the letters.

    7. _____

EXERCISES

NAME _____ DATE _____ SCORE _____

EXERCISE 1   Select the correct verb from each pair in parentheses, and write it in the space at the right.

1. I need to *(teach, learn)* how to use the computer for desktop publishing.

2. Finally, Jimmy *(taught, learned)* how to write a computer program.

3. Will you be *(teaching, learning)* at the university this semester?

4. You can *(teach, learn)* how to play a musical instrument.

5. *(Teach, Learn)* the rules of the road before applying for your driver's license.

6. You can *(teach, learn)* yourself how to ride a bike.

7. Adam wanted to *(teach, learn)* how to conduct interviews so he could work in the Personnel Department.

8. We had hoped to *(teach, learn)* people how to resolve conflicts at the workshop.

9. He *(taught, learned)* several of us how to prepare a ·newsletter on the computer.

10. *(Teach, Learn)* me how to be a better speller.

1. _____
2. _____
3. _____
4. _____
5. _____
6. _____
7. _____
8. _____
9. _____
10. _____

EXERCISE 2   Select the correct verb from each pair in parentheses, and write it in the space at the right.

1. We sat in the back so that we could *(let, leave)* early.

2. If you want to *(let, leave)* before 5 o'clock, then you'll need to work without a break this afternoon.

3. *(Let, Leave)* me help you with those packages.

4. Our supervisor *(lets, leaves)* us leave early if we come to work early.

5. I need to *(let, leave)* the office by 4 o'clock today.

6. *(Let, Leave)* Brenda prepare the report for the council meeting.

7. Yes, Mr. Tatro *(let, leave)* us use the faculty lounge for our meeting.

8. *(Let, Leave)* those library books here, and I'll take them back for you.

9. You can *(let, leave)* her use the car tomorrow.

10. He was just *(letting, leaving)* the house when I called.

1. _____
2. _____
3. _____
4. _____
5. _____
6. _____
7. _____
8. _____
9. _____
10. _____

EXERCISE 3   Select the correct verb from each pair in parentheses, and write it in the space at the right.

1. Will you please *(bring, take)* me a blanket from upstairs.

2. The committee will *(bring, take)* action on that item next week.

3. Please *(bring, take)* the mail when you come.

4. Father was *(bringing, taking)* home the groceries from the store.

5. *(Bring, Take)* a copy of the memo to Ms. Turner.

6. *(Bring, Take)* that typewriter to me when you come.

7. You're welcome to *(bring, take)* as many cookies as you want.

8. When you are finished typing the letter, please *(bring, take)* it to Mr. Jones for his signature.

9. *(Bring, Take)* the letter and make five photocopies of it for distribution among the managers.

10. *(Bringing, Taking)* home the groceries was something I did not plan to do today.

1. _____
2. _____
3. _____
4. _____
5. _____
6. _____
7. _____
8. _____
9. _____
10. _____

EXERCISE 4   Select the correct verb from each pair in parentheses, and write it in the space at the right.

1. How has the change in plans *(affected, effected)* you?   1. _____
2. The last-minute call for more desks will *(affect, effect)* our shipping
   schedule.   2. _____
3. Can you *(affect, effect)* a change in the way the work is done?   3. _____
4. What is the *(affect, effect)* of the change?   4. _____
5. What will the *(affects, effects)* be on your production schedule?   5. _____
6. We will all be *(affected, effected)* by the results of the storm.   6. _____
7. How did the layoffs *(affect, effect)* your department?   7. _____
8. When the contract takes *(affect, effect)*, we will no longer have flextime.   8. _____
9. An increase in plane fares will *(affect, effect)* the company's traveling
   policy.   9. _____
10. How does the new policy *(affect, effect)* your teaching schedule this spring?   10. _____

EXERCISE 5   Select the correct verb from each pair in parentheses, and write it in the space at the right.

1. Please *(borrow, lend)* me a hand with these boxes.   1. _____
2. You may not *(borrow, lend)* the car this evening; I will be using it.   2. _____
3. The manager agreed to *(borrow, lend)* the new employee $25 until he could
   get to the bank.   3. _____
4. Try not to *(borrow, lend)* money from your relatives.   4. _____
5. Would you be willing to *(borrow, lend)* me some money until Friday?   5. _____
6. Did she ask to *(borrow, lend)* those files from you?   6. _____
7. My sister may *(borrow, lend)* my clothes anytime since we are the same
   size.   7. _____
8. I learned never to *(borrow, lend)* him anything because he does not return the
   items.   8. _____
9. *(Borrowing, Lending)* from others is not a good practice.   9. _____
10. Suzie is forever *(borrowing, lending)* people her things.   10. _____

EXERCISE 6   Have you mastered the troublesome verbs? Let's see. In the space provided write a sentence using the given verb.

1. learn   _____
2. teach   _____
3. leave   _____
4. let   _____
5. bring   _____
6. take   _____
7. affect   _____
8. effect   _____
9. borrow   _____
10. lend   _____
11. learning _____
12. affects   _____
13. taught   _____
14. borrow   _____
15. take   _____

Adjectives

LESSON 26

DESCRIPTIVE WORDS   You have already heard that adjectives are descriptive words—they describe or modify nouns or pronouns.

The small, red loose-leaf manual is the programmer's.

Do you see how the words *the small, red loose-leaf* help to modify or describe the noun *manual?* They help bring *manual* into sharper focus by telling us more about the *manual. The* tells us it is a specific *manual,* not just any book. *Small* tells us something about its size; it is not a large book. *Red* tells us its color—not the green or the blue loose-leaf manual but the *red* one. And *loose-leaf* tells us something about the way *the small, red* manual is bound.

Let's look at another example of how adjectives help bring nouns and pronouns into sharper focus:

These electronic typewriters will be purchased. The subject *typewriters* (a noun) is modified by *These electronic. These* answers the question, Which typewriter? *Electronic* answers the question, What kind?

Beware!   Nouns frequently "disguise" themselves as adjectives when the nouns are used to modify other nouns or pronouns. Don't be fooled—look to see *how the noun is used.*

The company that bought this factory has its headquarters in New York. *New York* is a noun (a proper noun, in fact); it names a particular place.

A New York company has bought this factory. Here, *New York* is used to modify the noun *company;* thus *New York* is an adjective in this sentence.

Pronouns, too, can disguise themselves as adjectives:

These were very interesting. *These* is a pronoun—it takes the place of a noun.

These books were very interesting. *These* is an adjective in this sentence because it modifies the noun *books.* It does *not* replace a noun here.

Each of these books was very interesting. *Each* is a pronoun.

Each book was very interesting. Here, *each* modifies *book,* so *each* is an adjective.

CHECKUP 1   Underline the adjectives in each of the following sentences. Then write the total number of adjectives in each sentence in the space at the right.

1. San Antonio has lovely restaurants.   1. <u>1</u>
2. Human freedom exists in daily life.   2. _____
3. He writes romance novels.   3. _____
4. Studio apartments are available in large cities.   4. _____

A, AN, AND *THE*   *A, an,* and *the* are called *articles.* Perhaps you never notice, but whenever you use *a* or *an,* you are referring to something *indefinite.* Whenever you use *the,* you are referring to something *definite.*

If we wait, a clerk will come soon. *A* clerk—indefinite—*any* clerk.

She is the clerk who waited on us. *The* clerk—definite—a specific clerk, *the* clerk who waited on us, not any other clerk.

Use *a* before words that begin with a consonant (or consonant sound) or with the sound of a long *u*:

a clerk   a student   a teacher   a classroom
a hole   a hook   a dictionary a project
a uniform   a unit   a university a union
a one-hour class (Do you hear the consonant sound *w* in *one?*)

Use *an* before words that begin with a vowel or vowel sound (except the long *u* sound) or with a silent *h*:

an apple   an executive   an umbrella   an event
an heir   an hour   an honor (You don't hear the *h* because it's silent.)

DESCRIPTIVE ADJECTIVES
Descriptive adjectives are picture-making words, such as *big* and *small, short* and *tall, dull* and *lively, dark* and *bright, happy* and *sad, good* and *bad, poor* and *rich, low* and *high,* and so on.

The *optimistic* report disclosed *unexpected* profits that were gained from an *exciting new* venture. *Optimistic, unexpected, exciting,* and *new* are descriptive adjectives. *The* is an article.

CHECKUP 2   Underline the descriptive adjectives in the following sentences, and circle the articles *a, an,* and *the.*

1. ⓣThe newspaper ad asked for ⓐan experienced secretary.
2. Dr. Jones was a full professor and an eminent scholar of American history.
3. On a steamy August morning, I took a ten-speed bike for a ride in the downtown park.
4. We hired a general contractor to build a cedar closet in the downstairs bedroom.

POSSESSIVE ADJECTIVES
The pronouns *my, his, her, our, your, their, its,* and *whose* are adjectives whenever they modify nouns.

My office is on the fifteenth floor. *His* office is on the tenth floor. *My* and *his* are possessive adjectives.

THIS, THAT, THESE, AND THOSE
When used alone, *this, that, these,* and *those* are pronouns. When they modify nouns, of course, they are adjectives (called *demonstrative adjectives*).

Those are Harold's brochures. Pronoun. *Those* brochures are Harold's. Adjective—*those* modifies *brochures.*

LIMITING ADJECTIVES
Limiting adjectives refer to quantity. They are frequently numbers such as *two, ten, first,* and *fifth;* but they are also "quantity words," such as *few, several,* and *many.* Obviously, they tell "how much."

Only *three* rooms were repainted. *Three* is a limiting adjective.

Very *few* people were present. *Few* is a limiting adjective.

CHECKUP 3   Underscore once any possessive adjectives in the following sentences. Underscore twice any limiting adjectives. Circle the demonstrative adjectives *this, that, these,* and *those.*

1. My cousin will be attending the computer workshop ⓣthis month.
2. His work load increased this year for several reasons.
3. Her efforts on your behalf helped in getting the manager to take a second look at that problem.
4. A few controllers have voiced their opinions about those accounts.

NAME _____ DATE _____ SCORE _____

EXERCISE 1   Decide how many adjectives are in the following sentences. Underline each adjective, and circle each article (*a, an,* or *the*). Then write the total number of adjectives in each sentence in the space at the right. (*Hint:* Be sure to include possessive adjectives, such as *my* and *our,* and limiting adjectives, such as *two, tenth, few,* and *all.*)

1. My physics professor was lecturing one day on the scientific laws.   1. _____
2. One day at lunch our ecumenical group of doctoral students discussed the Sunday sermon.   2. _____
3. My college students asked if I would base their grades on relative performance instead of raw scores.   3. _____
4. In a large brown paper bag, combine cracker crumbs, iodized salt, and cayenne pepper.   4. _____
5. A combination of peanut oil and oriental spices gives this dish its unique flavor.   5. _____
6. Mark was perched on a low stool sipping a cup of hot tea while watching the birch logs burn in the old fireplace.   6. _____
7. It was a lovely spring day, and the bright red roses were dangling from the white trellis.   7. _____
8. By early June, the rich fields of winter wheat sprouted lush carpets of grain.   8. _____
9. Leading medical authorities point to strong evidence that eating foods low in fat is good for young adults.   9. _____
10. A desolate highway median became a setting for colorful wildflowers.   10. _____
11. The small boy heard his aged father say that he was starting an exercise program.   11. _____
12. Freshmen athletes know the importance of making healthful choices and avoiding reckless behavior.   12. _____
13. Tim was lying on the leather couch with a cold cloth on his hot forehead.   13. _____
14. Two red pencils were lying on the oak desk.   14. _____
15. My roommate Chad and I walked to the corner store for two cold sodas.   15. _____
16. I discussed my forthcoming European vacation with my two best friends.   16. _____
17. Bruce took the foam sleeping pad and spread it on the grassy hillside.   17. _____
18. His quick eye caught the slight movement in the new snow.   18. _____
19. Her younger brother took great pride in his scholastic achievements.   19. _____
20. The bedroom walls are paneled in wood veneer.   20. _____

EXERCISE 2   Underline only the demonstrative adjectives (*this, that, these,* and *those*), possessive adjectives, and limiting adjectives in the following sentences. (Remember that limiting adjectives refer to quantity.) Then write the total number of demonstrative, possessive, and limiting adjectives in each sentence in the space at the right.

1. This winter semester your older sister will be enrolled in my history class.   1. _____
2. That book and several others belong to her older brother.   2. _____
3. Two of these language classes will be taught by your former teacher.   3. _____

4. I would like to borrow three of those books from your friend. 4. _____

5. My new supervisor is related to my neighbor. 5. _____

6. Whose pen is lying on my desk? 6. _____

7. Those boxes have been here for several days. 7. _____

8. Her subordinates have won these awards two years in a row. 8. _____

9. This panel consists of five women who work with my mom. 9. _____

10. Their boss ordered ten new computers for the office. 10. _____

11. Those three typewriters arrived several days ago. 11. _____

12. That opinion was expressed by his colleague only a few weeks before the research paper was published. 12. _____

13. Was that your first experience with voice mail? 13. _____

14. These individuals will be handling all our telephone calls. 14. _____

15. That crate contains five paintings from his dad. 15. _____

16. Many presidents prepare their vice presidents to take over their positions someday. 16. _____

17. Several plans were adopted by his sister who works for an attorney. 17. _____

18. This weekend I would like to visit my sister and then my cousin. 18. _____

19. Whose turn is it to mail these letters? 19. _____

20. That operator said it was her opportunity to move on. 20. _____

21. Can you handle all his calls this morning? 21. _____

22. Few companies offer all their employees bonuses these days. 22. _____

23. That clerk sold 200 computers in one week. 23. _____

24. Please supervise their work all week. 24. _____

25. His flight to New York took only two hours. 25. _____

EXERCISE 3   Use each word listed below in a sentence. (Make sure that you use each as an adjective, not as a noun or as a verb.)

1. long _____

2. Chicago _____

3. first _____

4. third _____

5. those _____

6. four _____

7. enclosed _____

8. my _____

9. advertised _____

10. these _____

11. afternoon _____

12. tenth _____

13. his _____

14. low _____

15. progress _____

16. expensive _____

17. last _____

18. efficient _____

19. red _____

20. maximum _____

More About Adjectives

PROPER ADJECTIVES   Proper adjectives are words formed from proper nouns; for example, *Shakespearean* (from *Shakespeare*), *Platonic* (from *Plato*), *English* (from *England*), *American* (from *America*), *German* (from *Germany*), and so on.

CHECKUP 1   After each proper noun, write the proper adjective formed from it.

1. Poland **Polish** _____
2. Japan _____
3. France _____

4. Canada _____
5. Italy _____
6. Germany _____

DOUBLE ADJECTIVES   Sometimes two or more adjectives may be used to describe a word. For example, to describe a luxury car that is new, you would probably say "a new luxury car." To describe a house that is modern and spacious, you would say "a modern, spacious house." And to describe a building that is ten stories high, you would say "a ten-story building."

Did you notice that nothing separates *new* and *luxury*, that a comma separates *modern* and *spacious*, and that a hyphen joins *ten* and *story*? Let's see why.

WHEN TO USE A COMMA   Use a comma between adjectives that modify the *same noun*. As a test, see if you could say *and* between the adjectives and reverse the order of the adjectives without changing the meaning of the description.

a modern, spacious house Both *modern* and *spacious* modify the same noun, *house*. You could say "a house that is modern *and* spacious"; thus the comma is correct. You can also reverse the order of the adjectives and say "a house that is spacious and modern."

a superb, meticulous accountant Both *superb* and *meticulous* modify the same noun, *accountant*: "an accountant who is superb *and* meticulous."

You cannot say "a new *and* luxury car" because it makes no sense. The reason is simple: *luxury* modifies *car*, but *new* modifies both *luxury* and *car*. Thus, no comma is used.

CHECKUP 2   Decide if you would use a comma at the point marked (?) in each of the following sentences. Write *Yes* or *No* in the space at the right. (*Remember:* If *and* is not appropriate, then a comma is not appropriate either.)

1. Jerry bought her a miniature (?) German shepherd.
2. The story of his long (?) dull journey put everyone to sleep.
3. Upon her return from the war, a warm (?) enthusiastic crowd greeted Mary at the airport.
4. Their annual (?) holiday party will be given next week.
5. Myles works on a large (?) isolated ranch in Wyoming.

1. **No** _____
2. _____
3. _____
4. _____
5. _____

WHEN TO USE A HYPHEN   We frequently look for shortcuts—even in our speech. Thus we usually say "a five-room house" rather than the longer "a house that has five rooms"; we say "a 3-gallon container" rather than "a container that holds 3 gallons"; and so on. When we build up adjectives and place them before nouns, we usually need a hyphen to show that the words work together as *one unit,* as in *five-room house* and *3-gallon container*. But we do not always need the hyphen when the words *follow* the noun, because the words usually read clearly without the hyphen:

BEFORE THE NOUN	AFTER THE NOUN
an *up-to-date* list	a list that is *up to date*
a *high-level* manager	a manager at a *high level*
a *soon-to-be-released* movie	a movie that is *soon to be released*
an *out-of-town* guest	a guest from *out of town*

As you see, the hyphens are needed before the nouns to make the compound adjectives read clearly. When they follow the nouns, the phrases read quite clearly without the hyphens.

Some other words, however, are hyphenated *all the time*:

BEFORE THE NOUN	AFTER THE NOUN
an *air-conditioned* room	a room that is *air-conditioned*
a *tailor-made* suit	a suit that is *tailor-made*
a *soft-spoken* friend	a friend who is *soft-spoken*
a *tax-exempt* note	a note that is *tax-exempt*

Read these again carefully, and try to see why the hyphens help make these phrases clearer. As you do so, notice that many of these compounds have past participles (*-conditioned, -made, -spoken*).

Because such words would usually be confusing wherever they appear in a sentence, they are listed with hyphens in a dictionary. "Temporary" compounds, such as *3-gallon* and *five-room* are *not* listed in the dictionary.

CHECKUP 3   Decide if you would use a hyphen at the point marked (?) in each of the following sentences. Write *Yes* or *No* in the space at the right. Use a dictionary if your instructor permits.

1. The blue(?)eyed carpenter had decided to go into business for himself.   1. **Yes**
2. She is a well(?)known person in our community.   2. _____
3. The worn(?)out equipment will be replaced by the end of the year.   3. _____
4. The most(?)exciting event was the appearance of the country singer.   4. _____

Exceptions, Exceptions, Exceptions!   We do *not* use hyphens to join proper adjectives:

a *New York* law firm	*North American* ski resorts
the *Supreme Court* decisions	a *Los Angeles* school
many *United States* companies	three *Fifth Avenue* merchants

The reason is simple: The hyphen is not needed. The hyphen is also not needed for compounds that are so well known that the hyphens would provide no help:

a *high school* reunion	her *life insurance* agent
two *real estate* offices	my *social security* payments
a *12 percent* raise	two *10 percent* increases

CHECKUP 4   Decide if you would use a hyphen at the point marked (?) in each of the following sentences. Write *Yes* or *No* in the space at the right.

1. The well(?)known consultant receives $2,500 a day for his expertise.   1. **Yes**
2. Our annual(?)national convention will be held in New Orleans next year.   2. _____
3. Her five(?)year contract will expire at the end of the month.   3. _____
4. The Jefferson High(?)School band performed at the ceremony.   4. _____

EXERCISES

NAME _____ DATE _____ SCORE _____

EXERCISE 1   Decide if you would use a comma at the point marked (?) in each of the following sentences. Write *Yes* or *No* in the space at the right. (*Remember:* If *and* is not appropriate, then a comma is not appropriate either.)

1. A prominent journalist was the keynote speaker at the annual (?) state convention.

   1. _____

2. The long (?) tiring trip through the mountains left us exhausted.

   2. _____

3. Please use the second (?) business envelope for mailing those contracts.

   3. _____

4. This soft (?) plush carpeting was installed by Henley Brothers.

   4. _____

5. Our manager is a reserved (?) calm individual who likes to work with people.

   5. _____

6. Are you sure you want those three (?) electric mowers moved to the basement?

   6. _____

7. The obnoxious (?) loud client wanted to see our manager.

   7. _____

8. An excellent (?) exciting movie is now playing at United Artists.

   8. _____

9. This dark (?) dreary room reminds me of a cave.

   9. _____

10. The new (?) spring fashions are already being delivered to the store.

   10. _____

EXERCISE 2   Decide if you would use a hyphen at the point marked (?) in each of the following sentences. Write *Yes* or *No* in the space at the right. Use a dictionary if your instructor permits.

1. Are you interested in getting part(?)time help for the summer?

   1. _____

2. Kyle signed a contract for four(?)years.

   2. _____

3. Had you heard that he signed a four(?)year contract with the Dodgers?

   3. _____

4. The new(?)computer system is ready for installation.

   4. _____

5. Calvin, our life(?)insurance agent, has been with Surity Insurance for many years.

   5. _____

6. Mr. Termi is the highest(?)paid employee at the bank.

   6. _____

7. Marci's short(?)term goal was to learn French in six weeks.

   7. _____

8. Tom is so successful because he is a well(?)organized individual.

   8. _____

9. The family decided to buy a five(?)bedroom house so that each child would have his or her own bedroom.

   9. _____

10. The ugly(?)red carpet was put in the basement where no one would see it.

   10. _____

EXERCISE 3   Insert hyphens where necessary in each of the following sentences. Then write the hyphenated word in the space at the right. If a sentence is correct, write *OK*.

1. The long winded speaker spoke for two hours and just about put everyone to sleep.

   1. _____

2. His supervisor asked for an up to date progress report on the building.

   2. _____

3. Elsie is a soft spoken woman who loves to entertain friends.

   3. _____

4. Several serious errors were made in the final report.

   4. _____

5. What a relief it was to get out of the 90 degree weather.

   5. _____

6. The bank was able to give us a two month grace period.

   6. _____

7. The well known athlete was seen in television commercials endorsing various products.

   7. _____

8. The real estate office is closed on weekends.

8. _____

9. The friendly looking clerk had received the Outstanding Salesperson Award.

9. _____

10. We were given step by step instructions on how to operate the machine.

10. _____

11. The lumber company said that there was no charge for delivery within a 50 mile radius.

11. _____

12. Be sure to add only high grade oil to the engine of your car.

12. _____

13. The builder was given a five month extension.

13. _____

14. We thought we were going to get an 8 percent increase.

14. _____

15. While serving on the review board for a national journal, I received a book length article to review.

15. _____

EXERCISE 4   Rewrite each word group so that it is a hyphenated compound adjective.

1. A cake of two tiers   _____
2. A stamp that is 30 cents   _____
3. A container that holds 2 pints   _____
4. A proposal of 500 pages   _____
5. A lease of 99 years   _____
6. A speed limit of 55 miles per hour   _____
7. A goal for a long term   _____
8. A fee of 60 cents   _____
9. A building of ten stories   _____
10. A report that is organized well   _____
11. A person who is trained well   _____
12. A meeting held at a high level   _____
13. A sale that will last for one day   _____
14. A book that is written well   _____
15. An improvement that is much needed   _____

EXERCISE 5   Use each of the following adjectives or adjective phrases in a sentence. Be sure to use each as an adjective.

1. high-level   _____
2. Canadian   _____
3. democratic   _____
4. deep, wide   _____
5. high-ranking   _____
6. 5 percent   _____
7. English   _____
8. five-minute   _____
9. up-to-date   _____
10. well-constructed   _____
11. well-mannered   _____
12. cold, rainy   _____
13. off-the-record   _____
14. long-range   _____
15. accurate   _____

Comparing Adjectives

A MATTER OF DEGREE   As you have seen, adjectives allow us to describe things: a *late* delivery; an *early* schedule. But they also allow us to *compare* our descriptions:

a *later* delivery   an *earlier* schedule
the *latest* delivery   the *earliest* schedule

Forms such as *late/later/latest* and *early/earlier/earliest* represent the three forms of comparisons of adjectives. *Late* and *early* are positive forms—they describe *one* thing. *Later* and *earlier* are comparative forms—they are used to compare *two* things. *Latest* and *earliest* are superlative forms—they express the highest degree of *late* and *early*. Let's look at each.

LATE/EARLY—THE POSITIVE DEGREE   *Late* and *early* are positive—they describe *one* thing:

They attended a *late* meeting. *Late* is positive; it describes one *meeting*.

He planned to get an *early* start. *Early* is positive; it describes one *start*.

LATER/EARLIER—THE COMPARATIVE DEGREE   Together, *late* and *later* or *early* and *earlier* allow us to compare two things.

The *late* show starts at 10 p.m.; the *later* show begins at midnight. *Later* is used in a comparison of two shows: one is *late;* the other, *later*.

If only two dates are available, I prefer the *earlier* one. *Earlier* is used in a comparison of two dates.

Forming the Comparative Degree   Most adjectives form the comparative degree by adding *-er* to the positive form:

long + er = longer   fast + er = faster   clear + er = clearer   young + er = younger

Of course, adjectives that end in *e* or *y* are "special":

late + er = later (drop one *e*)   happy + er = happier (change *y* to *i*, then add *er*)

Most adjectives of two syllables or more do not "sound right" if *-er* is added to the positive form. For these adjectives, we use the word *more* or the word *less* instead of *-er: more cheerful* or *less cheerful* (NOT: cheerfuler); *more eager* or *less eager* (NOT: eagerer).

LATEST/EARLIEST—THE SUPERLATIVE DEGREE   Together, *late, later,* and *latest* or *early, earlier,* and *earliest* allow us to compare three or more things.

José came *late (early)* to the meeting. Brian arrived *later (earlier)*. Dee was the *latest (earliest)* to arrive.

Forming the Superlative Degree   Add *-est* to form the superlative degree of an adjective:

POSITIVE	COMPARATIVE	SUPERLATIVE
long	long + er = longer	long + est = longest
clear	clear + er = clearer	clear + est = clearest

Likewise, whenever you would use *more* (or *less*) to form the comparative, you would use *most* (or *least*) to form the superlative.

POSITIVE	COMPARATIVE	SUPERLATIVE
cheerful	more cheerful	most cheerful
eager	more eager	most eager

Remember: Use the positive form when only *one* thing is described, use the comparative form when *two* things are compared, and use the superlative form when *three or more* things are compared.

CHECKUP 1
Decide which adjective form is correct—positive, comparative, or superlative. In the space at the right, write the correct form of the adjective given in parentheses.

1. Sales for February were *(high)* than sales for March.
2. Of all the plays I have seen, this one was the *(good)*.
3. That document is of *(poor)* quality than the one you have.
4. You are *(famous)* for your ideas on management techniques.

1. __higher__
2. _____
3. _____
4. _____

Beware! Some adjectives cannot be compared in the regular sense because they are absolute. Examples are such words as *alive, alone, complete, correct, dead, empty, final, finished, full, ideal, perfect, right, round, square, straight,* and *unique.* Absolute adjectives may show comparison by using *more nearly* or *most nearly.*

This glass is *more nearly* full than that one.

Your assignment was the *most nearly* correct of them all.

GOOD, BETTER, BEST—THE IRREGULARS
Good is probably the most famous of the adjectives to which you cannot add *-er* and *-est*—here are some others:

POSITIVE	COMPARATIVE	SUPERLATIVE	POSITIVE	COMPARATIVE	SUPERLATIVE
bad	worse	worst	little	less	least
far	farther	farthest	many	more	most
good	better	best	much	more	most

DOUBLE TROUBLE
As you've seen, some adjectives add *-er* to make their comparative forms; others use the word *more* (or *less*). Never use both *-er* and *more* (or *less*).

Frankly, we need a *better* machine. (NOT: a *more better* machine.)

Summit Mail provides *faster* service. (NOT: *more faster* service.)

Likewise, never use both *-est* and the word *most* (or *least*).

We need the *latest* price list. (NOT: the *most latest* price list.)

Summit Mail provides the *fastest* service. (NOT: the *most fastest* service.)

CHECKUP 2
Select the correct adjective form from each pair in parentheses, and write it in the space at the right.

1. Theresa is *(kinder, more kind)* than Allison.
2. Mr. Miller is the *(less, more less, most less, least)* likely candidate of all.
3. Of our two choices, the first one is the *(better, more better, best)* one.
4. This is by far the *(easy, more easy, easiest)* task of all.

1. __kinder__
2. _____
3. _____
4. _____

EXERCISES

NAME _____ DATE _____ SCORE _____

EXERCISE 1   In the spaces at the right, write the comparative form of the adjective given in parentheses.

1. Of the two letters he had written, the first one was *(bad)*.   1. _____
2. Which of the two watches is *(small)*?   2. _____
3. The second applicant was *(skillful)* than the first one.   3. _____
4. I would like to buy the *(expensive)* watch because it is guaranteed for one year.   4. _____
5. Which of the two brothers is *(old)*?   5. _____
6. This telephone system is *(new)* than that one.   6. _____
7. That desk is *(near)* to the window than this one.   7. _____
8. This silk fabric is *(fine)* in texture than the cotton fabric.   8. _____
9. My desk is *(sturdy)* than Bonnie's.   9. _____
10. Sam thought that the music at the Holiday Playhouse was *(lively)* than that at the Lincoln Inn.   10. _____

EXERCISE 2   In the space at the right, write the superlative form of the adjective given in parentheses.

1. This has to be the *(old)* building in town.   1. _____
2. She hired the applicant who had the *(little)* number of errors on the typing test.   2. _____
3. This was the *(ideal)* solution to the problem.   3. _____
4. They did not want to buy the *(cheap)* chair in the store.   4. _____
5. That has to be the *(hot)* tamale I've ever eaten.   5. _____
6. Are you the *(young)* in your family?   6. _____
7. The professor asked for the *(current)* magazine available.   7. _____
8. Of all the short stories I read today, yours was the *(interesting)*.   8. _____
9. Mr. Morgan was the *(qualified)* of all the interviewees.   9. _____
10. They wanted to order the *(heavy)* card stock that we had.   10. _____

EXERCISE 3   Decide which adjective form is correct—positive, comparative, or superlative. In the space at the right, write the correct form of the adjective given in parentheses.

1. Everyone agreed that Barry's recommendation was *(good)* than Angela's.   1. _____
2. He happens to be the *(kind)* person I know.   2. _____
3. The *(old)* building in the city is now up for sale.   3. _____
4. Which of the two typewriters is in *(bad)* shape?   4. _____
5. The prices of our products are not *(high)*.   5. _____
6. Because we went shopping after work, we were *(late)* for dinner at the club.   6. _____
7. Of the three actresses, she was the *(beautiful)*.   7. _____
8. At one time it was the *(long)* expansion bridge in the world.   8. _____
9. Be sure that the cord is *(strong)* enough to hold the papers together.   9. _____
10. We agreed that Harriet's ideas was *(good)* than Bob's.   10. _____

EXERCISE 4   In the space at the right, write the correct form of the adjective in parentheses. Absolute adjectives may be used in your answers.

1. Who did the *(little)* amount of work in the office?   1. _____
2. Elaine was the *(neat)* of the two workers.   2. _____
3. Daniel's grades were *(high)* in science.   3. _____
4. Peter is the *(good)* mechanic in the plant.   4. _____
5. The woman who won the comedy contest was the *(funny)* of all the contestants.   5. _____
6. Of all the alternatives given, Andrew's was the *(creative)*.   6. _____
7. I would like to buy something that is *(strong)* than what I have now.   7. _____
8. Mom wanted a *(modern)* kitchen than what she currently has.   8. _____
9. That's the *(early)* appointment I can give you.   9. _____
10. Our Model K-14 desk is the *(durable)* product we make.   10. _____

EXERCISE 5   Decide which adjective form is correct—positive, comparative, or superlative. In the space at the right, write the correct form of the adjective given in parentheses.

1. Our president wanted a *(firm)* chair than the one she now has in her office.   1. _____
2. What is the *(short)* distance to your house from the office?   2. _____
3. The committee members agreed that Annette's solution was a *(good)* one.   3. _____
4. They felt that the new employee was the *(lazy)* person in the office.   4. _____
5. He was by far the *(tall)* man on the team.   5. _____
6. That solution is *(good)* than the one we heard this morning.   6. _____
7. Phillip lives a lot *(close)* to me than Lamar does.   7. _____
8. That room seems to be the *(dark)* one in the house.   8. _____
9. The keynote speaker at the national convention was the *(informative)* one I heard all day.   9. _____
10. This is the *(happy)* I have ever seen her.   10. _____

EXERCISE 6   Write the comparative and superlative degrees for the following adjectives.

POSITIVE	COMPARATIVE	SUPERLATIVE
1. bad	_____	_____
2. low	_____	_____
3. attractive	_____	_____
4. talented	_____	_____
5. correct	_____	_____
6. fine	_____	_____
7. tall	_____	_____
8. long	_____	_____
9. cold	_____	_____
10. little	_____	_____
11. great	_____	_____
12. poor	_____	_____
13. accurate	_____	_____
14. wise	_____	_____
15. sincere	_____	_____

Really? Surely. Carefully!

THE -ly WORDS—ADVERBS   Not all *-ly* words are adverbs, but most of them are. Adverbs (like *usually, finally,* and *completely*) modify verbs and adjectives. Let's look at a few examples.

The sales representatives *finally* finished their call reports. *Finally* is an adverb. It modifies the verb *finished.*

We asked them to solve these *unusually* difficult problems. *Unusually* is an adverb. It modifies the adjective *difficult.*

A *highly* qualified employee is difficult to find. *Highly* is an adverb. It modifies the adjective *qualified.*

CHECKUP 1   Underline the adverb in each of the following sentences. Then in the space at the right, write the word that the adverb modifies.

1. Our supervisor <u>readily</u> agreed to our requests.
2. Mr. Bailey wanted to sign the letters immediately.
3. They often played baseball in the park.
4. You were frequently recommended for the promotion.
5. It was her responsibility to raise the flag daily.

1. **agreed** _____
2. _____
3. _____
4. _____
5. _____

HOW? WHEN? WHERE?   Adverbs answer the questions *how, when, where, how much,* and *how often.* Let's see how they do so. Some of the adverbs that answer the question *how* are *quietly, quickly, loudly,* and *efficiently.* Most of these adverbs end in *-ly.*

The students spoke *quietly* in the library. Spoke how? *Quietly. Quietly* is an adverb modifying the verb *spoke.* How did the students speak? *Quietly.*

Because of the cold winds, shoppers walked *quickly.* Walked how? *Quickly. Quickly* is an adverb modifying the verb *walked.* How did the shoppers walk? *Quickly.*

When?   Most of the adverbs that answer the questions *when* or *how often* do not end in *-ly: often, once, twice, always, late, never,* and *seldom.* However, they do the same job the *-ly* adverbs do.

Committee meetings were called *often.* We have committee meetings *frequently.* In these sentences, *often* and *frequently* are both adverbs. *Often* modifies the verb *called,* and frequently modifies the verb *have.* Committee meetings are called when? *Often.* We have committee meetings when? *Frequently.*

Where?   Many of the adverbs that answer the question *where* also do not end in *-ly: everywhere* and *anywhere, forward* and *backward, up* and *down, above* and *below, here* and *there,* and so on.

We moved *forward* with our plans. Moved where? *Forward. Forward* is an adverb modifying the verb *moved.*

How Much?   Adverbs that answer the questions *how much* or *in what degree* usually modify adjectives and other adverbs: *almost, exceedingly, fully, most, too, very, little, so, enough,* and so on.

This was the *most* respected report we ever issued. How much respected? *Most* is an adverb modifying the adjective *respected.*

The early statistics give us *exceedingly* little to go on. How much to go on? *Exceedingly* is an adverb modifying the adjective *little.*

CHECKUP 2   Underline the adverb in each of the following sentences. Then in the space at the right, write the question that the adverb answers.

1. We had the maintenance people move <u>forward</u> with the repairs.   1. **where** _____
2. Many of the employees worked quietly in their offices.   2. _____
3. He was always late for his dental appointments.   3. _____
4. That was the most exciting book I've read.   4. _____
5. She calmly walked across the busy highway.   5. _____

VERY WELL!   Adverbs can also modify other adverbs.

The analyst knows her programming *well.* Knows programming how? Knows it *well. Well* is an adverb modifying the verb *knows.*

The analyst knows her programming *very well. Well* is still an adverb. It modifies the verb *knows. Very* is also an adverb. It modifies the adverb *well.* How well? *Very* well.

ADJECTIVE OR ADVERB?   Some adjectives and adverbs have the same forms. In the examples below, note how each adjective modifies a noun and how each adverb modifies a verb:

ADJECTIVE	ADVERB
A *late* train	he arrived *late*
an *early* bus	she came *early*
my *best* suggestion	I like it *best*

Of course, all words that end in *-ly* may look like adverbs, but there are some adjectives that end in *-ly* too:

friendly receptionist	*elderly* men	*costly* items	*timely* tips
lively messengers	*early* warning	*worldly* items	*lonely* person
motherly advice	*lovely* dress	*ghostly* tale	*cowardly* deed

Use your dictionary whenever you are not sure.

Beware!   Several frequently used adverbs have two acceptable forms.

close, closely	Look close or look closely.	quick, quickly	Come quick or come quickly.
deep, deeply	Cut deep or cut deeply.	slow, slowly	Drive slow or drive slowly.
direct, directly	Ship direct or ship directly.	loud, loudly	Talk loud or talk loudly.

CHECKUP 3   Underline the adverbs in the following sentences. Then in the space at the right, indicate whether each adverb modifies a verb *(V)*, an adjective *(ADJ)*, or another adverb *(ADV)*. (Hint: Some sentences have more than one adverb.)

1. She smiled <u>sweetly</u> at the photographer.   1. **V** _____
2. He was very seldom prepared for a presentation.   2. _____
3. We bought some very fine quality paper for our résumés.   3. _____
4. Do you attend these meetings very often, Darlene?   4. _____
5. Ginger works efficiently and competently.   5. _____
6. They were directly involved in the court proceedings.   6. _____
7. We bought some extremely fragile glassware at the outlet store.   7. _____
8. Carol met frequently with her staff to discuss marketing plans.   8. _____

NAME _____ DATE _____ SCORE _____

EXERCISE 1
Underline the adverbs in the following sentences. Then write the adverbs in the spaces at the right.

1. The librarian asked the students to study quietly.
2. Never had I heard such a long commencement address.
3. You'll do well on your exams if you prepare for them.
4. The dispatcher promised that he would ship the goods immediately.
5. I memorized the material quickly.
6. I was at the barbershop yesterday for a haircut.
7. Speak clearly over the telephone so that the other person can hear you.
8. Please arrive promptly at 8 o'clock.
9. We looked everywhere for those files.
10. Have you seen Mike lately?

1. _____
2. _____
3. _____
4. _____
5. _____
6. _____
7. _____
8. _____
9. _____
10. _____

EXERCISE 2
Underline the adverbs in the following sentences. Then in the space at the right, indicate whether each adverb modifies a verb *(V)*, an adjective *(ADJ)*, or another adverb *(ADV)*. (**Hint:** Some sentences may have more than one adverb.)

1. Monica repeatedly stressed the need to be concise when writing letters.
2. It was a very convenient time to take a vacation.
3. The computer was installed by a highly qualified technician.
4. He sometimes works in the office.
5. Janice is always very prepared for her seminars.
6. Mickey, here is the information you requested.
7. Diane eagerly awaited news from the company.
8. We need to analyze this problem further.
9. They waited patiently for the test results to be announced.
10. They were working efficiently to evacuate the area.

1. _____
2. _____
3. _____
4. _____
5. _____
6. _____
7. _____
8. _____
9. _____
10. _____

EXERCISE 3
Underline the adverbs in the following sentences. Then write the adverbs in the spaces at the right. (**Hint:** Some sentences may have more than one adverb.)

1. Did she know that you left early?
2. Today I plan to water the office plants.
3. The manager distinctly said that we could leave soon.
4. Don was fully aware of the consequences of his actions.
5. Please be sure to quote us the stock prices accurately.
6. You may work on that report tomorrow.
7. Place the papers neatly on the desk.
8. The supervisor wanted to further discuss the problem in the lab.
9. Our guests arrived sooner than we had anticipated.
10. We searched everywhere for his misplaced keys, and we could not find them in any of the usual places.

1. _____
2. _____
3. _____
4. _____
5. _____
6. _____
7. _____
8. _____
9. _____
10. _____

EXERCISE 4

Underline the adverb in each of the following sentences. Then in the space at the right, indicate whether the adverb modifies a verb *(V)*, an adjective *(ADJ)*, or another adverb *(ADV)*.

1. The maintenance people thoroughly cleaned the warehouse.   1. _____
2. The highly recommended applicant was doing excellent work.   2. _____
3. It seems to me that the consultant is paid very well for his services.   3. _____
4. Walk quietly as you go down the halls in the hospital.   4. _____
5. Mom gingerly took the cookies off the stainless steel cookie sheet.   5. _____
6. Close the jar tightly so that the food stays fresh.   6. _____
7. We frequently travel throughout Europe during the summer.   7. _____
8. Is 2 o'clock a very convenient time for us to meet?   8. _____
9. You can draw those lines vertically.   9. _____
10. She was in the garden delicately picking flowers for her centerpiece.   10. _____

EXERCISE 5

Select the correct word from each pair in parentheses, and write it in the space provided.

1. Margaret thought she did *(fair, fairly)* well on her final exam.   1. _____
2. Are you *(fair, fairly)* sure you can finish the report by noon?   2. _____
3. The word processor installed *(late, lately)* works just fine.   3. _____
4. Study the questions *(slow, slowly)* so that you will do well on the exam.   4. _____
5. The people in the audience *(quick, quickly)* took their seats.   5. _____
6. The cover letter asked the respondents to return the questionnaire
   (direct, directly).   6. _____
7. Students were asked to line up *(short, shortly)* for the procession.   7. _____
8. *(Right, Rightly)* you can change your name if you want to.   8. _____
9. Juan *(quick, quickly)* grabbed the child from the path of the cyclist.   9. _____
10. The dancers *(slow, slowly)* glided across the stage.   10. _____

EXERCISE 6

Use each of the following adverbs in a sentence.

1. immediately _____
2. frequently _____
3. satisfactorily _____
4. previously _____
5. clearly _____
6. truly _____
7. directly _____
8. closely _____
9. efficiently _____
10. cheerfully _____

EXERCISE 7

After each adjective, write the adverb formed from it.

1. correct _____   6. calm _____
2. eager _____   7. careful _____
3. complete _____   8. close _____
4. personal _____   9. loud _____
5. sure _____   10. nice _____

Comparing Adverbs

THE THREE DEGREES   Like adjectives, adverbs have three degrees of comparison: the positive, the comparative, and the superlative degrees.

>   Positive: Bob keyboards the agendas *fast*. He works *efficiently*.

>   Comparative: Sue keyboards her agendas *faster* than Bob. She works *more efficiently* than he.

>   Superlative: Betty keyboards her agendas the *fastest*. She works *most efficiently*.

The three degrees of the adverb *fast* are *fast, faster,* and *fastest*. The three degrees of the adverb *efficiently* are *efficiently, more* efficiently, and *most* efficiently. As you will see in this lesson, the three degrees of adverbs are formed in the same way the three degrees of adjectives are formed.

FAST/EFFICIENTLY—THE POSITIVE DEGREE   The adverbs *efficiently* and *fast* are positive—each describes one thing.

>   **Bob keyboards his agendas** *fast*. **He works** *efficiently*. *Fast* and *efficiently* are positive forms. *Fast* describes how Bob keyboards. *Efficiently* describes how Bob works.

FASTER/MORE EFFICIENTLY—THE COMPARATIVE DEGREE   Together, *fast* and *faster* or *efficiently* and *more efficiently* allow us to compare two things.

>   **Bob keyboards the agendas** *fast*. **Sue keyboards the agendas** *faster*. *Faster* is used in a comparison of two things: keyboarding *fast* and keyboarding *faster*.

>   **Bob works** *efficiently*. **Sue works** *more efficiently*. *More efficiently* is used in the comparison of two things: working *efficiently* and working *more efficiently*.

Forming the Comparative Degree   We form the comparative degree for adverbs just as we do for adjectives. We add *-er* to the positive form.

>   fast + er = faster   slow + er = slower

Or we use the words *more* or *less:*

>   more cheerfully   or   less cheerfully   more amusing   or   less amusing

All *-ly* adverbs use the words *more* or *less*. None of them can add *-er* without sounding strange. Also, never add both *-er* and *more* (or *less*) to a word.

>   loud   louder   more loudly   less loudly

CHECKUP 1   In the space at the right, write the comparative form of the word given in parentheses.

1. Louise and Kevin seem *(happily)* married than Suzanne and Lenny.
2. The seniors watched the game *(closely)* than the freshmen did.
3. I arrived early; however Gilberto arrived *(early)*.
4. She spoke *(assertively)* to the store clerk than her mother did.

1. **more (or less) happily**
2. _____
3. _____
4. _____

FASTEST/MOST EFFICIENTLY—THE SUPERLATIVE DEGREE

Together, *fast, faster,* and *fastest* allow us to compare three or more things. Also, *efficiently, more efficiently,* and *most efficiently* allow us to compare three or more things.

Bob keyboards his agendas *fast,* but Sue keyboards her agendas *faster.* However, Betty keyboards them the *fastest* of them all. Three things are being compared. *Fastest* is the superlative form.

Bob *works efficiently.* Sue works *more efficiently.* However, Betty works the *most efficiently.* Three things are being compared. *Most efficiently* is the superlative form.

Forming the Superlative Degree

Just as you add *-er* to form the comparative, you add *-est* to form the superlative.

POSITIVE	COMPARATIVE	SUPERLATIVE
high	higher	highest
loud	louder	loudest

Likewise, whenever you would use *more* (or *less*) to form the comparative, use *most* (or *least*) to form the superlative.

POSITIVE	COMPARATIVE	SUPERLATIVE
cheerfully	more cheerfully	most cheerfully
	less cheerfully	least cheerfully

WELL, BETTER, BEST—THE IRREGULARS

Remember the adjectives *good/better/best?* Now make sure you know *well/better/best* and the other "irregulars":

POSITIVE	COMPARATIVE	SUPERLATIVE
badly	worse	worst
far	farther	farthest
far	further	furthest
little	less	least
much	more	most
well	better	best

DOUBLE TROUBLE

Be sure that you don't "double" your comparisons by saying things like "most best," "more better," "more louder," "more sooner," "more faster," "more slower," "more earlier," or "more softer."

CHECKUP 2

Decide which adverb form is correct—the positive, the comparative, or the superlative. In the space at the right, write the correct form of the adverb given in parentheses.

1. Of all the machines in this room, this one works *(badly)* of all.
2. Marcia writes well, but Harvey writes *(well).*
3. Tim complains about the additional work *(much)* than Rick does.
4. Are you sure he can run *(fast)* than you?
5. You wrote that last paragraph very *(clear).*
6. The service at this restaurant is *(good)* than it used to be.
7. Food prices are *(high)* than they were a year ago.
8. She is the *(fast)* member of the track team.
9. A basement is the *(safe)* place to be during a tornado.
10. Kirk planned to arrive *(early)* for the ceremony.

1. **worst** _____
2. _____
3. _____
4. _____
5. _____
6. _____
7. _____
8. _____
9. _____
10. _____

EXERCISES

NAME _____ DATE _____ SCORE _____

EXERCISE 1   In the spaces at the right, write the comparative form of the adverb given in parentheses.

1. This phone rings *(quietly)* than that one.   1. _____
2. In departmental meetings, Susan speaks *(softly)* than Michiko.   2. _____
3. Of the two hikers, Bess walks *(slowly)* than Carrie.   3. _____
4. The latest figures show that car sales for this month are declining *(rapidly)* than they did for last month.   4. _____
5. This keyboard works well, but that keyboard works *(well)*.   5. _____
6. Andrew calculated the percentages *(rapidly)* than I expected.   6. _____
7. Frank arrived *(late)* than Arnold for the meeting with Mr. Thompson.   7. _____
8. This printer works *(fast)* than the one we have; I think we should buy it. 8. _____
9. Miles can answer your questions *(well)* than I can.   9. _____
10. Your writing is *(clear)* than what it had been.   10. _____

EXERCISE 2   In the spaces at the right, write the superlative form of the adverb given in parentheses.

1. Of all the new employees, Charlene works *(hard)*.   1. _____
2. Sonita is the *(fast)* typist we have in the office.   2. _____
3. This car runs *(smoothly)* of all our rental cars.   3. _____
4. All our printers work well, but this model works *(well)*.   4. _____
5. Of all the people who worked on the sale, Martha had done the *(much)*. 5. _____
6. Some proposals were bad, but this one has to be the *(badly)*.   6. _____
7. This gift was wrapped *(carefully)* of all the gifts.   7. _____
8. Our marketing manager advised us to pursue several new markets *(aggressively)*.   8. _____
9. The work was performed satisfactorily by two employees, but the work was performed *(satisfactorily)* by the group.   9. _____
10. We liked Jerlyn because she worked *(efficiently)* of all the employees.   10. _____

EXERCISE 3   Decide which adverb form is correct—positive, comparative, or superlative. In the spaces at the right, write the correct form of the adverb given in parentheses.

1. Daniel worked *(well)* with his colleagues than Peter did.   1. _____
2. This letter is written *(concisely)* than the one written by Jim.   2. _____
3. You seem to wrap the gifts *(fast)* than Janet.   3. _____
4. She fell from the ladder but she was not *(serious)* injured.   4. _____
5. Which of the three presidential candidates answered the reporter's question *(satisfactorily)*?   5. _____
6. Our present boss speaks to us *(kindly)* than our former boss.   6. _____
7. The broken water pipe ruined the *(real)* expensive furniture.   7. _____
8. Our team was *(well)* prepared than the other team.   8. _____
9. We thought the first skit was *(amusing)* than the second.   9. _____
10. We stopped *(sudden)* to avoid an accident.   10. _____

11. It couldn't be *(badly)* than what it was. 11. _____
12. Several guests arrived late, but Scott arrived *(late)* of all. 12. _____
13. This has to be your *(well)* work yet. 13. _____
14. He accepted the news even *(well)* than we thought he would. 14. _____
15. Our newest printer runs so *(quiet)* that we hardly hear it. 15. _____

EXERCISE 4   In each sentence, replace the question mark with an adverb. Write the adverb in the space at the right.

1. Her supervisor spoke (?) of her work. 1. _____
2. (?) we'll be able to leave for San Francisco. 2. _____
3. The company publishes the report (?). 3. _____
4. You were (?) right in assuming that we would not work on Memorial Day, which is a national holiday. 4. _____
5. (?) all the work has been completed by the night shift. 5. _____
6. We will (?) pack the boxes so that they will not be damaged in shipment. 6. _____
7. (?) is the day that we will start production of the new model. 7. _____
8. Ms. James (?) attends our weekly staff meetings. 8. _____
9. I believe that Bob is a (?) worker than Jorge. 9. _____
10. As soon as I heard the news, I (?) called my supervisor. 10. _____
11. We were told to (?) check the annual reports for any misspelled words. 11. _____
12. The shipment should have gone out (?). 12. _____
13. The manager wanted (?) progress reports from us. 13. _____
14. After the writing seminar, the engineers wrote more (?). 14. _____
15. That was (?) what he meant by that statement. 15. _____

EXERCISE 5   Write the comparative and superlative degrees for the following adverbs.

POSITIVE	COMPARATIVE	SUPERLATIVE
1. little	_____	_____
2. steadily	_____	_____
3. clearly	_____	_____
4. well	_____	_____
5. hard	_____	_____
6. badly	_____	_____
7. nearly	_____	_____
8. much	_____	_____
9. distinctly	_____	_____
10. fast	_____	_____
11. often	_____	_____
12. smart	_____	_____
13. strangely	_____	_____
14. gladly	_____	_____
15. important	_____	_____
16. carefully	_____	_____
17. slow	_____	_____
18. quickly	_____	_____
19. concisely	_____	_____
20. silently	_____	_____

Some Troublemakers

PLACEMENT OF WORDS   Be careful where you place modifiers. A misplaced adjective or adverb can change the meaning of a sentence or be confusing to the reader. Pay particular attention to the words *almost, ever, first, hardly, merely, last, just,* and *only*.

Only I told Ann about the announcement. *Only I*—no one else told Ann about the announcement.

I told *only* Ann about the announcement. I told *only Ann*—not Bill, not Harry, not Bob—about the announcement.

I told Ann about the announcement *only*. I told Ann about the announcement *only*—not about anything else. Remember: Place modifiers close to the words they modify.

CHECKUP 1   Rewrite the sentences below to eliminate misplaced modifiers or unnecessary repetitions.

1. Only give the call to Ms. Bussard; don't give it to anyone else.
   Give the call to Ms. Bussard only.

2. We lost the Oldani account almost.

3. Mr. Anderson just asked about the sales figures and nothing else.

DOUBLE NEGATIVES   Surely you remember the rule about double negatives: Do not use two negatives (*no, not, never, none, nowhere, don't, doesn't, won't,* and so on) together in a sentence. But do you remember that the words *scarcely, rarely, hardly, but,* and *barely* have negative meanings?

She could *barely* lift the heavy package. (NOT: She *couldn't barely* lift the heavy package.)

He could *hardly* wait to hear the news. (NOT: He *couldn't hardly* wait to hear the news.)

I have *no* markers to use as manuscript highlighters. (NOT: I *haven't got no* markers to use as manuscript highlighters.)

We *haven't* seen anyone in the computer room. (NOT: We haven't seen *no* one in the computer room.)

Rather than use *none* or *nothing* with negative expressions, use the positive words *any* or *anything*. Remember that two negatives cancel each other and make a positive statement.

AVOID UNNECESSARY REPETITIONS   Do not use an adverb to express a meaning already contained in the verb. Here are a few common redundancies (the adverb in parentheses in each case is unnecessary):

clear (off)   drop (down)   finish (up)   recline (back)   refer (back)   reply (back)   return (back)

CHECKUP 2   The sentences that follow contain double negatives or unnecessary repetitions. In the space provided, rewrite each of the following sentences to eliminate the double negative or unnecessary repetition.

1. They didn't have nothing more to say.
   They didn't have anything more to say.

2. Please finish up your work, or you'll be late.

3. You can sort out these papers.

_____

4. I haven't no money for you.

_____

ADVERB OR ADJECTIVE?

Sometimes you may wonder whether to say "She looked *angry*" or "She looked *angrily*." Which is correct, the adjective *angry* or the adverb *angrily*? Here's a test that will help you decide. Substitute one of the "being" verbs *(am, is, are, was, were)* for the verb in the sentence:

She *is (angry, angrily)*.

Which one makes more sense, "She is *angry*" or "She is *angrily*"? Obviously, the adjective *angry* makes sense; the adverb *angrily* does not. In all such sentences, choose the adjective when the "being" verb can be substituted. Let's see another example:

Your pie *tastes (delicious, deliciously)*.

Substitute the being verb *is* for *tastes*:

Your pie *is* delicious. Your pie *is* deliciously.

Which would you say? The adjective *delicious*, of course, is correct. Besides *taste* and *look*, some other verbs that may cause confusion are *feel, smell, sound, grow, appear*, and *seem*. As you see, then, whenever a being verb can be substituted, an adjective must follow because the adjective then modifies the subject (a noun or a pronoun). *An adverb cannot modify a noun or a pronoun!*

CHECKUP 3

Decide if the adjective or the adverb in each pair in parentheses is correct. Write the correct word in the space at the right. (Remember to substitute a "being" verb to help you make your choice.)

1. Denise Jones appeared to be very *(quiet, quietly)* throughout the meeting.　　1. <u>quiet</u>
2. He looked quite *(angry, angrily)* after he read the commission's findings.　　2. _____
3. These apples taste very *(sweet, sweetly)* to me.　　3. _____
4. Jim appeared *(sudden, suddenly)*, accompanied by several friends.　　4. _____

SURE AND *SURELY*; *BAD* AND *BADLY*

Sure and *bad* are adjectives that modify nouns and pronouns. They should not be used as adverbs. *Surely* and *badly* are adverbs modifying verbs, adjectives, and adverbs.

Here's a *sure* way to fix it. The adjective *sure* modifies the noun *way*.

She was *surely* excited about the trip. *Surely excited* or *very excited*—not *sure excited*. The adverb *surely* modifies the verb *excited*.

Use *bad* with the verbs *look* and *feel* in expressions such as these:

She feels *bad* about the move. (NOT: She feels *badly*.)

She looked *bad* after the accident. (NOT: She looked *badly*.)

BUT: She was *badly* hurt after the accident. (*Badly* is an adverb modifying the verb *hurt*.)

CHECKUP 4

Select the correct word from each pair in parentheses, and write it in the space at the right.

1. Our controller looked *(sad, sadly)* after she announced the cutbacks.　　1. <u>sad</u>
2. Irene was *(sure, surely)* relieved when she learned that her transfer was postponed.　　2. _____
3. Charles felt *(bad, badly)* that he could not help you.　　3. _____

EXERCISES

NAME _____ DATE _____ SCORE _____

EXERCISE 1   Rewrite each of the following sentences three times. Each time, change the position of the word *only* so that you also change the meaning of the sentence.

1. Only our secretary can file those papers.

_____
_____
_____

2. Only the supervisor attended the meeting in the morning.

_____
_____
_____

3. Only you are permitted to enter the building on Saturday.

_____
_____
_____

EXERCISE 2   Rewrite the sentences below to eliminate any misplaced modifiers or any unnecessary repetitions.

1. Please raise up your hand when you have a question.

_____

2. Give only a copy of the letter to Dan. (And to no one else.)

_____

3. Sandy just asked about the call to Chicago. (And nothing else.)

_____

4. The manager refunded our money for the broken vase cheerfully.

_____

5. Several of the respondents returned the completed questionnaires immediately.

_____

6. He referred back to his opening statement several times.

_____

7. You may recline back in your chair.

_____

8. Let's cooperate together so we can finish this project by noon.

_____

EXERCISE 3   Rewrite each of the following sentences so that each sentence contains only one negative element. (*Remember:* Avoid two negatives in one sentence.)

1. Don't you ever want for nothing?

_____

2. I haven't no respect for him.

_____

3. He didn't never think about that.

_____

4. I can't hardly tell that you made a mistake.

_____

5. I can't help but wonder about his actions.

_____

6. My aunt didn't give me none of her furniture.

_____

7. You can't hardly afford to go to college.

_____

8. There wasn't scarcely enough room for everyone.

_____

EXERCISE 4

For each sentence, decide which word in parentheses is correct—the adjective or the adverb. Write the correct word in the space at the right. (Remember to substitute a "being" verb to help you make your choice.)

1. Nadia did very (good, well) on her final examinations.   1. _____
2. This fudge tastes (delicious, deliciously).   2. _____
3. You (sure, surely) want to have at least two alternatives.   3. _____
4. When we woke in the morning, the fog seemed very (dense, densely).   4. _____
5. I felt (bad, badly) that I could not attend the meeting.   5. _____
6. The cookie tasted (good, well).   6. _____
7. Jane said the interview went (good, well).   7. _____
8. After working 15 hours, she felt (tired, tiredly).   8. _____

EXERCISE 5

Select the correct word from each pair in parentheses, and write it in the space at the right.

1. There hadn't been (no, any) calls for me.   1. _____
2. We received (good, well) information from the accountant.   2. _____
3. The new employee works (independent, independently).   3. _____
4. I (could, couldn't) hardly see the movie from where I sat.   4. _____
5. Phillip proofread the report very (careful, carefully).   5. _____
6. He (can, can't) hardly tell the difference in quality between the two
   fabrics.   6. _____
7. They (have, haven't) only to give a month's notice before they leave. 7. _____
8. He was sure that he was not hurt (bad, badly).   8. _____

EXERCISE 6

Underline any modification errors in the following sentences. Then write your corrections in the spaces at the right. If a sentence is correct, write OK.

1. Does this well water taste peculiarly to you?   1. _____
2. He smiled and remarked to the staff, "This is sure a terrific way to end our
   fiscal year!"   2. _____
3. Our new secretary, Leah, was able to type the report accurate.   3. _____
4. They haven't had no luck in getting people to join their organization. 4. _____
5. They were feeling bad that they could not be present for your graduation. 5. _____
6. Detective Ramirez examined the oddly shaped package careful.   6. _____
7. The hospital food was surprisingly good.   7. _____
8. The quarterback directed his teammates good.   8. _____
9. Kristen sang the national anthem beautiful.   9. _____
10. Please drive careful.   10. _____
11. That pie you served last night was delicious.   11. _____
12. We felt badly that we could not stay longer.   12. _____

More Troublemakers

USE *OTHER* OR *ELSE!* In many comparisons we use the word *than* with the comparative degree.

This job is better *than* any other I have had. This job is better *than* all the other jobs I have had.

Don't forget to include the word *other* or *else* when comparing one thing with a group of which it is a part. Without *other* or *else,* the sentences have different meanings:

She is smarter than anyone in our class. Without *else,* the sentence means that she is *not* in "our class."

She is smarter than all the people in our class. Without *other,* the sentence means that she is *not* in "our class." The words *other* and *else* show that the person or thing is being compared *with others of the same group.* Without *other* or *else,* we show that we are comparing someone or something with a person or thing from a *different* group.

CHECKUP 1 The words *other* or *else* are missing from the following sentences. Use a caret (˄), as in the example, to show where you should insert the appropriate word. Then write the correct word in the space at the right.

1. Our branch office is larger than any˄branch office in the company.　　　1. __other_____
2. In my opinion, Sally works harder than any employee.　　　2. _____
3. Rob is stronger than anyone at the gym.　　　3. _____
4. The president receives a larger salary than anyone in the company.　　　4. _____
5. Martin writes more memos than any manager in the company.　　　5. _____

REAL AND REALLY All of us hear people say "That was a *real* good movie" and "Dave just bought a *real* nice car" and so on. *Real* is wrong in such sentences because *real* is an adjective; you should say "*really* good," "*really* nice," and so on. Why? Because the adverb *really* is needed to modify the adjectives *good* and *nice*. So whenever you hear someone say "*real* good" or "*real* nice," remember that it should be "*really* good" or "*really* nice."

We were *really* expecting you to be on time today. (adverb)

His *real* concern was our welfare. (adjective)

I FEEL *WELL* You have already learned that *good* is an adjective and that *well* is an adverb. True—but there is an exception. When referring to health, use *well*, not *good:*

He slept longer than usual because he did not feel *well*. (NOT: feel *good*.)

Are you feeling better? Yes, I am *well*, thank you. (NOT: I am *good*.)

CHECKUP 2 Underline any incorrect uses of *good/well* or *real/really* in the following sentences. Then write your corrections in the spaces at the right. If a sentence is correct, write *OK*.

1. Matt can speak good on any topic.　　　1. __well_____
2. After being sick for several days, Laurie is real happy to be feeling well.　　　2. _____

3. The electricians worked really hard rewiring the old house.   3. _____

4. Adrian called in sick today; he wasn't feeling good.   4. _____

5. We attended a real important meeting with the officers of the company.   5. _____

ADVERBS THAT JOIN

Conjunctive adverbs, a special class of adverbs, join two independent clauses. (An independent clause has a subject and a verb and can stand alone as a complete sentence.)

Our supervisor accepted our recommendations; *however,* **she modified two of them.** Two independent clauses are joined by the conjunctive adverb *however.* A semicolon precedes the conjunctive adverb *however.* A comma follows it.

Several employees agreed to work through their lunch hours; *consequently,* **they were allowed to go home earlier.** An independent clause precedes the conjunctive adverb *consequently.* Another independent clause follows it.

Note that a semicolon (;) usually separates the two independent clauses. A comma generally follows the conjunctive adverb—but not always. In fact, sometimes the conjunctive adverb does not immediately follow the semicolon, as in the following sentences.

Mr. Anderson, our personnel director, agreed to pay our airfare to the convention; we offered, *therefore,* **to pay the registration fee.** A semicolon separates the two independent clauses. Two commas separate the adverb *therefore* from the rest of the sentence, showing that there is a slight pause surrounding *therefore.* Read the sentence aloud to notice the pause.

Mr. Anderson, our personnel director, agreed to pay our airfare to the convention; we *therefore* **offered to pay the registration fee.** The usual semicolon separates the two independent clauses, but no commas separate the adverb *therefore* because it should be read *without a pause.* Read the sentence aloud to see why no pause is needed.

The conjunctive adverbs *then* and *thus* usually need no commas.

They adjourned the meeting at 6 o'clock; *then* **we all went out for dinner.** No comma is needed after *then.*

Many adverbs join independent clauses; the following list contains some of the more commonly used ones:

accordingly	consequently	likewise	otherwise
nevertheless	furthermore	yet	thus
however	moreover	then	therefore
hence	notwithstanding	besides	also

CHECKUP 3

Decide which conjunctive adverb best replaces the question mark in each of the following sentences. Write your choice in the space at the right, and be sure to include the necessary punctuation before or after it. (*Note:* More than one answer may be correct.)

1. We didn't sell enough boxes (?) we were not eligible for the award.   1. **; consequently,** _____

2. Krista has been an accountant for many years (?) she is capable of completing my income tax forms.   2. _____

3. They would like to join us (?) they have some errands to run first.   3. _____

4. First, remove the cover (?) add the toner cartridge.   4. _____

5. You need to be ready by 5 o'clock (?) they will leave without you.   5. _____

6. Larry bought shrubs for around the building (?) he bought flowers for the planters.   6. _____

EXERCISES

NAME _____ DATE _____ SCORE _____

EXERCISE 1   The words *other* or *else* are missing from the following sentences. Use a caret (∧) to show where you should insert the appropriate word. Then write the correct word in the space at the right.

1. Carrie has received more government grants than anyone in the department.

2. Detroit is larger than any city in Michigan.

3. Her phone rings more often than any phone in this office.

4. The state of Iowa harvests more corn than any state in the Midwest.

5. Todd had better grades than anyone in his class.

6. That book sold better than any book on gardening.

7. This steel chair from Hayworth is more comfortable than any chair I have used.

8. Charlie runs faster than anyone on his football team.

9. Lynn sells more billboard advertising space than any employee at Adams Advertising.

10. Kathleen brings in more catering business than anyone at the hotel.

11. Jan has covered more town meetings for the newspaper than any reporter on the staff.

12. Ramon contributed more research than anyone on the research team.

1. _____
2. _____
3. _____
4. _____
5. _____
6. _____
7. _____
8. _____
9. _____
10. _____
11. _____
12. _____

EXERCISE 2   Underline any incorrect uses of *good/well* or *real/really* in the following sentences. Then write your corrections in the spaces at the right. If a sentence is correct, write *OK*.

1. Whatever Joel does, he does good.

2. Are you real interested in buying the property on Gull Lake?

3. The old mansion held up fairly well.

4. The apples we bought at the orchard were extremely well.

5. Mom always used real butter when she made her Christmas cookies.

6. Bob Meyers is a real good writer of proposals and contracts.

7. The people in the sales department work good together.

8. Arthur did a real good job of painting the house inside and out.

9. The professor researched the topic real well before writing an article for the journal.

10. We were proud of our basketball team; they played so good together.

11. With only two days in which to complete the report, Kelly had to work really hard.

12. Jean was surprised at how good she felt only a week after her surgery.

1. _____
2. _____
3. _____
4. _____
5. _____
6. _____
7. _____
8. _____
9. _____
10. _____
11. _____
12. _____

EXERCISE 3   Decide which conjunctive adverb best replaces the question mark in each of the following sentences. Write your choice in the space at the right, and be sure to include the necessary punctuation before or after it. (*Note:* More than one answer may be correct.)

1. Dan wanted to attend the football game (?) he had to do his homework first.

2. An agenda item for the directors meeting was communication (?) all the communication specialists were invited to attend the meeting.

3. First, we visited Spain (?) we flew over to France before returning home.

1. _____

2. _____

3. _____

4. While in Hong Kong we bought two custom-made suits (?) we bought shirts to go with them.

4. _____

5. The budget was reduced (?) we had to curtail our spending.

5. _____

6. We only needed 18¾ yards of material (?) we bought 20 yards.

6. _____

7. Five of us wished to attend the meeting (?) our manager said only three of us could go.

7. _____

8. No one on the committee wished to be the chairperson (?) the senior member appointed someone.

8. _____

9. The mason wanted to leave early (?) he worked through his lunch hour.

9. _____

10. A heated debate ensued over the proposed changes (?) the committee members remained adamant about their plans.

10. _____

11. The collator on the copy machine was broken (?) we had to collate the report by hand.

11. _____

12. We knew that several people had prior commitments (?) we scheduled the meeting for Tuesday.

12. _____

EXERCISE 4   Use each of the following conjunctive adverbs in a sentence. Be sure to punctuate the sentences correctly.

1. consequently _____

2. therefore _____

3. then _____

4. moreover _____

5. however _____

6. furthermore _____

7. accordingly _____

8. thus _____

9. yet _____

10. nevertheless _____

11. otherwise _____

12. however _____

EXERCISE 5   This exercise will review your ability to use adjectives and adverbs correctly. Underline any errors in the following sentences. Then write your corrections in the spaces at the right. If a sentence is correct, write OK.

1. The young children were behaving very bad in the grocery store.

1. _____

2. Debbie speaks loud when she talks to customers.

2. _____

3. The high school soccer team played extremely good today.

3. _____

4. Diane feels miserable after having had the flu for three days.

4. _____

5. Tim said he would be able to finish the report easy within the hour.

5. _____

6. The Seattle plant sells freshly salmon.

6. _____

7. The company made her a real good offer and she accepted it.

7. _____

8. If we are to work together, then we must get along better.

8. _____

9. Sandy couldn't hardly wait to see her returning son.

9. _____

10. Can you find a well way to write this report?

10. _____

11. Please sign your name legible on the form.

11. _____

12. In our opinion, Jane Ann works well with others in her unit.

12. _____

13. Dan was surely to win the top prize for academic achievement.

13. _____

14. Terri was feeling badly about the misplaced file.

14. _____

15. Weren't there no messages for me while I was gone?

15. _____

For, By, and Of—
The Preposition

PREPOSITIONS   Words such as *in* and *to, from* and *by, around* and *about,* and *between* and *among* are prepositions. But there are many more prepositions! Here is a list of the ones we use most often:

about	above	across	after	against	among	around
at	before	behind	below	beneath	beside	between
beyond	by	down	during	except	for	from
in	into	like	of	off	on	over
past	through	throughout	to	toward	under	underneath
until	up	upon	with	within	without	near

Now, what exactly do they *do*? They tell us—specifically—what the relation is between things or between people. For example: All the following sentences have the same subject *(report)* and the same verb *(is),* yet each tells us something different about the relationship between *report* and *desk.* How? By using different prepositions.

The report is *on* the desk. *On* tells us the specific relationship.

The report is *under* the desk. Quite different from *on* the desk!

The report is *in* the desk. *In*—not *on,* not *under* the desk.

CHECKUP 1   Underline the prepositions in each of the following sentences. Then write the total number of prepositions in each sentence in the space at the right.

1. Take the pen on my desk, and sign the letter in the blue folder.   1. __2__
2. The items in this box are from my mother, who lives across the street from us.   2. _____
3. Between you and me, I did not enjoy staying with my cousin during my two-week vacation.   3. _____
4. Please return the library books that are on the shelf, under the table, and against the window.   4. _____
5. To make more room, place the desk near the wall, move the chair to the side, and put the sofa against the table.   5. _____

PREPOSITIONAL PHRASES   As you've seen, a noun or a pronoun always follows a preposition: "to *Mrs. Smith,*" "except *her,*" and so on. Together the preposition plus the noun (or pronoun) make up a phrase—a *prepositional* phrase, of course. Sometimes words may modify the noun in a prepositional phrase, but the preposition is always first and the noun (or pronoun) is always last. Look at the prepositional phrases that follow:

on your desk *On* is the preposition; the noun *desk* is the object of the preposition; and *your* modifies the noun *desk.*

to Ms. Jones *To* is the preposition; the noun *Ms. Jones* is the object of the preposition.

Beware!   When the word *to* is followed by a verb, it is an infinitive phrase and not a prepositional phrase. Infinitive phrases begin with an infinitive—*to sell* cars, *to score* points, and so on.

The visiting executives want *to play golf* with their hosts. *To play golf* is an infinitive phrase. *With their hosts* is a prepositional phrase.

CHECKUP 2   Underline the prepositional phrases in the following sentences. Write the noun or pronoun that is the object of each preposition in the space at the right. Then circle any words that modify the objects of the prepositions. One of the prepositional phrases has two objects. Can you find that phrase?

1. (On) Monday, the manager will be in (the) office all week.   1. <u>**Monday, office**</u>
2. Members of the committee were invited to stay for lunch.   2. <u>   </u>
3. Between you and me, I plan to take Monday off.   3. <u>   </u>
4. Mr. Clarkson wants to give us a demonstration of the printer.   4. <u>   </u>
5. I would not be able to complete the project without your help.   5. <u>   </u>

HOW PREPOSITIONAL PHRASES ARE USED

Prepositional phrases can be used as adjectives or as adverbs. Adjectives modify nouns and pronouns—right? So, if a prepositional phrase modifies a noun or a pronoun, you'll know that the phrase is an *adjective* phrase:

The exhibitors *from Australia* left today. Since the prepositional phrase *from Australia* modifies the noun *exhibitors,* it must be an adjective phrase.

Most *of the travelers* were flying South. Since the phrase *of the travelers* modifies the pronoun *most,* it must be an adjective phrase.

Likewise, if a prepositional phrase modifies a verb, an adjective, or another adverb, you'll know the phrase is an *adverb* phrase because adverbs modify verbs, adjectives, and other adverbs.

Casey is looking *for a new law partner.* The prepositional phrase, *for a new law partner,* modifies the verb *is looking,* so the phrase must be an adverb phrase.

He is most productive *in the afternoons.* The prepositional phrase, *in the afternoons,* modifies the adjective *productive.* It is, therefore, an adverb phrase.

CHECKUP 3   Underline the prepositional phrases in the following sentences. Then tell whether each phrase works as an adjective or adverb by writing *ADJ* or *ADV* in the spaces at the right. Some of the sentences may have more than one prepositional phrase.

1. Many of the files from his office were taken to City Hall.   1. <u>**ADJ, ADJ, ADV**</u>
2. Throughout the day, we watched the news on television.   2. <u>   </u>
3. Two of the attorneys wanted a trial by jury.   3. <u>   </u>
4. The doctor is looking at the test results carefully.   4. <u>   </u>
5. Members of the surgical team were exhausted after the ten-hour operation.   5. <u>   </u>

CHECKUP 4   Use each of the following prepositional phrases correctly in a sentence.

1. between you and me   **Between you and me, I am disappointed in the results of the study.**
2. on the table   <u>   </u>
3. except for her   <u>   </u>
4. within the company   <u>   </u>
5. toward the entrance   <u>   </u>
6. at the end   <u>   </u>
7. among the crowd   <u>   </u>
8. after next week   <u>   </u>

EXERCISES

NAME _____ DATE _____ SCORE _____

EXERCISE 1   Underline the prepositional phrases in each of the following sentences. Then write the total number of prepositions in each sentence in the space at the right. (*Remember:* When the word *to* is followed by a verb, it is an infinitive and not a preposition.)

1. You can give one of these copies to Mr. Holling.   1. _____
2. Linda placed the papers on the desk, on the chair, and on the table.   2. _____
3. Several of the nurses were on call during the night.   3. _____
4. The members of the jury listened to the instructions of the judge.   4. _____
5. You can divide those papers between you and him.   5. _____
6. After visiting several of her relatives, Marie returned to the West Coast. 6. _____
7. From his office on the top floor, Tom had an excellent view of the city. 7. _____
8. While in the hospital, Aaron received many cards from his friends.   8. _____
9. After the holidays, you will be able to find many sale items in the stores. 9. _____
10. I expect to receive an answer from Jim within the hour.   10. _____

EXERCISE 2   Underline the prepositional phrases in the following sentences. In the spaces at the right, write the noun or pronoun that is the object of each preposition. (*Note:* Some sentences may have more than one prepositional phrase.)

1. Only one of the executives is in the office.   1. _____
2. He greeted us at the door with a grin on his face.   2. _____
3. After lunch it will be too late to go to the store.   3. _____
4. Visitors from the West were touring cities in the East.   4. _____
5. In his retirement speech, he spoke highly of the company.   5. _____
6. Beneath the blue water in the Caribbean, we saw many beautiful fish.   6. _____
7. They were basking under the sun on a sandy beach in California.   7. _____
8. The baseball player hit the ball into left field.   8. _____
9. We waited at the airport to see our friends from France.   9. _____
10. Stephanie proofreads the manuscript with accuracy.   10. _____

EXERCISE 3   Underline the prepositional phrases in the following sentences. Then tell whether each phrase works as an adjective or adverb by writing *ADJ* or *ADV* in the spaces at the right.

1. The pitcher threw the ball over the batter's head.   1. _____
2. Miriam practices the piano for two hours each day.   2. _____
3. Can people live on the moon?   3. _____
4. Hide the gift behind the plant.   4. _____
5. Many of the guests lived in a neighboring town.   5. _____
6. She was ready to go to the shopping mall with her friends.   6. _____
7. After the performance, we congratulated Rosemary.   7. _____
8. Before the meeting, Gerald agreed to work with us.   8. _____
9. The plant for the sick patient came from Blossoms Unlimited.   9. _____
10. The chairperson promised us her support for the drive.   10. _____

EXERCISE 4   Use each of the following prepositional phrases correctly in a sentence.

1. around the medical building

_____

2. after her arrival

_____

3. near the desk

_____

4. between you and me

_____

5. in this carton

_____

6. throughout the entire meeting

_____

7. to the date

_____

8. of our survey

_____

9. at the airport

_____

10. from the nurses

_____

EXERCISE 5   Add a modifying adjective phrase to each of the nouns or pronouns listed below.

1. lights	1. _____	11. conversation	11. _____
2. weeds	2. _____	12. convention	12. _____
3. help	3. _____	13. boxes	13. _____
4. memo	4. _____	14. shelves	14. _____
5. keys	5. _____	15. reviews	15. _____
6. house	6. _____	16. everyone	16. _____
7. supervisors	7. _____	17. news	17. _____
8. wires	8. _____	18. facts	18. _____
9. tools	9. _____	19. printer	19. _____
10. samples	10. _____	20. town	20. _____

EXERCISE 6   Add a modifying adverb phrase to each of the verbs listed below.

1. leave	1. _____	11. place	11. _____
2. come	2. _____	12. send	12. _____
3. go	3. _____	13. comply	13. _____
4. refer	4. _____	14. whispered	14. _____
5. arrived	5. _____	15. meet	15. _____
6. left	6. _____	16. sit	16. _____
7. put	7. _____	17. call	17. _____
8. compiled	8. _____	18. move	18. _____
9. waited	9. _____	19. walk	19. _____
10. helped	10. _____	20. served	20. _____

Common Preposition Errors

BETWEEN YOU AND *ME*   Pronouns that are objects of prepositions must be in the objective case, of course. Some people think that "between you and me" *sounds* wrong, so they say "between you and *I*." *Me* is correct.

> He said to divide the work *between you and me. Me,* the object of the preposition *between,* is correct.

AMONG/BETWEEN   Use *among* when speaking of three or more persons or objects. Use *between* when speaking of two persons or objects.

> They shared the lottery winnings *among the five of them.* *Among* is correct because more than two people are involved.

> *Between the two of us,* we should be able to find a solution. *Between* is correct because only two people are involved.

ONE TOO MANY   Some prepositions, such as *off, up, out, in,* and *on,* can also function as adverbs. (See the discussion of unnecessary repetitions in Lesson 31.) Some of us add adverbs and prepositions where they are not needed. In each of the following word groups, the preposition functioning as an adverb is not necessary.

> clear *off*   clean *up*   dust *off*   wipe *off*   off *of*   opposite *to*   near *to*

> Wipe *off* the counter, please. *Off* is not needed; omit it.
> We could not help *from* hearing what she said. *From* is not needed; omit it.

> Other repetitions to avoid are *rise up, fill up,* and *finish up.*

AT THE END   You may have heard that sentences should not end with prepositions. In conversations you may hear people using prepositions at the end of a sentence, but in formal writing you should avoid these expressions.

> Whom shall I give the report *to?* In formal writing, change to read: To whom shall I give the report?

CHECKUP 1   Underline any incorrect uses of pronouns or prepositions in the following sentences. Then write your corrections in the spaces at the right. Write *omit* if the preposition should be omitted.

1. Between the three of us, we should be able to find a solution.   1. __Among_____
2. Where is she at?   2. _____
3. John and me were responsible for editing the manuscript.   3. _____
4. I couldn't help from hearing that Joann wants a transfer.   4. _____

FROM (NOT OFF OF)   *Off of* is always wrong. Sometimes *off* is enough, as you saw earlier; other times, the word *from* is really intended.

> We borrowed a book *from* the professor. (NOT: *off of* the professor.)
> Did the comptroller receive the reports *from* the department managers? (NOT: *off of* the department managers.)

DIFFERENT FROM (NOT DIFFERENT THAN)

Be careful to use *different from* in sentences such as these:

> This computer is *different from* the one that was demonstrated. (NOT: *different than.*)

> This invoice number is *different from* the one recorded in the complaint. (NOT: *different than.*)

BESIDE AND BESIDES

Beside means "next to"; *besides* means "in addition to." These words should not be used interchangeably.

> The president sat *beside* the vice president at the meeting. (*Next to* the vice president.)

> *Besides* the plaque, she was also presented with a $5,000 check. (*In addition to* the plaque.)

COMPARE TO AND COMPARE WITH

For in-depth comparisons and an analysis of similarities and differences, use *compare with*. For comparisons that are not in depth or that merely suggest a similarity, use *compare to*.

> *Compared to* yesterday's sales totals, today's are terrific. A comparison that is not in depth.

> As part of her dissertation, Nadine *compared* teaching methodologies of the 1940s *with* those of the 1990s. An in-depth comparison.

IDENTICAL WITH (NOT TO)

Be sure to use *identical with*. A common error is using *identical to*.

> The dress pattern should be *identical with* the original design. (NOT: *identical to* the original.)

RETROACTIVE TO (NOT FROM)

Use *retroactive to*. A common error is using *retroactive from*.

> Her salary increase was *retroactive to* July 1. (NOT: *retroactive from* July 1.)

SPEAK TO, SPEAK WITH

Use *speak to* to indicate that you're telling something to someone. Use *speak with* to indicate that you're discussing something with someone.

> The supervisor *spoke to* him about the spelling errors in his correspondence. The supervisor *told* him something about the errors.

> The supervisor *spoke with* the entire staff about the need to avoid spelling errors in their correspondence. The supervisor *discussed* this important topic with them.

COULD HAVE

Neither *could* nor *have* is a preposition, of course, but many people say "could have" so that it sounds like "could've." Consequently, some people write *could of!* Always write *could have*.

> They *could have* had three copies. (NOT: *could of* had.)

CHECKUP 2   Underline any incorrect uses of prepositions in the following sentences. Write your corrections in the spaces at the right. If a sentence is correct, write *OK*.

1. I could of bought the book for $5. 1. **have** _____
2. Our manager compared April sales to March sales. 2. _____
3. Merit pay was retroactive from January 1. 3. _____
4. Raymond wanted to borrow a book off of Ms. Towers. 4. _____
5. This bank is different than the one downtown. 5. _____
6. Her office is besides mine. 6. _____
7. I spoke with my neighbors about the block party. 7. _____
8. Their plan is identical to the one you proposed. 8. _____

EXERCISES

NAME _____ DATE _____ SCORE _____

EXERCISE 1
Underline any incorrect uses of pronouns or prepositions in the following sentences. Then write your corrections in the spaces at the right. Write *omit* if the preposition should be omitted.

1. I do not know whom Mr. Klaus gave the contract to. 1. _____
2. Between you and I, I am applying for the opening in the Research Department. 2. _____
3. The journals are to be distributed between the three lawyers. 3. _____
4. They could not help from seeing what was going on in their department. 4. _____
5. Whom did Pamela give the medical report to? 5. _____
6. I really don't know where she is at. 6. _____
7. You may take a copy of the report off of the desk. 7. _____
8. Have you seen where Jason went to? 8. _____
9. Please divide the work among the two of you. 9. _____
10. That district will be divided evenly between the five sales representatives. 10. _____

EXERCISE 2
Select the correct word from each pair in parentheses, and write it in the space at the right.

1. They should *(have, of)* written to us sooner about the problem. 1. _____
2. It was arranged so that the president would sit *(beside, besides)* the philanthropist. 2. _____
3. That fabric is different *(from, than)* the one that was ordered. 3. _____
4. The winnings were shared *(among, between)* the five team members. 4. _____
5. Let's just divide the work between you and *(I, me)*. 5. _____
6. I would like to speak *(to, with)* you about your lateness. 6. _____
7. The union negotiated to have the pay increase retroactive *(to, from)* July 1. 7. _____
8. Burt said that the letter should be identical *(with, to)* the one that was written by Mr. Colson. 8. _____
9. Compared *(to, with)* yesterday's figures, today's are excellent. 9. _____
10. *(Beside, Besides)* receiving a certificate, the winner was awarded a $50 savings bond. 10. _____

EXERCISE 3
Underline any incorrect uses of pronouns or prepositions in the following sentences. Then write your corrections in the spaces at the right. If a sentence is correct, write *OK*.

1. One other person beside me will make a presentation at the meeting. 1. _____
2. Ask if your salary increase will be retroactive from the first of the year. 2. _____
3. The doctor spoke with the interns about the emergency room procedures. 3. _____
4. That dress is identical with mine. 4. _____
5. At the reception, John was standing besides Mr. Nolan. 5. _____
6. Between the six of us, we should be able to come up with several solutions. 6. _____
7. When we tallied our totals at the end of the day, John's totals were different than mine. 7. _____
8. Do you know which office is identical with his? 8. _____
9. William could of seen the report by now. 9. _____
10. They differ from us on that issue. 10. _____

EXERCISE 4

Decide if the word in italics is an adverb or a preposition. (*Remember:* An adverb tells how, when, or where. A preposition shows the relationship between its object and another word in a sentence.) Tell whether each word works as an adverb or a preposition by writing *ADV* or *PREP* in the space at the right.

1. Here's the document that Ms. Olsen wants us to send *to* the hospital.   1. _____
2. We had the freedom to move *about* the building unescorted.   2. _____
3. We should know the answer *within* three weeks.   3. _____
4. After she came *to*, she recognized her parents.   4. _____
5. The Purchasing Department orders supplies *from* DeNoyer Office Supplies.   5. _____

EXERCISE 5

In the space provided, complete each sentence by writing a prepositional phrase to modify the italicized word. (Remember to include a period in your answer.)

1. Please place the *papers*   1. _____
2. Give the *certificates*   2. _____
3. The will stipulated that the property be *divided*   3. _____
4. Here are the *results*   4. _____
5. The information was *gathered*   5. _____

EXERCISE 6

Rewrite the following sentences so that the preposition is either used correctly or omitted.

1. Whom are you voting for?

   _____

2. We couldn't find the boxes that these came in.

   _____

3. Do you know where he went to?

   _____

4. I would like to borrow that off you.

   _____

5. Where did you see her at?

   _____

EXERCISE 7

Use each of the following prepositional phrases in a sentence.

1. between you and me   _____
2. beside the typewriter   _____
3. within the hour   _____
4. during our lunch break   _____
5. for the position   _____
6. through the double doors   _____
7. among the first to arrive   _____
8. to him   _____
9. for Michael and me   _____
10. upon my return   _____
11. with Ms. VonHaften   _____
12. toward Fifth Avenue   _____
13. except me   _____
14. behind the building   _____

Phrases

WHAT IS A PHRASE?   A phrase is a group of related words that does *not* have a subject and a predicate. (The predicate, as you know, is the verb and its modifiers that tell what the subject does.)

to the supervisor   No verb is in this prepositional phrase; *supervisor* is the object of the preposition *to*.

Remember that and you will remember that a phrase—prepositional or otherwise—does not have a subject and a verb. Remember, too, that prepositional phrases can be used as nouns, adverbs, or adjectives.

From my office to the Municipal Building **is a five-minute walk.** The prepositional phrase *From my office to the Municipal Building* is used as a noun; it is the subject of the verb *is*.

The woman *with the attaché case* is his wife. The prepositional phrase *with the attaché case* is used as an adjective; it modifies the noun *woman*.

Today we drove *to the lake*. The prepositional phrase *to the lake* is used as an adverb. Went where? *To the lake*.

Besides prepositional phrases there are infinitive phrases, participial phrases, and gerund phrases.

INFINITIVE PHRASES   *To run* and *to walk, to sit* and *to stand, to read* and *to write*—all are infinitives. An *infinitive*, as you see, is simply the word *to* plus a verb. An infinitive phrase is a phrase consisting of an infinitive (*to* plus the verb) and any modifiers it may have.

***My goal is to move to the city by winter*.** The infinitive *to move* starts the phrase *to move to the city by winter*. This phrase is an infinitive phrase. Note that the complete infinitive phrase includes two prepositional phrases—*to the city* and *by winter*—which modify the infinitive *to move*.

Beware!   Do not confuse an infinitive phrase with a simple prepositional phrase starting with the preposition *to*. Prepositional phrases do not have verbs. For example:

to the office   to him   to the park   to the game

Infinitive phrases have verbs. For example:

to invite friends   to write memos   to prepare dinner

CHECKUP 1   Underline the infinitive phrase in each of the following sentences. Then write just the infinitive in the space at the right. (*Caution:* Watch for *to* used as a preposition!)

1. I plan <u>to give</u> my ticket to him.
2. We wanted to leave the office early so that we could go to the concert.
3. To save money was his goal.
4. Do you have any ideas about how to solve the problem?
5. I plan to arrive before noon.
6. To reject their offer seems unkind.

1. **to give**
2. _____
3. _____
4. _____
5. _____
6. _____

PARTICIPIAL PHRASES

Remember participles? A participle is a verb form that is used as an adjective. Words such as *walking* and *running, typing* and *filing, standing* and *sitting* are present participles. The past participles for these words are *walked, ran, typed, filed, stood,* and *sat.* Let's see how phrases that begin with present participles or past participles can be used as adjectives—that is, used to describe.

Running to the bus stop, **Ms. Pulaski caught the 7:15 on time.** Do you see how *running to the bus stop* describes *Ms. Pulaski?* Because it describes a noun, this phrase works as an adjective. *Running* is a present participle.

The accounting records, *inspected by several auditors,* **were judged to be accurate.** The phrase *inspected by several auditors* describes *the accounting records,* of course. *Inspected* is a past participle.

Beware! To avoid confusion, be sure that the introductory participial phrase is followed by a word that it can logically modify.

CONFUSING:

Running down the stairs, my toe caught in the carpet. The *toe* was not running down the stairs. The participial phrase, *running down the stairs,* cannot logically modify *toe.*

CORRECT:

Running down the stairs, I caught my toe in the carpet. *I* was running down the stairs.

CHECKUP 2

Underline the participial phrase in each of the following sentences. Then write the participle in the space at the right.

1. <u>Emphasizing grammar</u>, the English class was offered to all freshmen.
2. Being a surgical nurse, Carrie subscribed to several professional medical journals.
3. Persuaded by his parents, Norman applied for admission to several colleges.
4. Left in charge of the office, Ms. Butler had to make the night deposit.
5. Given the circumstances, Ellen acted wisely.
6. Encouraged by my family, I returned to school.

1. <u>**Emphasizing**</u>
2. _____
3. _____
4. _____
5. _____
6. _____

GERUND PHRASES

A gerund is a verb form ending in *-ing* that is used as a noun. A gerund phrase is a phrase consisting of a gerund and its modifiers.

Working in the evening **is tiring.** *Working in the evening* acts as a noun; it is the subject of the verb *is.* (You can substitute a pronoun for this phrase: It is tiring. Thus *working in the evening* must be a noun.)

My favorite task at work is *assembling those report figures.* *Assembling those report figures* acts as a noun. (Can you replace the *-ing* phrase *assembling those report figures* with a pronoun? Yes: *My favorite task is this.* Therefore the *-ing* phrase *assembling those report figures* is a noun.)

CHECKUP 3

Underline the *-ing* phrase in each of the following sentences. For each *-ing* phrase that works as an adjective, write the word that the phrase modifies. For each *-ing* phrase that works as a noun, write the verb for that noun.

1. <u>Serving his country</u> was an honor.
2. Making 32 points was his outstanding achievement that evening.
3. Traveling throughout the West, Donald saw many beautiful scenes.
4. Earning a scholastic scholarship proved that Barry's studying hard was not in vain.
5. Comparing these statistics is tedious work.
6. Revising the sales report is a real challenge.

1. <u>**was**</u>
2. _____
3. _____
4. _____
5. _____
6. _____

EXERCISES

NAME _____ DATE _____ SCORE _____

EXERCISE 1   Underline the infinitive phrase in each of the following sentences. Then write just the infinitive in the space at the right. (*Caution:* Watch for *to* used as a preposition!) Some sentences may have two infinitive phrases. Others may have none—write *none* if this is the case.

1. Are you sure you want to invest that much money in stocks?   1. _____
2. Ray asked to take a week's vacation before Christmas.   2. _____
3. The surgeon was asked to operate on the patient immediately.   3. _____
4. Please give the report to Ms. Crenshaw before you leave the office.   4. _____
5. The children wished to spend their money on candy.   5. _____
6. When will it be time to leave for the opera?   6. _____
7. The women wanted to play bridge; the men wanted to play dominoes.   7. _____
8. The professor helped the student to find a summer job.   8. _____
9. I needed to vote before the polls closed.   9. _____
10. Are you ready to go shopping?   10. _____

EXERCISE 2   Underline the participial phrase in each of the following sentences. Then write the word that it modifies in the space at the right.

1. Serving on the committee, Jane learned much about local issues.   1. _____
2. Hurrying to catch the bus, Robert fell.   2. _____
3. Watching the late movie on television, they fell asleep.   3. _____
4. Skipping breakfast earlier that morning, Amy was hungry by 10 o'clock.   4. _____
5. Acting as a butler in the play, Harold gave a convincing performance.   5. _____
6. Reduced because it was soiled, the dress was a bargain at $40.   6. _____
7. Left to his own resources, Jeff was able to build the bookcase alone.   7. _____
8. Entering the elevator, Joe removed his hat.   8. _____
9. Provided they pay their own registration fee, the two women could attend the workshop.   9. _____
10. Having been told that the flight was canceled, Janice decided to change her travel plans.   10. _____

EXERCISE 3   Underline the gerund phrase in each of the following sentences. Then write the verb for that phrase in the space provided.

1. The counselor advises sending applications for financial aid early.   1. _____
2. Asking your supervisor for a raise was not prudent.   2. _____
3. Taking telephone messages was not his idea of fun.   3. _____
4. Writing letters to former students is very time-consuming.   4. _____
5. Running for a political office requires a lot of money.   5. _____
6. Providing children with clothing is very expensive.   6. _____
7. Earning a college education was his main goal.   7. _____
8. Proofreading the manuscript proved easier than she had expected.   8. _____
9. Managing the office demonstrated his leadership style.   9. _____
10. Rejecting the application was not easy.   10. _____

11. The caterer suggested serving the dessert after the awards presentation. 11. _____
12. He began writing his résumé when the project ended. 12. _____
13. Coaching the team took more than he anticipated. 13. _____
14. We considered leaving before the speeches. 14. _____
15. Reaching an agreement is our most important task. 15. _____

EXERCISE 4   Underline the infinitive, participial, and gerund phrases in the following sentences. In the space at the right, identify the phrase as infinitive, participial, or gerund.

1. The employees wanted to leave by 8 o'clock. 1. _____
2. Printing the final pages was a relief. 2. _____
3. Speaking in a quiet tone, the nurse calmed the anxious patient. 3. _____
4. Walking five miles each day, the athlete hoped to stay in shape. 4. _____
5. Selling real estate was Chris's career goal. 5. _____
6. Where did you want me to put these items? 6. _____
7. Knowing all the answers made the student feel confident. 7. _____
8. Hungry for a homemade pie, Jill asked her mom to bake her one. 8. _____
9. We stayed to help Marion get the job finished. 9. _____
10. Having good directions helped Jean find the hospital. 10. _____
11. Playing softball is her favorite leisure activity. 11. _____
12. We were asked to arrive promptly at 7 o'clock. 12. _____
13. Revising her résumé was a priority. 13. _____
14. Dan was hired to answer the phones. 14. _____
15. Watching that movie made me want to travel. 15. _____

EXERCISE 5   Use each phrase given below as the beginning of a sentence. Complete the sentence in your own words, adding punctuation as necessary.

1. Sitting on the porch swing _____
2. Seeing the cat in the window _____
3. Traveling in the South _____
4. Entering the stadium _____
5. Listening to the music _____
6. Answering the classified ad promptly _____
7. Painting for 12 hours _____
8. Traveling around the world _____
9. Having a teaching assistant _____
10. Left in charge of the children _____
11. Studying for the exam _____
12. Considering the current situation _____
13. Estimating the costs beforehand _____
14. Rejecting the proposal _____
15. Reserving a table _____
16. Choosing a career _____
17. Repairing the engine _____
18. Leaving in a hurry _____
19. Buying a home _____
20. Running in the park _____

Conjunctions Are Joiners!

WHAT DO THEY JOIN?   Conjunctions are words that *join*. (Use the word *junction*—a place where two roads join—to remind you that the conjunctions *join*.) This lesson covers two kinds of conjunctions—coordinating conjunctions and correlative conjunctions.

COORDINATING CONJUNCTIONS   Of the seven coordinating conjunctions, the four common ones are *and, but, or,* and *nor*. The other three—*yet, for,* and *so*—are used infrequently. Coordinating conjunctions join two or more of the same things.

Two or more nouns:

assistants, managers, *and* supervisors   Brian, Joel, *or* David

Two or more pronouns:

he *and* I   you, her, *or* me

Nouns and pronouns (considered the same for this purpose):

Gary *and* he   Joanne, Jay, *or* him

Two or more adjectives:

slow *and* deliberate   quick *but* cautious

Two or more phrases:

to run *or* to jog   proofreading manuscripts, editing documents, *and* revising reports

Two or more clauses:

I came; I saw; *and* I conquered.
Our manager greeted the new employees, visited each department, *and* called everyone by name.

Here's a chart to help you decide which coordinating conjunction to use:

USE	FOR	EXAMPLE
and	addition	Tom and Mary will go.
but	contrast	He is fast but sloppy.
or	choice	We can stay or leave.
nor	opposite	I didn't call, nor has he called.

CHECKUP 1
Underline twice the conjunction in each of the following sentences, and write it in the space at the right. Then underline once the items that the conjunction joins.

1. Harvey and Dale were working together on the project.
2. The speaker was witty and charming.
3. You or he may attend the convention in Spokane.
4. The fabric was attractive but expensive.
5. Stocks and bonds were being sold that day.

1. **and**
2. _____
3. _____
4. _____
5. _____

CHECKUP 2
Conjunctions are missing from the following sentences. Use a caret (∧) to show where you should insert each conjunction. Then write the appropriate conjunction in the space at the right. The first one has been done for you.

1. The shoes were comfortable∧not attractive.
2. Sheila Robert were moving to New York City.
3. During our lunch hour we wanted to run to walk.
4. The secretary typed the report quickly accurately.
5. Please give this letter to Mr. Baxter his secretary.

1. **but**
2. _____
3. _____
4. _____
5. _____

CORRELATIVE CONJUNCTIONS
Correlative conjunctions are used in pairs, but once again, they join the same things. Common pairs of correlative conjunctions are *both/and, either/or, neither/nor, not only/but also,* and *whether/or.*

both quickly *and* accurately — *both/and* join two adverbs

either you *or* me — *either/or* join two pronouns

neither tall *nor* short — *neither/nor* join two adjectives

not only Mary *but also* him — *not only/but also* join a noun and a pronoun. Remember that nouns and pronouns are considered the same thing as far as conjunctions are concerned. (*Note:* sometimes *also* is omitted in *not only/but also.* For example: Not only was Marta late, but she had forgotten to bring the lunch.)

whether for him *or* for you — *whether/or* joins two prepositional phrases

Careful!
Subjects joined by conjunctions should not cause any problems in verb choice—*if you are careful!*

Either Sharon or her daughters have the key. *Have agrees with the subject closer to it, daughters (her daughters have).*

Either her daughters or Sharon has the key. *Has agrees with the subject closer to it—in this case, Sharon (Sharon has).*

Doesn't she or I merit it? Don't I or she merit it?

Eddie or you were to receive it. You or Eddie were to receive it.

CHECKUP 3
Conjunctions are missing from the following sentences. Use a caret (∧) to show where you should insert each conjunction. Then write the appropriate conjunction in the space at the right.

1. Either you∧he will need to give the presentation.
2. Not only Brian his assistant are gone for the afternoon.
3. They will neither walk jog when the humidity is so high.
4. We are not only going shopping going to lunch.
5. David couldn't decide whether to quit to take a leave of absence.
6. See if either Jack Linda is on vacation next week.
7. Not only you your sister is applying for the job.

1. **or**
2. _____
3. _____
4. _____
5. _____
6. _____
7. _____

EXERCISES

NAME _____ DATE _____ SCORE _____

EXERCISE 1   Underline twice the conjunction in each of the following sentences, and write it in the space at the right. Then underline once the items that the conjunction joins.

1. Ruth and Paul both work in the emergency room at the hospital.   1. _____
2. The office assistant prepared the report quickly and accurately.   2. _____
3. The dress was inexpensive but attractive.   3. _____
4. You can start by filing the correspondence or by typing the reports.   4. _____
5. Deb was responsible for hiring and firing employees.   5. _____
6. The president and vice president were both in their offices.   6. _____
7. The manager or his assistant will sign the contract.   7. _____
8. They can either accept or reject our offer.   8. _____
9. Applicants are tested and interviewed before being hired.   9. _____
10. The meeting was held to decide whether to raise prices or to keep them at the same level.   10. _____
11. Was the pipe made of plastic or steel?   11. _____
12. The engineers were not sure whether they would be leaving on Monday or Tuesday.   12. _____
13. It doesn't matter whether we turn left or right.   13. _____
14. She was admired for her loyalty and her courage.   14. _____
15. Mary could be transferred to our Chicago office or our Detroit office.   15. _____
16. Our accountant wanted to know about our fixed and current assets.   16. _____
17. Amanda worked conscientiously and carefully.   17. _____
18. The co-chairpersons for the convention were Drs. Haggerty and O'Brien.   18. _____
19. We were in and out of the cold lake water in seconds.   19. _____
20. Mr. and Mrs. Wilson will arrive about 4 o'clock this afternoon.   20. _____

EXERCISE 2   Each of the following sentences needs a pair of conjunctions—but one of the pair is missing from each sentence. Use a caret (ʌ) to show where the missing conjunction belongs; then write it in the space provided.

1. Either you Lowell will be working for Mr. Martin this afternoon.   1. _____
2. I have neither seen heard from Ramon.   2. _____
3. We will not only borrow your van fill it with gas.   3. _____
4. Michael had not decided whether to get a job to start work on a master's degree.   4. _____
5. They decided to sell their cottage by the lake both because it required too much yard work because the taxes were too high.   5. _____
6. Either we will work on the project this afternoon, we will forget about it.   6. _____
7. Neither this book that book will be acceptable to the school board.   7. _____
8. Gary neither asked for received a sabbatical.   8. _____
9. Not only Dr. Ghani Dr. Yaeger spoke at the commencement ceremony.   9. _____
10. The doctor had to decide whether to operate to prescribe medication.   10. _____

EXERCISE 3

Conjunctions are missing from the following sentences. Use a caret (∧) to show where you should insert each conjunction. Then write the appropriate conjunction in the space at the right.

1. Reading the operator's manual is essential, most employees ignore it.
2. Members of the class enjoyed their reunion reminisced about their years in high school.
3. The inventor of the new stain remover was not only wealthy friendly.
4. Ten years ago she was pretty, now she is somewhat thin and pale.
5. Jim Martin is a professor his wife is a surgeon.
6. The store was having a moving sale, it seemed that the prices were the same as they had been before the sale.
7. Deliver the goods by Friday I will place the order with another company.
8. Neither Harry William was happy with their father's decision.
9. Paula wanted her to proofread the manuscript carefully quickly.
10. Ernesto wanted to go on the trip, he didn't have the money for it.
11. Tim will work either for you for him.
12. He moved to Arizona because of the dry climate, his health did not improve.
13. They couldn't decide whether to stay an extra day to leave the following morning.
14. We need to proofread not only the letters the memos.
15. Neither he his wife is eligible for promotion to associate professor.

1. _____
2. _____
3. _____
4. _____
5. _____
6. _____
7. _____
8. _____
9. _____
10. _____
11. _____
12. _____
13. _____
14. _____
15. _____

EXERCISE 4

Use each of the following conjunctions correctly in a sentence. Be sure to use proper punctuation.

1. both/and _____
2. not only/but also _____
3. either/or _____
4. whether/or _____
5. neither/nor _____
6. and _____
7. but _____
8. or _____
9. for _____
10. nor _____

EXERCISE 5

Complete the following sentences by adding an appropriate conjunction and a second related group of words. Also, be sure to include the punctuation at the end of each sentence.

1. It was late already, _____
2. Our manager asked people to work overtime, _____
3. The human resources director was willing to hire someone without experience, _____
4. We ordered the merchandise in March, _____
5. The receptionist at the hospital answers the telephone _____
6. You may stay if you want to, _____
7. I have not gone, _____
8. We can stay here tonight, _____

Clauses

WHAT'S IN A CLAUSE?   A clause is a group of words containing a subject and a predicate and used as part of a sentence. Clauses that can stand alone are called *independent clauses;* clauses that do not express a complete thought and cannot stand alone are called *dependent clauses.*

Because he ordered five items is a clause. It has a subject *(he)* and a predicate *(ordered)* but does not express a complete thought. This clause is dependent; it is not a sentence.

He ordered five items This clause can stand alone. It is independent; it could be a sentence.

Both examples are clauses. Yet, as similar as they appear to be, these clauses are different. What makes one a sentence and the other not a sentence? The answer is the word *because.* The word *because* makes us expect more. It is a conjunction. Its purpose is to join one clause with another clause.

Because he ordered five items, he received a discount. Here the clause *because he ordered five items* is connected to another clause—*he received a discount.* Without that other clause, the *because* clause is incomplete. It is not a sentence. It cannot stand alone; it is a dependent clause. It needs help. It needs an independent clause, a clause that can stand alone, to complete its meaning. Let's look at two dependent clauses. Note that each one does not express a complete thought. They are not sentences.

before we leave for the conference   while I'm at work

Combined with independent clauses these dependent clauses form complete sentences.

Before we leave for the conference, I would like to phone the office.

Sherry will watch the children while I'm at work.

SUBORDINATING CONJUNCTIONS   Independent clauses are also called main clauses. Dependent clauses are also called subordinate clauses. Subordinate conjunctions connect independent clauses with dependent clauses to form sentences. Listed below are some of the common subordinating conjunctions:

after	although	for	so that	unless	whether	as if	than
until	while	as	if	once	that	when	whenever
because	since	though	where	before	so	till	whereas

Whenever you see these subordinating conjunctions, you will know that they introduce *dependent clauses.* You will know, too, that they join these dependent clauses to independent clauses (because dependent clauses need help from independent clauses).

Beware!   A dependent clause does not always appear at the beginning of a sentence.

After they met for eight hours, he was tired. The dependent clause *after they met for eight hours* appears at the beginning of the sentence. (A comma shows where this clause ends.)

He was tired *after they met for eight hours.* Here, the same clause is used at the end of the sentence. (No punctuation is needed in this sentence because the clause appears at the end of the sentence.)

It is easy to spot a dependent clause wherever it appears because it begins with a subordinating conjunction, such as *after, if, as,* or *when.*

CHECKUP 1
Decide if the following groups of words are independent, that is, if they are sentences. If so, write *S* in the space at the right. If the words form a dependent clause, write *NS* for *no sentence.*

1. Because we were willing to go to the store.   1. __NS_____
2. No, we haven't had a chance to see the demonstration yet.   2. _____
3. While you were gone from the office.   3. _____

Now underline the dependent clause in each of the following sentences. In the space at the right, write the subordinating conjunction that joins the dependent clause to an independent clause.

4. We were exhausted <u>after we returned from a camping weekend.</u> 4. __after_____
5. They will be glad to see you when you return from Africa.   5. _____
6. You need training before you can do that job.   6. _____

NOUN CLAUSES
Clauses work in different ways. They can serve as nouns, as adjectives, or as adverbs. A clause works as a noun when it serves as the subject of a sentence, when it is the object of a verb, and so on.

Meg said *that we should all agree. That we should all agree* is the object of the verb *said.*

That he chose Donna to chair the committee is a good sign that she will be promoted. *That he chose Donna to chair the committee* is the subject. The verb is *is.*

For an easy way to test whether a clause is a noun clause, just try to replace the clause with a pronoun. Because a noun can be replaced by a pronoun, a noun clause can also be replaced by a pronoun.

This is a good sign that she will be promoted. The pronoun *this* can replace the noun clause *that he chose her to chair the committee* in the previous example.

ADJECTIVE CLAUSES
Adjective clauses describe—they modify nouns or pronouns. Frequently, adjective clauses begin with *who, whom, whose, which,* and *that.*

Bobby, *who has been with the company for three years,* is our new director. The clause *who has been with the company for three years* is used as an adjective. It modifies the noun *Bobby.* The clause has its own subject *(who)* and its own verb *(has been).*

ADVERB CLAUSES
Like adverbs, adverb clauses modify verbs, adjectives, and other adverbs. The clause is joined to the word it modifies by a subordinating conjunction, such as *after, although, because,* and *while.*

We'll work on that newsletter *when we have time.* Let's work on that newsletter when? *When we have time.* This adverb clause modifies the verb *work.*

They were pleased *when we donated the painting.* The adverb clause *when we donated the painting* modifies the adjective *pleased.*

She types faster *than he types. Faster* is an adverb. It modifies the verb *types.* The adverb clause *than he types* modifies the adverb *faster.* It has a subject *(he)* and a verb *(types).*

CHECKUP 2
Underline the dependent clauses in the following sentences. Then in the spaces at the right identify each dependent clause as a noun clause *(N),* an adjective clause *(ADJ),* or an adverb clause *(ADV).*

1. They elected a person <u>who shared their same views.</u>   1. __ADJ_____
2. Pat said that we should all go to the conference.   2. _____
3. Jill's book, which was written in three months, sold over a million copies. 3. _____
4. Jason worked on the project when he had time.   4. _____

EXERCISES

NAME _____ DATE _____ SCORE _____

EXERCISE 1   Decide if the following groups of words are independent—that is, if they are sentences. If so, write *S* for each sentence in the space at the right. If the words form a dependent clause, write *NS* for *no sentence.*

1. We'll be free to leave after we finish the work.   1. _____
2. So that we can hire an extra person to help with the project. 2. _____
3. Because they had signed the document.   3. _____
4. If you are leaving, may I use your office.   4. _____
5. While the medical staff was meeting.   5. _____
6. When your lawyer is here.   6. _____
7. Until I hear from my accountant, I will not comment on the case. 7. _____
8. Since that was over several years ago.   8. _____
9. Whether or not you believe the story.   9. _____
10. When the supervisor approached us.   10. _____

EXERCISE 2   Underline the dependent clause in each of the following sentences. In the space at the right, write the subordinating conjunction that joins the dependent clause to an independent clause.

1. Since you have been gone for over three weeks, we thought you would not
   return.   1. _____
2. Send me a copy of the list when you have completed it.   2. _____
3. Gary, who lives in Washington, D.C., will be our moderator.   3. _____
4. These are the projects that you researched for us.   4. _____
5. We appreciate the help that you gave our friends.   5. _____
6. I'm not sure where she went.   6. _____
7. When you hear about their plans, please let me know.   7. _____
8. Ask someone who worked on the project to give you the details. 8. _____
9. When we leave for Europe, we'll be sure to let you know.   9. _____
10. The doctor who treated her was Dr. John Arnold.   10. _____

EXERCISE 3   Underline the dependent clauses in the following sentences. Then in the spaces at the right identify each dependent clause as a noun clause *(N)*, an adjective clause *(ADJ)*, or an adverb clause *(ADV)*.

1. Products that sell well come from the United States.   1. _____
2. Do you know what time it is?   2. _____
3. Joan is confident that she will be promoted.   3. _____
4. Please ship that box, which contains the copy paper they ordered. 4. _____
5. Jim said that we were all invited to the show.   5. _____
6. Friends who are like Jean are wonderful.   6. _____
7. Ray played the piano better than Linda did.   7. _____
8. Cars that are very reliable are listed in this consumer newsletter. 8. _____
9. We assign our assistants where they are needed at the moment. 9. _____
10. The painters, whom were hired three days ago, finished the job in record
    time.   10. _____

11. That you help others in need is a recommended practice. 11. _____

12. Ms. Grossinger manages people much better than Mr. Howard does. 12. _____

13. Call me when you have the financial statements complete. 13. _____

14. The doctor, whose husband works with me, prescribed a medication for my headaches. 14. _____

15. Norbert said that we were all invited to his party. 15. _____

16. What she does after work is not our business. 16. _____

17. Please mail that letter, which contains Bob's check. 17. _____

18. The employee, whom you saw at the meeting, works in Accounting. 18. _____

19. The sample packets were more than we wanted. 19. _____

20. He plays the guitar whenever he can. 20. _____

21. Where she went after the conference is a mystery to us. 21. _____

22. That you send a thank-you note to your host is a good practice. 22. _____

23. The amount that you shipped was more than we ordered. 23. _____

24. After he received the report, Mr. Humphries felt better able to respond to their suggestions. 24. _____

25. The budget director indicated that the funds could be made available. 25. _____

EXERCISE 4   Each of the following sentences contains an incomplete clause. (The first word of each clause is in italics.) Complete each clause by writing your answer in the space provided. Do not add any punctuation. (The type of clause required is indicated in parentheses at the end of each sentence.)

1. *Who* _____ is a secret at this time. (noun)

2. The reason Martha receives more money is *that* _____. (noun)

3. Carolyn deserves merit pay *because* _____. (adverb)

4. Ms. Nottingham, *who* _____, has been with the company for over five years. (adjective)

5. The woman *who* _____ is a wonderful companion. (adjective)

6. The employee *whom* _____ is Darrell's friend. (adjective)

7. *Whoever* _____, please bring back some milk. (noun)

8. Here is a copy of *what* _____. (noun)

9. Joe is confident *that* _____. (adverb)

10. He is the one *who* _____. (adjective)

EXERCISE 5   Use each of the following dependent clauses in a sentence.

1. After you finish that report, _____

2. Before you return that wrench, _____

3. Because we will be leaving on Wednesday, _____

4. While we are gone, _____

5. If you would like to stay, _____

6. Since I joined the company, _____

7. Although enrollment has increased, _____

8. While you were consulting with Mr. Potter, _____

9. When you purchased the equipment, _____

10. Because we need additional information, _____

11. Whenever you decide to leave, _____

12. Unless they hear from you today, _____

13. Before a deadline is set, _____

14. Until sales improve, _____

Lost and Found Department

THREE-PIECE MEN'S SUITS!   Have you ever seen a man in three pieces? No? Well, take a look at the following ad.

Three-Piece Men's Suits on Sale!

What is intended, of course, is "Men's Three-Piece Suits." Since *three-piece* modifies *suits,* it must be placed closer to *suits.* Let's see another example of the ridiculous things that can happen when a word is misplaced (in the following example, it's the word *only*):

Miss Jamison only went to the seminar. Apparently Miss Jamison didn't *listen;* she didn't *sit;* she didn't *talk.* She "only *went.*" The sentence should read, "Only Miss Jamison went to the seminar."

Sometimes entire phrases are misplaced:

The gift is for an employee who is going to retire in this box. Can you imagine someone retiring *in a box?* Hardly probable.

The gift in this box is for an employee who is going to retire. Better now. The gift, not the employee, is in the box.

When you look over your writing, always check for any "lost" or "misplaced" modifiers. Place them close to the words they modify.

CHECKUP 1   Underline any misplaced words or phrases in the sentences below. Use a caret (∧) to show where you should insert each misplaced word or phrase. (You need not show any necessary changes in capitalization or punctuation.)

1. The market <u>only</u> sells fish on Friday∧
2. The supervisor asked Geraldine to write the report twice.
3. All the supervisors almost attended the meeting.
4. Several of the callers asked for red women's dresses.

BEWARE OF DANGLING PARTICIPLES   A participle—an *-ing* or *-ed* phrase—that begins a sentence must modify the person or thing doing the acting, *the subject.* Always place the phrase as close as possible to the noun or pronoun that it modifies. When the phrase is not near its modifier, it is said to *dangle.* Sometimes these dangling expressions can be humorous, as shown in the following examples.

Entering the subway, his hat got caught in the turnstyle. Did the hat enter the subway? No! He did.

In most cases you can correct the dangling modifier by making the subject of the sentence the doer of the action expressed by the *-ing* or *-ed* phrase.

Entering the subway, he caught his hat in the turnstyle. The doer of the action expressed by the *-ing* phrase is *he. He* is the subject of the sentence.

Having been caught in the rain, the umbrella was opened by Jane. It sounds as though the umbrella was caught in the rain, doesn't it? *Umbrella* is the subject of the sentence. The verb *was opened* is in the passive voice. (A verb is in the passive voice when its subject is acted upon. A verb is in the active voice when the subject is doing the action.)

Sometimes you can correct a dangling modifier by changing the sentence from passive voice to active voice:

Having been caught in the rain, Jane opened her umbrella. *Jane,* the doer of the action, is the subject of the sentence. The verb *opened* is in the active voice.

CHECKUP 2   Rewrite each of the following sentences to correct the dangling modifiers.

1. Carrying a tray of food, Danny's toe caught on the wire.
   Carrying a tray of food, Danny caught his toe on the wire.

2. Damaged during shipment, we returned the furniture to the store.

   _____

3. While swatting the wasp, my car went off the road.

   _____

MISPLACED CLAUSES   Unfortunately, modifiers can be misplaced in more ways. Be very careful where you place clauses beginning with *that.*

We saw a diamond in the window of a store near our building *that weighed 4 carats.* What weighed *4 carats?* The *building?* No, the diamond weighed 4 carats. The sentence should be rewritten:

We saw a diamond that weighed 4 carats in the window of a store near our building. Or: We saw in the window of a store near our building a diamond that weighed 4 carats.

In sentences with *which* clauses, the clauses should be close to the words they modify.

The calculator has small numerals, which we had also ordered from the store in our building. The *which* clause is close to *numerals;* did we order the *numerals?* No, we ordered the *calculator.*

The calculator, which we had ordered from the store in our building, has small numerals. Here, the *which* clause properly modifies *calculator. Which* clauses are separated by commas; *that* clauses are not.

In the stockroom, Tom, you will find three cartons on the bottom shelf. Please bring me the carton that is marked "1991 Taxes." Without the clause *that is marked "1991 Taxes"* how would Tom know which of the three cartons he should choose? *Please bring me the carton* does not, by itself, give Tom all the information he needs. *The carton that is marked "1991 Taxes"* separates that carton from the other two so that there can be no confusion. The *that* clause is essential; it should not be separated by commas.

Tom helped me to go through the tax papers in the carton, which contained more than I had expected. Would this sentence be confusing without the *which* clause? No, it would not, because the *which* clause offers extra information. Use commas to set off extra information in *which* clauses.

CHECKUP 3   Underline any misplaced clauses in the following sentences. Use a caret (∧) to show where you should insert each misplaced clause. (You need not show any necessary changes in capitalization or punctuation.)

1. Please give the report∧to Ms. Simpson <u>that you prepared.</u>
2. Carl ran five miles daily to stay fit wearing a sweatsuit.
3. Our committee meeting was to be held at the Southside Inn, which was canceled.

Replace the question mark in each of the following sentences with either *which* or *that.* Then write the correct word in the space at the right. Use a caret (∧) to indicate where any commas may be needed.

4. There are many CD players from which to choose. The model (?) we recommend is HiFi.

   4. __**that**_____

5. Mr. Tatro's birthday party (?) we all attended was a surprise.

   5. _____

6. The building (?) has been for sale for three months was sold last week.

   6. _____

EXERCISES

NAME _____ DATE _____ SCORE _____

EXERCISE 1   Rewrite each of the following sentences to correct the dangling modifiers.

1. Leaving in a hurry, the reports were left on my desk.

_____

2. Having been delayed at the airport, the meeting had already begun when we arrived.

_____

3. Declaring their independence, freedom was gained by the citizens.

_____

4. Lifting the heavy boards, his back was injured.

_____

5. Left alone in the office, the sudden noise scared her.

_____

6. When only a small boy, my father took me to the airport.

_____

7. Trying not to panic, the burning building was exited by them.

_____

8. Selling flowers, a woman approached her.

_____

9. Lying on the beach, the water refreshed her.

_____

EXERCISE 2   Decide which sentence in each pair shows the correct placement of modifiers, and write the letter of your choice in the space at the right.

1. a. To satisfy each of us, the supervisor requested our advice.
   b. To satisfy each of us, our advice was requested by the supervisor.   1. _____
2. a. By practicing the piano for hours, perfection was achieved by him.
   b. By practicing the piano for hours, he achieved perfection.   2. _____
3. a. While interviewing applicants, the lights went out in her office.
   b. While she was interviewing applicants, the lights went out in her
      office.   3. _____
4. a. While he was coming up the stairs, he noticed the lovely painting.
   b. Coming up the stairs, the painting looked lovely to him.   4. _____
5. a. Comparing the totals carefully, we found discrepancies.
   b. Comparing the totals carefully, discrepancies were found.   5. _____
6. a. Approved by the vice president, the Purchasing Department placed the
      order.
   b. Approved by the vice president, the order was placed by the Purchasing
      Department.   6. _____
7. a. To prepare the graphic aids, a computer is necessary.
   b. To prepare the graphic aids, I will need a computer.   7. _____
8. a. They watched the news on television eating their dinner.
   b. Eating their dinner, they watched the news on television.   8. _____
9. a. Absorbed in the movie, the time passed quickly for us.
   b. Absorbed in the movie, we found that the time passed quickly.   9. _____

10. a. Never having been to Germany, we had an exciting trip.
    b. Never having been to Germany, the trip was exciting for us.   10. _____

EXERCISE 3
Each of the following sentences contains dangling modifiers and misplaced words, phrases, or clauses. Rewrite each sentence correctly in the space provided. Be sure to place the modifier as close as possible to the word it modifies.

1. Arriving late that evening, a message was left on the door.

   _____

2. The president had a large envelope talking to Mr. Fritag.

   _____

3. Eating my sandwich, the officer asked me to move my car.

   _____

4. To work in this cluttered room, a table is needed.

   _____

5. Walking to the hospital that afternoon, an ambulance went by.

   _____

6. Return the books to Dr. Targowski on my desk.

   _____

7. While trying to repair my computer, they arrived.

   _____

8. Opening the office door, her attaché case caught on the knob.

   _____

9. To finalize our plans, a meeting was held that afternoon.

   _____

10. Having approved the requisition, it was sent to the Purchasing Department.

    _____

11. Is that the coat I told you about from Lears?

    _____

12. While trying to paint the house, the water main broke.

    _____

EXERCISE 4
Combine the two sentences in each pair below by using the italicized words in one sentence as a modifier in the other. See the example below.

0. Darlene worked late in the office. She was *editing a manuscript.*
   Editing a manuscript, Darlene worked late in the office.
   _____

1. Our manager found the answer. She was *looking through her notes.*

   _____

2. The tourists were happy. They were *seeing beautiful sites.*

   _____

3. Mr. Hopkins interviewed the applicant. Mr. Hopkins was *sitting down.*

   _____

4. She was *answering the phone.* She let the file fall to the floor.

   _____

5. They enjoyed their dinner. They were *listening to music.*

   _____

6. The customer was satisfied. She was *receiving a refund.*

   _____

Common Conjunction Errors

A SQUARE PEG IN A ROUND HOLE?   As you know, a square peg doesn't belong in a round hole; it belongs in a square hole. When conjunctions do not join the same things—two or more nouns, two or more verbs, two or more adjectives, two or more adverbs, and so on—you have a square peg in a round hole. Parallel ideas should be expressed in parallel form.

The legal secretaries typed *quickly* and *with accuracy*. The conjunction *and* joins an adverb *(quickly)* to a prepositional phrase *(with accuracy)*. A square peg in a round hole! Unparallel form.

The legal secretaries typed *quickly* and *accurately*. Now *and* joins two adverbs—*quickly* and *accurately*. Better, isn't it? It's in parallel form.

It is usually quite simple to make sure that conjunctions join the same things.

The contract was *illegible, lengthy,* and *it is awkward*. *Illegible* and *lengthy,* both adjectives, are joined to *it is awkward,* which is not an adjective. A square peg is in a round hole. Unparallel form.

The contract was *illegible, lengthy,* and *awkward*. Now three adjectives are joined. Much better! It's in parallel form.

The editor *read, revised,* and *put the manuscript in the mail*. *Read* and *revised* are the same tense (past), but *put* is a different tense (present). The conjunction joins two past tense verbs and one present verb. Parallelism is absent.

The editor *read, revised,* and *mailed* the manuscript. Now *and* joins three verbs in the same tense. Parallelism is present in the sentence.

These kinds of errors are also often made when pairs of conjunctions are used:

Either the order clerk delays the materials ***or*** ships them immediately. Look at what follows the conjunctions *either* and *or*. Are the *order clerk* and *ships* the same parts of speech? No. Parallelism is absent.

The order clerk *either* delays the materials *or* ships them immediately. What follows *either* and *or* are now the same things—verbs! The sentence is parallel.

CHECKUP 1   Each sentence below has some square pegs in round holes. Can you find them? Underline the words that make the sentence unparallel. Correct the sentence so that it is parallel. Write your answer in the space provided.

1. Either ask Hazel or Victor to research, write, and prepare the contract for the client.

   1. **Ask either** _____

2. Before you order the merchandise, you should not only ask the purchasing agent but also the controller.

   2. _____

3. Ms. Wingford was hired because she was enthusiastic and had intelligence.

   3. _____

4. We had all agreed that we would discuss neither the terms of the contract nor reveal the settlement amount.

   4. _____

5. The radiologist studied the X ray carefully and with competence.

   5. _____

Beware!   Two kinds of errors that you should be aware of when using conjunctions are the *run-on sentence* and the *comma splice.*

Dr. Pesce will retire next month we are having a party for him. This is a *run-on sentence*. Two independent clauses run into each other. The sentence has no comma and conjunction to join the two independent clauses.

Dr. Pesce will retire next month, we are having a party for him. This is a *comma splice*. It has only a comma joining the two sentences. A comma splices (joins) two independent clauses without a conjunction.

Correct run-on sentences and comma splices with a comma and a conjunction, a semicolon, or a period and a capital letter. The sentences below are written correctly:

Dr. Pesce will retire next month, and we are having a party for him. A comma and a conjunction join the two independent clauses.

Dr. Pesce will retire next month; we are having a party for him. A semicolon joins the two independent clauses.

Dr. Pesce will retire next month. We are having a party for him. A period and a capital letter are used to form two sentences.

CHECKUP 2   Indicate whether each of the following groups of words is a sentence with a comma splice; a run-on sentence; or a correct sentence. Write *comma splice, run-on,* or *OK* in the space provided.

1. The doctor in residency was exhausted he still worked 24 hours in the emergency room.
2. We attended the two-day workshop, it was excellent.
3. Several of us are taking an extended vacation; we're leaving July 1.
4. This is a serious problem, I would appreciate your help in investigating it.

1. **run-on**
2. _____
3. _____
4. _____

THAT, THAT, THAT   People often incorrectly use *because* and *where* instead of *that* to introduce clauses.

The reason is that they had to order the items. Use *The reason is that,* not *The reason is because.* Also avoid using *The reason why.*

I read in the newspaper that Eileen and Jim were married. Do not use *where* in place of *that.*

By the way, never use *being that.* Use *because, since,* or *as* instead.

Because Marty worked during his lunch hour, he left early. (NOT: *Being that Marty.*)

AS I SAID   In business writing and speaking, avoid the expression "like I said." *Like* is a preposition, and a prepositional phrase does not have a verb in it—remember? Use the word *as* instead.

As you said, I was happy. (NOT: Like you said.) *Like* cannot introduce a clause, and *as you said* is a clause. It has a subject *(you)* and a verb *(said).*

WITHOUT AND EXCEPT ARE PREPOSITIONS TOO   Like *like,* the words *without* and *except* are prepositions. Do not use them to introduce clauses. Use *unless* instead.

I won't go to the reception unless she goes too. (NOT: *except she goes too.*)

TRY TO   Sometimes conjunctions may be misused, as in the expression *try and.* *Try to,* not *try and,* is correct. The *to* is used in expressions like this to form part of an infinitive. See the examples below.

Let's try to finish this now. (NOT: *try and finish.*)

Check to see that we have the necessary forms. (NOT: *check and see.*)

EXERCISES

NAME _____ DATE _____ SCORE _____

EXERCISE 1 Each sentence below has some square pegs in round holes. Can you find them? Underline the words that make the sentence unparallel. Correct the sentence so that it is parallel. Write your answer in the space provided. In some cases, tell what word(s) you are omitting.

1. Our physician enjoyed tennis, golf, and playing volleyball.

1. _____

2. The second vice president is responsible for revising the operational guidelines and to hire employees.

2. _____

3. We were responsible not only for raising the funds but also to distribute them.

3. _____

4. Hiking is much more fun than going fishing.

4. _____

5. The nurse's duties were to provide the medication and checking the monitor.

5. _____

6. The intern's duties were to examine the patient, to order X rays if necessary, and prescribing medication.

6. _____

7. Mary was thrilled about her trips to Australia and going to New Zealand.

7. _____

8. Your tasks are to file the correspondence, to photocopy documents, and answering the telephone.

8. _____

EXERCISE 2 Underline the incorrect words in the following sentences. Then write your corrections in the spaces at the right. If the sentence is correct, write *OK*.

1. The reason I went to London is because I wanted to see Windsor Castle.

1. _____

2. Being that you are president, you are responsible for preparing the agenda for the meeting.

2. _____

3. Before you leave tonight, check and see that all the doors are locked.

3. _____

4. Except a signature is provided, we will not be able to leave the National Express package.

4. _____

5. Do you think those headings are appropriate for the medical report?

5. _____

6. Try and be here by 8 o'clock so that we can start work.

6. _____

7. We notice where you have been promoted to vice president of the Association for Nurses.

7. _____

8. Like Henry said, we should reach our fund-raising goal of $50,000.

8. _____

9. Andrea will try and visit the local hospitals.

9. _____

10. Being that you are the treasurer of the association, you are responsible for preparing the monthly financial report.

10. _____

EXERCISE 3 In each of the following sentences, identify the error by writing *run-on* or *comma splice*. Then rewrite the run-on sentences by adding a comma and a conjunction. Rewrite the comma splice sentences by adding a conjunction after the comma.

1. The marketing manager suggested a new campaign he recommended that it be implemented by September.

_____

_____

2. The new employees were unable to express themselves in writing, they were able to express themselves orally.

_____

_____

3. Last year's model car sold for $15,000 this year's model sells for $18,000.

_____

4. The students wanted to learn, they were willing to study hard.

_____

5. In observation research, observers use their senses to obtain firsthand information, they report only what they have observed.

_____

_____

6. Send your recommendations to me have candidates apply directly to my office.

_____

7. The body of the report consists of the introduction the text of the report contains the summary, conclusions, and recommendations.

_____

_____

EXERCISE 4

Correct each of the following sentences three different ways: (1) Use a period and a capital letter, (2) use a semicolon, and (3) use a comma and a conjunction.

1. We have plans to sell our home in Indiana we are hoping to buy a condo in Florida.

_____

_____

_____

2. The auditors canceled yesterday's meeting they rescheduled it for Thursday.

_____

_____

_____

3. Chem Products just announced a 3 percent increase this is its second price hike in two years.

_____

_____

_____

4. The order was called in at 8 a.m. it was delivered by 5 p.m.

_____

_____

_____

EXERCISE 5

Each of the following sentences contains an error in the choice of words or in the placement of conjunctions. Underline the errors, and write the corrections in the spaces at the right. You may add or delete words.

1. Try and beat our prices.   1. _____

2. Like he said, they will not have the time to work on the project. 2. _____

3. Being that it is already 1:30 p.m., we need to get back to the office. 3. _____

4. Did you read where they are appointing Mr. Drennan chief executive officer of the company?   4. _____

5. The food servers at Hogan's Restaurant are not only friendly but they also are courteous.   5. _____

6. Please check and see if our loan has been approved.   6. _____

Faulty Parallelism

Parallel structure means that sentence elements are alike in function and in construction. Let's study the following parallel examples:

Subjects: *Ms. Frazer* and *Mr. Godfrey* had (NOT: *Pam and Mr. Godfrey*)

Rob and *Marie* went (NOT: *Rob and Ms. Parker*)

men and *women* were (NOT: *men and ladies were*)

Verbs: The teacher *knew* the material and *presented* it well.

Infinitives: My father wanted *to see* and *to hear* the speaker.

Direct objects: The dean of the college wanted *a new building* and *a new associate dean*.

Indirect objects: We will buy *him* and *her* each a pen and pencil set.

Objects of prepositions: The copy is *for her* and *for him*.

Adjectives: *Three efficient* accountants and *two capable* clerks prepared the payroll.

Adverbs: The nurses worked *quickly* and *competently*.

Phrases: The financial planner looked *on the desk, in the files,* and *in the basket* for the missing bonds.

Dependent clauses: Please call *before you leave the office* and *when you arrive home.*

Independent clauses: *The letters were dated,* but *they were not signed.*

CHECKUP 1   Underline the elements in each of the following sentences that should be alike in function and in construction. In the space at the right, indicate whether these elements are used as subjects, verbs, adjectives, adverbs, or objects.

1. The Association of Nurses <u>planned</u> the seminar, <u>selected</u> the speakers, and <u>organized</u> the program.
2. The defense attorney and the prosecuting attorney were called into the judge's chamber.
3. The doctor wrote the treatment instructions clearly and legibly for her elderly patient.
4. The well-written and well-organized procedures manual helped the hospital interns.
5. Lola's ambition was to be a nurse or a medical doctor.

1. __verbs_____

2. _____

3. _____

4. _____

5. _____

WITH CONJUNCTIONS   Conjunctions must be followed by sentence elements of equal rank. When *either* is followed by a noun, *or* must be followed by a noun. When *not only* is followed by a verb, *but also* must be followed by a verb. If *neither* is followed by an adjective, then *nor* must be followed by an adjective. *Remember:* balance nouns with nouns, verbs with verbs, adjectives with adjectives, and so on.

Either Betty *or* Tom has the keys. (subjects)

The twins will *neither* write nor *call* when they are on vacation. (verbs)

We plan to play *either* tennis *or* golf this weekend. (objects)

When *not only* is followed by an infinitive phrase, *but also* must be followed by an infinitive phrase.

She asked *not only* to write the report *but also* to type it.

OUTLINES, LISTS, AND DISPLAYED ENUMERATIONS

Parallelism is especially important in outlines, lists, and displayed enumerations.

OUTLINE:

I. Kinds of Sentences According to Form
   A. Simple
   B. Compound
   C. Complex
   D. Compound-complex
II. Kinds of Sentences According to Function
   A. Declarative
   B. Interrogative
   C. Imperative
   D. Exclamatory

The outline is parallel. The items in roman numerals *I* and *II* are parallel with each other, and each of the subdivisions (*A* through *D*) is parallel with one another.

LIST:

As chairperson, your duties are to:

Call the meeting to order

Ask for the approval of the minutes

Ask for the treasurer's report

Ask for committee reports

Conduct new business

Adjourn the meeting

ENUMERATIONS:

The six elements of effective writing are:

1. Clarity
2. Conciseness
3. Courtesy
4. Confidence
5. Correctness
6. Conversational tone

Both of these lists are parallel. Each item in the first list begins with a verb. Each item in the second list is a noun; all the items in the list are enumerated.

With Grammatical Construction

Faulty parallelism occurs when joined items do not have equal grammatical form. Note the faulty parallelism in each of the following examples.

Her duties included *typing, taking dictation,* and *to answer the phone.* This is faulty parallelism because *typing* and *taking dictation* are present progressive tense and *to answer* is an infinitive.

To make a parallel construction clear, repeat an article, a preposition, an infinitive, or a pronoun.

Article: We had *a* letter and *a* telegram.

Preposition: Send the letter *to* Mark and *to* David.

Infinitive: She wanted us *to read* and *to criticize* the book.

Pronoun: Give the message to *my* father or *my* mother.

CHECKUP 2   In the space at the right, write the word or words that would make each of the following sentences parallel. Use a caret (∧) to show where the missing word should be inserted.

1. Please deliver these memos to people in the Research Division and∧the Marketing Division.

2. You may return the medical records to Dr. Stone or Dr. DeSilva.

3. Our workshop folders included a pencil, note pad, and an evaluation sheet.

4. Should I mail the application form to the student's home address or student's school address?

1. **in** _____

2. _____

3. _____

4. _____

EXERCISES

NAME _____ DATE _____ SCORE _____

EXERCISE 1   In the space at the right, indicate whether the italicized parallel elements are used as subjects, verbs, adjectives, adverbs, direct objects, infinitives, indirect objects, or phrases.

1. The purchasing agent was *tall, dark,* and *handsome.*   1. _____
2. The head nurse gave *Judy* and *John* responsibilities in the emergency room.   2. _____
3. *He* and *she* are both ready to be spectators at the sporting event.   3. _____
4. Dr. Rinehard *lectured* and *tested* students on the benefits of blood testing.   4. _____
5. The tour guide took us *around the castle, into the rooms,* and *beyond the courtyard.*   5. _____
6. I advised her to prepare the report *quickly* and *accurately.*   6. _____
7. Have you taken *economics* or *statistics* yet?   7. _____
8. The *teacher* and the *principal* agreed to have the students plan the assembly.   8. _____
9. Charlie *recognized* and *identified* the suspect in court.   9. _____
10. Marlene wanted *to edit* and *to proofread* her own work.   10. _____

EXERCISE 2   Rewrite each sentence so that its elements are parallel. If the elements of a sentence are already parallel, write *OK*.

1. Francine's responsibilities were to arrange the flowers, water the plants, and ordering the supplies.

_____

2. These lounge chairs are better for beauty, for appearance, and they are comfortable.

_____

3. Her new job promises to be exciting and a challenge.

_____

4. Professor Gossman told the students to read the chapter, to answer the end-of-chapter questions, and be preparing for a test.

_____

5. Revising, revising, and to revise again are essential to good writing habits.

_____

6. If you would like an *A* on your paper, you need to spell the words correctly and punctuation sentences correctly.

_____

7. Because of the time and because of the company, she wanted to go home.

_____

8. First, he completed the application; secondly, he signed his name; and third, he made a copy of it for his files.

_____

9. Both Joanne and Jerome will be working at the Career Fair.

_____

10. The director of nursing not only visited our hospital in New York City but also Boston.

_____

11. Either Homer or Doris will represent us at the meeting.

_____

12. Her hobbies are playing the piano and the collection of stamps.

_____

EXERCISE 3

Insert or delete words to make the following sentences parallel. Use a caret (∧) to show where words should be inserted. Place in parentheses those words that should be deleted. In the spaces at the right, write the inserted or deleted words. If the sentence is correct, write *OK*.

1. Martin said that he would leave about 8 a.m. and he would call when he arrived at his destination.

1. _____

2. The company not only paid us every week but gave us a commission.

2. _____

3. They appreciate the overtime pay and health benefits.

3. _____

4. We were to judge the candidates on their ability to write and on their ability to work well with others.

4. _____

5. Either read the chapter or you will have to complete the study guide.

5. _____

6. Faye had to edit the article and proofread it.

6. _____

7. They took pictures of an elderly couple and child playing in the park.

7. _____

8. Either work today or you will have to work tomorrow.

8. _____

EXERCISE 4

Rewrite the following groups of words so that they are parallel. If the items are parallel, write *OK*.

1. either make one copy or five copies

_____

2. not only the reports but also letters

_____

3. whether to accept or reject the offer

_____

4. attend meetings, take notes, and prepare reports

_____

5. neither the judge or the lawyer

_____

EXERCISE 5

Use each of the grammatical elements listed below in a parallel sentence.

1. nouns

_____

2. verbs

_____

3. direct objects

_____

4. indirect objects

_____

5. adjectives

_____

6. adverbs

_____

7. phrases

_____

8. dependent clauses

_____

9. independent clauses

_____

10. objects of prepositions

_____

Using Punctuation Marks

THE PERIOD Use a period at the end of a declarative sentence.

Peg is the new administrative assistant.

She recommended that we adopt the plan.

Use a period at the end of an imperative command.

Proofread carefully so that we won't have any errors in the report.

Make an extra copy of the letter for me.

Use a period after an indirect question.

The Director of Nursing asked the nurses if they wanted to attend the seminar.

THE QUESTION MARK Direct questions end in question marks, not periods.

How long do you expect to be gone from the office?

Use a question mark to indicate a question within a sentence.

We can come late to the meeting, can't we?

You'll be able to come for dinner, won't you?

Some sentences sound like questions but are really polite requests or commands. Use periods, not question marks, at the end of such sentences.

Will you please prepare the materials for me. This is not really a question. It's a command—a polite request.

THE EXCLAMATION POINT In business and formal writing, very few sentences end in exclamation points. Use an exclamation point after a word, phrase, clause, or sentence to express strong feelings or emotions.

Congratulations on your promotion!

As you can see, then, most sentences end in periods. A few will end in question marks. Rarely does a sentence end in an exclamation point.

CHECKUP 1 Decide whether a period, a question mark, or an exclamation point belongs at the end of the following sentences. Insert the missing mark at the end of the sentence. In the spaces provided, write the names of the punctuation marks.

1. Mark asked if he could borrow the computer for about an hour.

2. Does anyone know where the Curry files are

3. May I please hear from you before July 1

4. That's fantastic, Julie

1. **period**

2. _____

3. _____

4. _____

OTHER USES OF PERIODS

Many abbreviations are written with periods, but there are probably as many written *without* periods.

a.m.	Ph.D.	gal	L (for *liter*)	Mrs.	Sr.	lb	km (for *kilometer*)
p.m.	Rev.	qt	cm (for *centimeter*)	Ms.	Esq.	yd	g (for *gram*)
c.o.d.	f.o.b.	pt	m (for *meter*)	Ave.	St.	Blvd.	Apt.
Mr.	Jr.	oz	mm (for *millimeter*)	Jan.	Feb.	Aug.	Sept.

In the list above, note that no extra space is used within abbreviations such as *c.o.d.* and *f.o.b.* because they would be harder to read with extra space. Also, note that abbreviations of units of measure, such as pounds *(lb)* and centimeters *(cm)*, are written without periods. Do not add *s* to form their plurals: 3 gal (NOT: gal*s*), 4 cm (NOT: cm*s*). In letters and memos, the full words are spelled out; the abbreviations are generally used in tables and in business forms.

Abbreviations in all-capital letters are usually written without periods.

CPA (for certified public accountant)   UN (for United Nations)

FCC (for Federal Communications Commission)   WNEW (the call letters of a radio station)

Another use of periods is after initials:

William *J.* Frawley, Jr.   Mr. and Mrs. John *V.* Morot   Joan *Q.* Lacey, M.D.

Periods are also used with amounts of money, with percentages, and with decimals.

The price of the oak desk that you asked about is *$145.99*.

Ann was thrilled when she learned that she received a *96.5* percent on her final examination in physics.

OTHER USES OF QUESTION MARKS AND EXCLAMATION POINTS

Question marks and exclamation points, too, can be used elsewhere; their positions are not limited to the ends of sentences.

He gave the supervisor (or was it the manager?) the itemized list of recommendations. Only the clause in parentheses is a question. Thus the question mark goes inside the parentheses.

Please ask Dr. Taylor—isn't she your department chair?—to approve this request.

Where shall we meet for lunch? Rizzo's? Repeat the question mark after each question.

Remind her to send the report to our office in Sterling, Illinois (not Sterling, Massachusetts!). Only the clause within parentheses is an exclamation, so it gets the exclamation point (not the entire sentence).

Not even the vice president—imagine!—has the authority to approve your request.

THE HYPHEN

Use the hyphen in compound words, in numbers, and in fractions.

Jules visited his *mother-in-law* on Thursday.   The students pegged him as a *show-off*.

The Browns were celebrating their *forty-third* wedding anniversary.

Over *two-thirds* of the audience agreed with the presenter.

Use the hyphen in most compound adjectives when they appear before the noun.

They work in a *five-story* building. (before the noun)

Beware!   Most compound adjectives that begin with *well* or *self* are hyphenated whether they precede or follow the noun—well-adjusted, well-spoken, self-made, self-taught, and so forth.

EXERCISES

NAME _____ DATE _____ SCORE _____

EXERCISE 1   Decide whether a period, a question mark, or an exclamation point belongs at the end of each of the following sentences. Insert the missing punctuation mark in the sentence. In the space provided, write the name of the punctuation mark.

1. Please proofread the contract for the attorney   1. _____
2. What's the difference between Model X and Model Y   2. _____
3. For heaven's sake, stop it right now   3. _____
4. If we finish our work by 3 o'clock, may we leave   4. _____
5. Carrie is very interested in math and science   5. _____
6. Congratulations on receiving the Outstanding Nurse Award   6. _____
7. You expect me to believe that line   7. _____
8. You told her the truth, didn't you   8. _____
9. Maggie's only response was that she was tired and didn't want to be
   disturbed   9. _____
10. Make copies of the report for each of the doctors and interns   10. _____
11. Are you volunteering for the Peace Corps   11. _____
12. No, you are not allowed to go   12. _____

EXERCISE 2   Decide where periods are necessary in the following sentences. Insert the missing periods where they belong. In the space at the right, indicate the total number of periods you used in each sentence.

1. Send the check to Mr E R Neubig at his home address   1. _____
2. Myra received her D D S degree from Michigan State University   2. _____
3. He wanted to be addressed as Mr Loyd Chiodo, Jr on all his correspondence   3. _____
4. On the invoice we were billed for 1 gal of turpentine and 1 pt of paint
   remover   4. _____
5. Station WKZO announced a tornado watch for several counties until 7
   p m this evening   5. _____
6. Ms Hilary requested that we send her mail to the following address for
   Sept and Oct: 204 S Second St, St Paul, MN 55102   6. _____
7. I was surprised to received a c o d package from Mr Hattington   7. _____
8. The Rev O'Keefe, who also has a Ph D in philosophy, will be the
   keynote speaker at the convention in St Louis   8. _____
9. Her grade point average at the end of the winter semester was almost
   90 percent—874 to be exact   9. _____
10. The office chair was under $100; it cost only $7999   10. _____
11. The meteorologist announced that the humidity reached a high of
    82 5 percent today   11. _____
12. Dr and Mrs Ferraro are moving to Mt Clemens in November   12. _____
13. Don Ralph will receive his M D degree in May   13. _____
14. The memo dated July 1 from M C Miller arrived about 2:30 p m   14. _____
15. Mr and Mrs R C Tavers were to be here by 8:15 a m   15. _____
16. Ms Arlington is one of the new CPAs for the Diedrick and Darcy Ac-
    counting Associates   16. _____

EXERCISE 3   Decide where question marks and exclamation points are necessary in the following sentences. Insert the missing marks where they belong. In the spaces at the right, indicate the total number of question marks and exclamation points you used in each sentence.

1. Yes We won $5,000 in cash and prizes   1. _____
2. Please ask Rhonda Boyd — isn't she in the Research Department — for her signature on this contract.   2. _____
3. William gave the surgeon (or was it the oncologist) the X rays.   3. _____
4. What a marvelous performance   4. _____
5. Did you by any chance happen to watch the news last night on television   5. _____
6. When will you be able to start work on the project for Ms. Okuda   6. _____
7. Oh That's beautiful   7. _____
8. Oh, yes We guarantee all our products for one year.   8. _____
9. Where were you when the announcement was made by the president   9. _____
10. Not even our boss — imagine — has the authority to sign the release.   10. _____
11. Leave that box where it is   11. _____
12. Congratulations You are the winner   12. _____
13. Will you be traveling to France this summer Germany Italy   13. _____
14. Would you please ask Mr. Parsons — isn't he your supervisor — to sign the release statement.   14. _____
15. When will you be able to finish the job How soon   15. _____
16. No You may not have the car, and that's final   16. _____
17. These are the papers you requested, aren't they   17. _____
18. Will the sales report be ready by June 15   18. _____

EXERCISE 4   Insert hyphens where necessary in the following sentences. Write the hyphenated words in the spaces provided. If no hyphen is required, write *OK*.

1. The firm moved its offices to the thirty third floor of the Hines Building.   1. _____
2. Over three quarters of the participants filled out the evaluation form.   2. _____
3. Glynna's brother was a show off.   3. _____
4. The company announced that it would be celebrating its twenty fifth anniversary in July.   4. _____
5. Her comment was made off the record.   5. _____
6. Three fourths of the representatives were back in Washington, D.C., this spring.   6. _____
7. The human resources director selected the applicant who was well groomed and well educated.   7. _____
8. The artist's portrait was hanging in the ten story museum.   8. _____
9. We recommended that a well balanced decision be made.   9. _____
10. One sixth of his estate went to his nieces and nephews.   10. _____
11. Gladys received one fourth of her grandmother's estate.   11. _____
12. Will we need a two thirds majority to pass the resolution?   12. _____
13. The well written report was mailed on Friday.   13. _____
14. Did the captain call a time out?   14. _____
15. Rosa did not mind the hand me downs from her older sister.   15. _____
16. Mary Louise's father in law is the mayor of the city of Portage.   16. _____
17. Jill is well known in her community for her volunteer work at the hospital.   17. _____
18. One third of the accounts had been closed.   18. _____
19. The items were high priced, so we did not purchase them.   19. _____
20. Robin's mother in law is a civil rights attorney.   20. _____

Using Commas

Commas are very commonly used in all writing—and for good reason. Without commas, our writing would be uninteresting or, sometimes, confusing.

Dr. Alberts graduated *cum laude.* She graduated from Yale University. She has a one-year appointment. She will teach speech and drama at Central University.

Each sentence above is technically correct. But, with commas the sentences could have been reworded as follows:

Dr. Alberts, who graduated *cum laude* from Yale University, has a one-year appointment to teach speech and drama at Central University.

Of course, it isn't always desirable to write one long sentence instead of three shorter ones, but when it is, you'll need commas.

COMMAS JOIN INDEPENDENT CLAUSES Independent clauses can be written as individual sentences, or they can be joined as one sentence. *Remember:* Two or more independent clauses joined by a coordinating conjunction *(and, but, or, for, nor, yet, or so)* make up a compound sentence.

Dan wrote a research paper on motivation. He submitted it for publication. Two independent clauses written as two individual sentences.

Dan wrote a research paper on motivation, and he submitted it for publication.

To check this, let's look at what follows the conjunction *and: he submitted it for publication.* Is this an independent clause? Yes, it is; therefore, the comma before *and* is correct.

Beware! Make sure that what follows *and* is indeed an independent clause. If it is not, then do not use a comma.

Dan wrote a research paper and submitted it for publication. No comma. Check to see if what follows the conjunction *and* is an independent clause: *submitted it for publication* is not an independent clause (it does not have its own subject), so we do not use a comma before *and*.

CHECKUP 1 Insert commas where necessary in the following sentences. Identify the coordinating conjunctions by writing them in the spaces provided. If a sentence is correct, write *OK*.

1. Mr. Onderlinde left the firm for several reasons, but he wasn't telling what they were.

   1. but _____

2. Ms. Horn enjoyed being a juror and she'll be happy to serve again if asked.

   2. _____

3. We can leave here about 10 a.m. or we can leave after lunch.

   3. _____

4. Several employees will need to work late tonight or to work Saturday until they are finished packing all the merchandise.

   4. _____

COMMAS JOIN DEPENDENT CLAUSES In Lesson 37 we saw that dependent clauses are frequently joined to independent clauses by subordinating conjunctions such as *after, because,* and *since.*
When the dependent clause is at the beginning of the sentence, use a comma after the clause. When the dependent clause is at the end of the sentence, the comma may or may not be needed.

After we had seen the model, we decided to buy a condominium. A comma separates the dependent clause *after we had seen the model* from the independent clause that follows.

We decided to buy a condominium *after we had seen the model.* No commas when the dependent clause *follows* the independent clause.

Ask her to meet with us *when the manager will be in the office.* No comma needed.

Ask her to meet with us at 9 a.m., *when the manager will be in the office.* The comma is needed here because the phrase *at 9 a.m.* and the clause *when the manager will be in the office* say the same thing. Because the clause is repetitious, we use a comma to set it off from the rest of the sentence.

Dependent clauses can also appear in the middle of sentences. When they do, two commas should be used:

I know that Mr. Robertson, *who was elected for his second term,* will do an outstanding job for the city. Two commas separate the dependent clause from the rest of the sentence.

THREE OF A KIND   Notice how we use commas to separate three or more items in a series.

Pat, Mary, and Cathy started their own business. Three items—(1) *Pat,* (2) *Mary,* and (3) *Cathy*—are separated by two commas. Note that a comma precedes the conjunction and that no comma comes after *Cathy,* the last item in this series.

We learned from the applicant's résumé that he had written two books, five articles, two workbooks, and three brochures. Here, four items are joined: (1) *two books,* (2) *five articles,* (3) *two workbooks,* and (4) *three brochures.* Note that commas are used between each of them. The last is preceded by both the comma and the conjunction *and.*

The president of the association notified members of the meeting, prepared an agenda, and mailed application forms to prospective candidates. Do you see three of a kind? They are (1) *notified members of the meeting,* (2) *prepared an agenda,* and (3) *mailed application forms to prospective candidates.*

INTRODUCTORY WORDS, PHRASES, OR CLAUSES   Use a comma after introductory words, phrases, or clauses. Use a comma after introductory words such as *yes, no, look, well, in fact, for example, however,* and *therefore.*

Yes, this is the way we are going to do it.

Use a comma after an introductory participial phrase.

Hearing the news of his promotion, we offered him our congratulations.

Beware!   Do not confuse a gerund (a verb form ending in *-ing* and used as a noun) phrase that is used as the subject of the sentence with an introductory participial phrase.

Running five miles a day strengthens his legs.

Use a comma after an introductory infinitive phrase.

To welcome home its servicemen and servicewomen, the town held a parade.

Use a comma after a prepositional phrase that has five words or more.

In the spring of next year, we will start construction on our house on the lake.

Do not use commas after introductory adverbs that refer to time or place (when, how often, where).

On May 1 we will have our grand opening.   *At the meeting* we'll discuss those topics.

EXERCISES

NAME _____ DATE _____ SCORE _____

EXERCISE 1   Insert commas where necessary in the following sentences. Identify the coordinating conjunction by writing it in the space provided. If a sentence is correct, write *OK*. (*Hint:* Make sure that you check to see if an independent clause follows the conjunction.)

1. I read the letter carefully and I found several glaring errors in it.

2. Noreen wanted increased responsibilities so she made an appointment with her supervisor to discuss her job description.

3. I could recommend Harold for the job or I could recommend Lillian.

4. Philip had been studying history but he changed his major to journalism.

5. The Vanderwalls were not interested in the architect's suggestions nor were they interested in the contractor's recommendations.

6. Dad built the house that we lived in and he also built the house that my aunt and uncle live in.

1. _____

2. _____

3. _____

4. _____

5. _____

6. _____

EXERCISE 2   Complete the following sentences by adding a conjunction and an independent clause in the space provided. (*Hint:* An independent clause can stand alone as a complete sentence.)

1. The carpenter had plenty of tools,

_____

2. The editor of our newspaper received her bachelor's degree from Boston College,

_____

3. We can go to the play at Miller Auditorium,

_____

EXERCISE 3   Complete the following sentences by adding a dependent clause in the space provided. (*Hint:* A dependent clause contains a subject and a verb but cannot stand alone as a complete sentence.)

1. We volunteered to work on Houses for Humanity

_____

2. The parents were busy painting the walls

_____

3. We were still unable to find the missing documents

_____

EXERCISE 4   In the following sentences insert commas where necessary, especially to set off dependent clauses. In the spaces at the right, indicate how many commas are necessary. Also identify the subordinating conjunctions by underlining them. If a sentence is correct, write *OK*.

1. Although we received an invitation to the wedding we were not able to attend.

2. Many of us are planning to take a tour of the city when we go to Denver for the convention.

3. While we have an excellent work environment our salaries are not that high.

4. Before you can receive the merchandise you ordered please complete the enclosed card to let us know what size you want.

1. _____

2. _____

3. _____

4. _____

5. After shopping for several hours we stopped for lunch at a neighborhood restaurant.

5. _____

6. Unless we hear otherwise from you we will make the reservations for a single room with the ocean view.

6. _____

7. The Lampmans decided to buy the car after they had taken the test drive.

7. _____

8. As you know we have had several inquiries about the product.

8. _____

9. Since you have been out of the office we have had very few visitors.

9. _____

10. When we reach our goal of $25,000 we will no longer have to solicit funds.

10. _____

EXERCISE 5   Look for three (or more) of a kind in each of the following sentences. Then insert commas where necessary. In the space at the right, indicate how many commas are necessary. If a sentence is correct, write *OK*.

1. The advertisement said applicants who were college graduates who had three years' experience and who had good communication skills were eligible for the marketing position.

1. _____

2. Among the gifts John bought on his European trip were chocolates from Belgium wool sweaters from England and linen from Ireland.

2. _____

3. Be sure to file the letters the memos the purchase orders and the contracts.

3. _____

4. Chris and Michael and Karen were hoping to see the elephants when they were on a safari in Africa.

4. _____

5. During the summer they had the house painted a new garage door installed and the garden expanded.

5. _____

6. Improvements in the hotel included a new heating system an alarm system and a sprinkler system.

6. _____

7. Among the many folk songs they played and sang were ballads hymns and spirituals.

7. _____

8. Beth has lived in Chicago Detroit Los Angeles and Seattle during the past three years.

8. _____

9. The restaurant serves soups salads and sandwiches for lunch.

9. _____

10. We donated canned goods clothing and blankets to the open shelter.

10. _____

EXERCISE 6   Insert commas where necessary in the following sentences. In the space at the right, indicate the number of commas you used. If a sentence needs no further punctuation, write *OK*.

1. In fact we already have five applicants for the position.

1. _____

2. No we really don't need any paper this month.

2. _____

3. Seeing the hospital reminded her of her appointment to see the doctor.

3. _____

4. To learn more about the computer I plan to attend a two-week workshop on how to use the computer effectively.

4. _____

5. By the fall of next year I will have lost ten pounds.

5. _____

6. When Kelly received her first paycheck she put it in the bank for her college expenses.

6. _____

7. At the stockholders' meeting the directors announced a 2-for-1 split of the stock.

7. _____

8. Hearing about the family's need for clothing we immediately donated clothing for them.

8. _____

9. Playing bridge for three hours helped her to relax.

9. _____

10. If you would like a copy of the letter please let me know.

10. _____

11. On April 1 we will move into our new house.

11. _____

12. Yes they have decided to accept our offer.

12. _____

Commas, Commas, and More Commas

PARENTHETICAL ELEMENTS   Use commas to set off parenthetical elements—words, phrases, and clauses that are unnecessary for the meaning of the sentence. Parenthetical elements are also called nonessential elements because they are not essential to the meaning of the sentence. To test whether elements are parenthetical, place parentheses around the elements. Does the sentence make sense without the elements? If so, then the elements are nonessential; they can be removed. If removing the elements changes the meaning of the sentence, then the elements are essential. Essential elements are not set off by commas.

Margo White, who is attending State University, will receive her bachelor's degree in May. The subordinate clause, *who is attending State University,* does not affect the meaning of the sentence. It is, therefore, a nonessential clause. Clauses that modify proper nouns are almost always nonessential.

Walt McClintock, an industrial arts instructor, will help the Clausens build their house. The adjective phrase, *an industrial arts instructor,* does not affect the meaning of the sentence. It is, therefore, a nonessential clause. Phrases that modify proper nouns are almost always nonessential.

ESSENTIAL ELEMENTS   Do not use commas to set off essential (not parenthetical) elements of a sentence.

The book *Hatteras* has been on the best-seller list for three months. The name of the book is essential to the meaning of the sentence. It is not set off by commas.

The state where I would like to live is North Carolina. The adjective clause, *where I would like to live,* is essential to the meaning of the sentence. It is not set off by commas.

CHECKUP 1   Insert commas in the following sentences. In the space provided, indicate how many commas are necessary. If the sentence is punctuated correctly, write *OK*. Also indicate whether the elements are essential or nonessential.

1. Carmen DeLato, a senior at South High School, has been awarded a Medallion Scholarship by the Commerce Association.
2. Her brother who was running in the park tripped and hurt himself.
3. The magazine *Flying Time* has a subscription rate of $15 a year.

1. **2, nonessential**
2. _____
3. _____

DESCRIPTIVE EXPRESSIONS   Use commas to set off descriptive expressions that provide nonessential information.

Bob Brozowski's latest book, *A Winning Attitude,* has sold over 500,000 copies. *Latest book* identifies exactly which book is meant. The title of the book merely adds nonessential information. Commas set off the title of the book.

Bob Brozowski's book *A Winning Attitude* has sold over 500,000 copies. The descriptive title is necessary to identify which book sold over 500,000 copies. Do not set off the descriptive title with commas.

CONTRASTING EXPRESSIONS   Parenthetical expressions used to show contrast are set off by commas. Generally these expressions begin with *not, but,* or *rather than.*

The nurses, *not the doctors,* were requested to attend the lecture.

We intend to go to the Midwest Convention, *but not until Friday.*

CHECKUP 2

Insert commas in the following sentences. In the spaces provided, write whether the italicized elements are essential or nonessential.

1. John's book *Organizing Your Thoughts* is being used as a textbook.
2. Kevin *rather than Scott* helped remove the boxes from the garage.
3. The cows and the sheep *and not the horses* were grazing on the hillside.
4. Her sister *not her mother* is in charge of the food bank.
5. We bought her novel *Country Roads* as a gift for my father.

2. **essential**
2. _____
3. _____
4. _____
5. _____

WITHOUT A DOUBT, IN OTHER WORDS, OF COURSE

Notice how commas are used to set off the italicized "interrupters" in the following excerpts.

Without a doubt, many of our students are planning to attend college. *Consequently,* we should offer classes that will challenge them. *For example,* we could offer algebra, chemistry, and German. *In addition,* we might consider offering physics, trigonometry, and Russian. We cannot, *of course,* offer all foreign languages. *For this reason,* we need to make some decisions.

Whenever you write such interrupters, make sure that you separate them with commas. Use one comma for interrupters that introduce a clause; use two commas for those that appear in the middle of a clause.

Consequently, we decided to accept their offer, but still we were not sure it was the best offer. One comma is used after *consequently,* which introduces the first independent clause.

Charles McLaughlin, *therefore,* needed an assistant, and he placed an advertisement for one in the local newspaper. Two commas are used around *therefore,* which appears in the middle of an independent clause.

Beware!

Sometimes expressions that are commonly used as "interrupters" do not interrupt; they can be important parts of the sentence.

Adrian, our manager, *certainly* knew what he was doing. No commas.

They *of course* understood what we had done. No commas.

However sure you may be, I suggest that you still ask permission. No comma after *however.*

There is *no doubt* that we will be awarded the contract. No commas.

When the words *thus* and *then* introduce a clause, they are usually written without commas.

He called the office to say he would be late; *then* he took the car over to the garage for repairs. No comma after *then.*

Thus I hope our discussion will end all the confusion. No commas.

CHECKUP 3

Decide if there are any interrupters in the following sentences. If so, insert commas to show how the interrupters should be separated. In the spaces at the right, indicate how many commas are necessary. If a sentence is correct, write *OK*.

1. The proposal, however, will not be completed until we have the figures from our engineers.
2. However the decision goes we will be supportive.
3. The candidate said he would obviously not run again for public office.
4. We concluded therefore that they were eager to begin the project.
5. In my opinion we should forget about signing the lease and just rent by the month.

1. **2** _____
2. _____
3. _____
4. _____
5. _____

EXERCISES

NAME _____ DATE _____ SCORE _____

EXERCISE 1   Insert commas in the following sentences. In the spaces provided, indicate how many commas are necessary. If the sentence is punctuated correctly, write *OK*. Also indicate whether the elements are essential or nonessential.

1. It is unsafe for a child to swim alone in the lake.
2. Darlene who is so talented is seeking a musical career.
3. Many people who immigrated to the United States came because they wanted freedom.
4. Barry's car which has over 50,000 miles on it needs new brakes.
5. The students who came to class yesterday met the visiting professor.
6. People who are conscientious are likely to succeed.
7. My only aunt who works in a candy factory rarely eats candy.
8. Alice Sonnenberg the firm's payroll clerk found an error on one of the checks.
9. Margo who ate her food quickly began to feel uncomfortable.
10. Our new Coldaire refrigerator which we bought for $800 is working beautifully.
11. Only one of our partners Ms. Crawford specializes in liability cases.
12. The house on the corner sold for $125,000.

1. _____
2. _____
3. _____
4. _____
5. _____
6. _____
7. _____
8. _____
9. _____
10. _____
11. _____
12. _____

EXERCISE 2   Insert commas where necessary in the following sentences. In the spaces provided, write whether the italicized elements are essential or nonessential.

1. Lisa Walden's latest book *Getting Your Ideas Down on Paper* has been adopted as a textbook by over 100 schools.
2. The seniors *and not the freshmen* were having a tailgate party before the football game.
3. The Chicago Bulls *not the Detroit Pistons* won the basketball tournament.
4. George Carlson's book *Coping With Stress* is recommended for those people who experience stress in their lives.
5. The contract for the painting of the exterior of the building was awarded to A&B Painting *and not Associated Painters*.
6. The Catalinas were traveling east to Connecticut, Rhode Island, and Massachusetts *but not Maine*.
7. Kent's proposal *"Analyzing the City's Water Supply"* was still being considered by the evaluation committee.
8. Sonia Honian's manuscript *"A Clear View of Our Representational Systems"* has been rejected several times already.
9. Dr. Flynn *rather than Dr. Barnaby* will be the new administrator of the hospital.
10. The lawyer's new article *"Writing Your Will"* will be published in the next issue of the journal.
11. When we were in California we visited many places *but not Disneyland*.
12. The Carters *but not the Freemans* will be attending the concert.

1. _____
2. _____
3. _____
4. _____
5. _____
6. _____
7. _____
8. _____
9. _____
10. _____
11. _____
12. _____

EXERCISE 3

Decide if there are any interrupters in the following sentences. If so, insert commas to show how the interrupters should be separated. In the space at the right, indicate how many commas are necessary. If a sentence is correct, write *OK*.

1. Fortunately we had enough money to buy a plane ticket.
2. The rain however will not dampen their spirits.
3. However you picture it it will still be more beautiful than the previous design.
4. I would in fact like to hire three more accountants after the first of the year.
5. In addition we will need five desks and five chairs.
6. There is no doubt that her children will be successful.
7. The piano concert by Van Cliburn was without a doubt the finest performance I had heard.
8. The names for example could be changed very easily.
9. First I want to commend you for your excellent report.
10. Cheryl certainly knew what she was getting into when she bid for that job.
11. We will however need the report by Monday.
12. In my opinion she deserves to be elected.
13. However you may wish to consider all points of view.
14. Of course we will be at your wedding.
15. Simon was certainly accurate in his assessment of the situation.

1. _____
2. _____
3. _____
4. _____
5. _____
6. _____
7. _____
8. _____
9. _____
10. _____
11. _____
12. _____
13. _____
14. _____
15. _____

EXERCISE 4

Write sentences using each of the following interrupters. Insert commas where appropriate.

1. without a doubt

_____

2. for example

_____

3. in addition

_____

4. In other words

_____

5. however

_____

6. therefore

_____

7. consequently

_____

8. certainly

_____

9. First

_____

10. no doubt

_____

11. In my opinion

_____

12. of course

_____

The Versatile Comma

DELIBERATE REPETITIONS   Nouns or noun phrases that rename or explain the immediately preceding noun or pronoun are called *appositives*. Appositives that are not essential are set off by commas. Appositives that are essential do not require commas. In the following sentences, note the deliberate repetitions.

Ms. Charlene Karstens, *our office manager,* is well liked by everyone in the office. Our office manager is *Ms. Charlene Karstens,* and we set off *our office manager* with commas because it repeats (in different words) the same information given by "Ms. Charlene Karstens." The expression *our office manager* is an appositive.

Both applicants, *Carole Collins and he,* will be interviewed this afternoon. *Carole Collins and he* is another way of saying *both applicants,* so it is set off with commas. Note that the nominative form *he* is correct because we could say "Carole Collins and *he* will be interviewed this afternoon." The expression *Carole Collins and he* is an appositive.

As you see, correct pronoun choice can be tricky in sentences such as those above. But if you omit part of the sentence and substitute the repetition that contains the pronoun, the choice becomes clear.

Please ask one of the new mail messengers, *either Ken or her. Either Ken or her* repeats the same information as *one of the new mail messengers.* Note that the correct pronoun choice for this sentence becomes obvious when you say "Please ask either Ken or her." (You would not say "Please ask she.")

Beware!   Do not set off with commas expressions that are essential to the meaning of the sentence.

The word *accommodation* is frequently misspelled.

Students often say "I don't know" when they haven't read the chapter.

The printer Roy Beck prepared the business cards for us.

Do not use a comma to set off closely related and one-word appositives.

We doctors agreed with the recommendation.

My cousin Rosemarie will be flying in from Kansas today.

Use a comma to separate words that are repeated in a sentence.

When you *study, study hard.* Note the comma in *study, study.*

CHECKUP 1   Decide if any commas are missing from the following sentences. Insert the missing commas in the sentences. Then write both the word that precedes each comma and the comma itself in the space at the right. If a sentence is correct, write *OK*.

1. We attorneys agreed to share research on similar cases.
2. Her sister-in-law Judge Grace Holmquist was reappointed by Governor Marley.
3. When you walk walk with confidence.
4. Both doctors Dr. Graham and she were commended for their work with AIDS patients.

1. __OK_____
2. _____
3. _____
4. _____

"YES, MS. NOBLES." "OF COURSE, MISS NOBLES."   When we speak directly to someone, whether in person, in writing, or on the phone, we often use that person's name. In writing, we use commas to separate the name of the person whom we are addressing from the rest of the sentence. Words used in direct address are parenthetical.

Yes, *Ms. Nobles,* your appointment is for Tuesday. Note the commas around the person's name.

COMMAS IN DATES, ADDRESSES, AND GEOGRAPHICAL ITEMS   In dates, commas help us to separate two consecutive numbers.

Dad signed the first contract on *March 15, 1992,* and the second one on *April 15, 1992.* Note that two commas are around the first *1992;* of course, only one comma is needed before the second *1992* because it is followed by a period.

We do not use commas when only the month and year are given in dates.

The *December 1992* issue is a s̟____ issue that highlights the major events of the year. (NOT: The *December, 1992,* issue.)

Frequently, dates are used as deliberate repetitions:

On Friday, *September 23,* we will have our first meeting. Note the commas around *September 23*—a deliberate repetition that specifies which Friday is intended.

In addresses, commas help us to identify the parts of the full address.

Mail a copy of the statement to *Mr. Craig Bell, 3432 West Monroe Street, Columbia, SC 29208,* before the end of the month.

In geographic items, use commas to set off the name of a state when it follows the name of the city. Also, use commas to set off counties.

We had hoped to visit relatives in *Spokane, Washington,* while we are out West.

The bank considered opening a branch in *Kansas City, Missouri.*
The Olsens would be moving to *Cass County, Michigan,* sometime in August.

TO SEPARATE ADJECTIVES   When two adjectives modify the same noun, use a comma to separate them.

Kelly is an honest, trustworthy employee. Note again that the word *and* can be used in place of the comma.

They had planned to purchase several new computers. No comma between the two adjectives *several* and *new* (both modify computers). Why? Because you cannot use the word *and* in place of the comma (*purchase several and new computers* does not make sense).

Always test to see whether you can substitute the word *and* for the comma. If you can, then the comma is correct. If you cannot, do not use a comma.

CHECKUP 2   Insert commas where necessary in the following sentences. In the space at the right indicate how many commas are necessary. If a sentence is correct, write *OK.*

1. No, Mr. Dixon, we have no employee by that name working here.   1. **2** _____
2. Please address the envelope to Ms. Geneva Lemley 408 Main Street Atlanta Georgia 30315.   2. _____
3. The March 1991 issue of *Forbes* was not in the library.   3. _____
4. The new inexpensive desk will be delivered on Tuesday June 15.   4. _____

EXERCISES

NAME _____ DATE _____ SCORE _____

EXERCISE 1   Decide which sentence in each of the following pairs is punctuated correctly. In the space provided, write the letter of the sentence that is correct.

1. a. Ms. Visser, I would appreciate your letting me know when Mr. Curtis arrives.
   b. Ms. Visser I would appreciate your letting me know when Mr. Curtis arrives.

1. _____

2. a. I found Edward's latest book, *Computing Made Easy,* very easy to read.
   b. I found Edward's latest book *Computing Made Easy* very easy to read.

2. _____

3. a. The new doctor is a compassionate, caring individual.
   b. The new doctor is a compassionate caring individual.

3. _____

4. a. That new energetic nurse in the emergency room studied at New York University.
   b. That new, energetic nurse in the emergency room studied at New York University.

4. _____

5. a. Ms. Bonnie Correll, our human resources director, explained the benefits to new employees.
   b. Ms. Bonnie Correll our human resources director explained the benefits to new employees.

5. _____

6. a. Caroline, would you please send copies of the report to the members of the board.
   b. Caroline would you please send copies of the report to the members of the board.

6. _____

7. a. Two nurses, Rita Holbrook and Bob Kimbrel volunteered to take people's blood pressure in the shopping mall.
   b. Two nurses, Rita Holbrook and Bob Kimbrel, volunteered to take people's blood pressure in the shopping mall.

7. _____

8. a. Judge Harrison is fair, enthusiastic, and effective.
   b. Judge Harrison is fair enthusiastic and effective.

8. _____

9. a. That information should be given to Ms. Derhammer our credit manager.
   b. That information should be given to Ms. Derhammer, our credit manager.

9. _____

10. a. Please ask one of the new workers Sean or Frances, about the mail delivery.
    b. Please ask one of the new workers, Sean or Frances, about the mail delivery.

10. _____

EXERCISE 2   Decide if any commas are missing from the following sentences. Insert the missing commas in the sentences. Then in the spaces at the right, indicate how many commas are necessary. If a sentence is correct, write *OK.* (*Hint:* Watch for deliberate repetitions.)

1. By February 1992 they will have installed the new furnace in the building.

1. _____

2. Rex tells me that his parents will be moving to Sioux City Iowa within the next few weeks.

2. _____

3. On Monday August 5 our Board of Directors will be meeting in San Diego California.

3. _____

4. Several new printers have been ordered for the Research Division.

4. _____

5. Her brother-in-law Dr. Ted Gomolak recently was hired as the superintendent of schools in Portage.

5. _____

6. No no that's not the way to make overhead transparencies.

6. _____

7. Of course Ms. Riley we have the materials ready for you to pick up.

7. _____

8. Barrien County Michigan is known as the Fruit Belt of the state.

8. _____

EXERCISE 3   Insert commas where necessary in the following sentences. Then in the spaces at the right, indicate how many commas are necessary. If a sentence is correct, write *OK*.

1. That intelligent efficient woman has been a law clerk for several years.

1. _____

2. Only one manager Ms. Barrington or Mr. Coggan can be gone during the holidays.

2. _____

3. The word *receive* is on the list of frequently misspelled words.

3. _____

4. Doctors are very very much in demand in a small rural area.

4. _____

5. Yes Ms. Smolinski I promise to be here before 8 o'clock tomorrow morning.

5. _____

6. The letter was dated February 23 1991 but we didn't receive it until March 15 1991.

6. _____

7. We nurses have had to work the night shift for three months now.

7. _____

8. I enjoyed working with Janette because she was witty enthusiastic and entertaining.

8. _____

EXERCISE 4   Correct the following sentences by inserting commas. In the spaces at the right, indicate how many commas are necessary. If a sentence is correct, write *OK*.

1. The district manager for Books Inc. Todd Castern is responsible for schools in Ohio Wisconsin Illinois Michigan and Indiana.

1. _____

2. Elizabeth was born on November 16 1935 and her sister was born on September 9 1938.

2. _____

3. The September 1991 issue of *Our Town* published an excellent article on the Crosby family.

3. _____

4. Her widowed aunt lives at 3249 South Mason Road Apartment 2B Melbourne Florida 32905.

4. _____

EXERCISE 5   Write sentences using the elements specified, and punctuate them correctly.

1. Three or more items in a series using *and*

_____

2. Three or more items in a series using *or*

_____

3. Two dates with consecutive numbers

_____

4. Repetition of *very, very*

_____

5. A direct address

_____

6. An address that includes a street number, city, state, and ZIP Code

_____

7. A repeated word

_____

8. A one-word appositive

_____

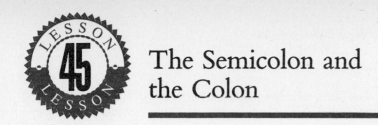

The Semicolon and the Colon

THE SEMICOLON   Do you remember the adverbs that join? In Lesson 32, you learned about conjunctive adverbs such as *accordingly, therefore,* and *however.* These adverbs are usually used to join two independent clauses. When they do join two independent clauses, semicolons are *always* used.

He entered the mail-order business in early 1980; however, he continued to operate several other businesses. The semicolon after *1980* is essential; it shows clearly where the first independent clause ends and the second one begins.

In the same way, semicolons are needed when a word or phrase, such as *for example, that is, on the contrary,* or *on the other hand,* is used to link the thoughts in two independent clauses.

She made several excellent suggestions; for example, she recommended that we sponsor a fund-raising drive for scholarships. The semicolon after *suggestions* shows where the first independent clause ends and the second one starts.

The semicolon also serves to join independent clauses in another way. Compare the next two examples:

The company's management decided to hire another 50 plant workers, but it wasn't sure how many additional office workers to hire. Here, two independent clauses are joined by the conjunction *but* plus a comma.

The company's management decided to hire another 50 plant workers; it wasn't sure how many additional office workers to hire. Here, a semicolon has replaced both the conjunction *but* and the comma.

In the preceding example, the semicolon replaces the conjunction *but* and a comma. It can also replace the conjunctions *and, or,* or *nor.*

Perhaps by this time you have already asked yourself, "Why not simply make each independent clause into a separate sentence?" Of course, you could do so and avoid using the semicolon, but when you want to show that two ideas are closely related, you may decide that semicolons provide the best means to show that close relationship.

One more case requires semicolons. Use a semicolon to separate items in a series when any of the items already contain commas.

The sales representative's territory included Providence, Rhode Island; Hartford, Connecticut; and Springfield, Massachusetts. The semicolons separate the three sites clearly.

CHECKUP 1   Insert semicolons or commas where necessary in the following sentences. Then in the spaces at the right, indicate how many semicolons and commas (total) are necessary.

1. Only Mr. Griffin supported our recommendation; the other officers of the company did not.

    1. <u>__1_____</u>

2. Dr. Margaret Pfizer is listed in several Who's Who publications for example she is listed in *Who's Who in the Midwest Who's Who in America* and *Who's Who of American Women.*

    2. <u>_____</u>

3. We recommended Giles Sandhal for the position however he was not interested in relocating at this time.

    3. <u>_____</u>

THE COLON

Colons are used after the salutations in business letters.

Ladies and Gentlemen: Dear Ms. Rockwell and Mr. Osterling:

A colon is also used after an independent clause to show that what follows *further explains* that clause.

He had only one reason for the change: business was expanding and more room was necessary. What follows the colon further explains what is meant by *one reason*. A semicolon would not be enough to show a relationship *this* close.

The semicolon shows that two ideas are related, but the colon shows a much closer relationship. A colon is used when what follows the colon *has already been suggested.* Often the words that appear before the colon are very obvious hints: *the following, as follows, these,* and so on. In general, whatever precedes the colon should be a complete sentence.

They needed the following information for their sales presentation: total sales for January, February, and March; estimated sales for April, May, and June; and projected sales for the second half of the year. The words *the following* tell you that an explanation or a listing will come after the colon.

Please bring the following items with you: warm clothing, walking shoes, and blankets.

Sometimes the list is typed on separate lines:

These three companies recently joined the Business Bureau:

1. Aero-Motive Manufacturing Company

2. First National Bank

3. National Waterlift Company

You will also see colons used after words such as *remember, hint,* and *caution.*

Remember: Look both ways before crossing the street.

Beware!   Do *not* use a colon to interrupt sentences. Never use a colon to separate a verb and its object or a preposition and its object.

The regional meetings were held in Boston, Chicago, and Los Angeles. (NOT: The regional meetings were held in: Boston, . . .)

Write to Dr. J. T. Phillips, 103 South Main Street, Sacramento, CA 95819. (NOT: Write to: Dr. J. T. Phillips . . .)

You are probably familiar with colons used in expressions of time:

at 7:30 a.m.   before 5:45 p.m.   after 7:30 p.m.

CHECKUP 2

Insert colons and commas where necessary in the following sentences. Then in the spaces at the right, indicate how many colons and commas (total) are necessary.

1. Remember: Our deadline for submitting the proposal is December 1.   1. __1_____

2. This is the equipment they requested for their presentation an overhead projector a screen and a podium.   2. _____

3. The meeting was to start at 815 a.m. and to adjourn at 1130 a.m.   3. _____

4. These are the employees we selected for merit pay Ray Rossi Kathleen Mahoney Bertha Swager and Hugh Hughes.   4. _____

EXERCISES

NAME _____ DATE _____ SCORE _____

EXERCISE 1   Decide which sentence in each of the following pairs is punctuated correctly. In the space at the right, write the letter of the sentence that is correct.

1. a. The seminar was a great success, over 200 people attended.
   b. The seminar was a great success; over 200 people attended.

   1. _____

2. a. Ms. Collick was made assistant vice president two years ago; today she is a senior vice president in the company.
   b. Ms. Collick was made assistant vice president two years ago, today she is a senior vice president in the company.

   2. _____

3. a. Thank you for your order for two dozen T-shirts, however, we would appreciate your completing the enclosed card to let us know what sizes you would like.
   b. Thank you for your order for two dozen T-shirts; however, we would appreciate your completing the enclosed card to let us know what sizes you would like.

   3. _____

4. a. As the computer systems expert, Yuri traveled to our branch offices in Lansing, Michigan; Elkhart, Indiana; and Moline, Illinois.
   b. As the computer systems expert, Yuri traveled to our branch offices in Lansing, Michigan, Elkhart, Indiana, and Moline, Illinois.

   4. _____

5. a. You should receive your order by February 15, we shipped it by National Parcel Service today.
   b. You should receive your order by February 15; we shipped it by National Parcel Service today.

   5. _____

EXERCISE 2   Insert semicolons and commas where necessary in the following sentences. Then in the spaces at the right, indicate how many semicolons and commas (total) are necessary.

1. Ms. Wagford has been promoted to manager she certainly deserves it.

   1. _____

2. Students were complaining about the many fees they had to pay namely the health fee the computer fee and the recreational fee.

   2. _____

3. The committee members were excited about having the survey completed they were however unhappy with the results.

   3. _____

4. Because of early retirements two positions will be available in the Art Department consequently we'll soon be announcing these positions.

   4. _____

5. The new procedures worked very well we had only five calls asking for clarification of them.

   5. _____

6. As you requested the original copy of the invoice was sent to your main office a copy of the invoice was sent to your branch office in Chicago.

   6. _____

7. The departmental faculty meeting is scheduled for Tuesday May 5 at 3 o'clock all faculty are requested to attend.

   7. _____

8. The bar graphs were designed by Stan Kallick the line graphs were designed by Shelley Bright.

   8. _____

9. Ms. Estkowski has the skills for the job furthermore she has the experience.

   9. _____

10. The receptionist at the doctor's office checked the appointment book no appointments were available until the first of next month.

    10. _____

11. The large purchase order was to be shipped to several locations namely Louisville Kentucky New Orleans Louisiana and Baltimore Maryland.

    11. _____

12. Anthony operated a paper plant for years however he also managed several other businesses.

13. Isabel developed skill in several winter sports namely downhill skiing cross-country skiing and ice skating.

14. Holiday weekends have always been times of increased numbers of traffic accidents therefore drivers should be especially careful during these times.

15. Today less than 20 percent of college students join fraternities and sororities several years ago the percentage was higher.

16. First she typed the long report for her manager then she typed several letters.

12. _____

13. _____

14. _____

15. _____

16. _____

EXERCISE 3

Insert colons and commas where necessary in the following sentences. In the spaces at the right, indicate how many colons and commas (total) are necessary.

1. The following faculty were selected to serve on the committee for curriculum development Drs. Cornwell Gotfryd Earle and Sherburn.

2. Here's a list of the items that we need for the project drawing paper a compass and a protractor.

3. Avoid these common redundancies in your writing *finish up over with* and *repeat again.*

4. Hint The document contains five misspelled words.

5. The Sherwoods were leaving on Flight 307 at 845 a.m.

6. Here's what she wanted for her birthday a laptop computer a printer and a modem.

7. His objective is clear He wants to help the poor the sick and the homeless.

8. The rule is simple Only 50 people are allowed in the pool at one time.

9. These are the countries we would like to visit England Scotland Ireland and France.

10. Albert needed to make a choice He could take the job either with the printing company or with the insurance company.

1. _____

2. _____

3. _____

4. _____

5. _____

6. _____

7. _____

8. _____

9. _____

10. _____

EXERCISE 4

Insert commas, semicolons, and colons where necessary in the following sentences. In the spaces at the right, indicate how many punctuation marks are necessary.

1. I wanted to see the play he wanted to see the movie.

2. His math and science scores were average however his reading and writing skills were above average.

3. The check hasn't arrived therefore the goods will not be shipped.

4. We had hoped to be in our new office on Monday August 1 1991 at 830 a.m.

5. Only the manager had the combination to the safe unfortunately she hadn't arrived yet.

6. This morning's meeting was at 830 this afternoon's meeting will be at 330.

7. Glenn hopes to attend Tulane University in New Orleans Louisiana this fall.

8. The play begins at 830 let's plan to leave about 730.

9. Please order the following items for the office three staplers one dictionary and twelve pens.

10. I appreciate your concern Millie I will let you know how the situation is resolved.

1. _____

2. _____

3. _____

4. _____

5. _____

6. _____

7. _____

8. _____

9. _____

10. _____

Dashes, Parentheses, and Brackets

THE DASH

The dash shares some of its uses with other marks of punctuation—the comma, the semicolon, and the colon. The dash shows more emphasis, however, than those other marks of punctuation. Here are a few examples of how the dash is used.

The vice president—as well as the president—was adamant in his decision to reject the merger offer. The dashes emphasize *as well as the president*. Commas would not be so emphatic.

Three of our manufacturing plants—the ones in Tuscaloosa, Little Rock, and Stillwater—are being renovated. Commas would be confusing because the phrase *the ones in Tuscaloosa, Little Rock, and Stillwater* already contains two commas.

Use a dash before a word or phrase that has been repeated for greater emphasis.

Dawn is busy—extremely busy—with the end-of-the-month reports for management. The dashes provide the needed emphasis.

Dashes provide more emphasis than a semicolon or a colon can.

He wants to have the meeting at 9:00 a.m.—in fact, he thinks 9:30 might be too late! The dash in this case provides more emphasis than a semicolon, although a semicolon would also be correct.

Our real estate agent told us the three most important factors in purchasing a home—location, location, location. A colon would be more formal but less emphatic.

Use a dash to set off a brief summary or before words such as *these*, *each*, and *all*.

Louis, Myles, and Patrick—each one knows how to operate the farm machinery.

PARENTHESES

Use parentheses to give the reader extra information. Just as dashes are used to emphasize material, parentheses are used to deemphasize material. Like dashes, parentheses enclose material that could be set off by commas.

To place your order today, call our toll-free number (800-555-3445). Here parentheses enclose a telephone number.

The will provided one thousand dollars ($1,000) for the Red Cross. Here parentheses are used to restate a dollar amount in figures.

The operator's manual provides complete instructions for assembling the lawn mower (see page 8). The parentheses enclose the independent clause *see page 8*.

The Springfield (Illinois) office houses our customer relations department. The parentheses here replace commas: *The Springfield, Illinois, office* would not be as clear.

The Oakville Company will merge with Springfield Metals (a Massachusetts firm); by now, both businesses have probably signed a letter of intent. The parentheses enclose nonessential information.

Use parentheses to enclose numbers or letters used to enumerate items within a sentence.

He agreed to the following terms: (1) a starting salary of $25,000, (2) a two weeks' vacation, and (3) a company car.

Use parentheses to enclose the abbreviation or acronym of an organization that immediately follows the full name of the organization.

The National Association for the Advancement of Colored People (NAACP) is having its annual convention in Atlanta, Georgia, this year.

CHECKUP 1   Insert any missing punctuation marks in the following sentences.

1. You may reach me at my toll-free number (800-555-6400).
2. Amanda as well as Sidney was positive we would receive the grant.
3. The Columbus Kentucky plant manufactures the cartons that we use for our products.
4. Two of the buildings the Skyrise and the Hytower were purchased by Financial Enterprises Inc.
5. Fifteen percent of his income went toward clothing see pie chart on page 8.

OTHER PUNCTUATION MARKS WITH PARENTHESES AND DASHES

Here are the *only* ways in which you can use other punctuation marks with dashes.

The Portage office is too crowded—isn't it?—for additional staff. The words within the dashes pose the question; thus the question mark goes before the second dash.

The Portage office is too crowded—definitely too crowded!—for additional staff. The exclamation point belongs only to the words within the dashes; thus it is placed before the second dash.

Now let's see how other punctuation marks may be used with parentheses.

The Portage office is too crowded (isn't it?) for additional staff. Only the words within the parentheses pose the question.

The Portage office is too crowded (definitely too crowded!) for additional staff. The exclamation point belongs only to those words within parentheses.

Unlike dashes, parentheses can be followed by other marks of punctuation.

He had to drive 30 miles (about 40 minutes). The period that ends the sentence *follows* the second parenthesis.

Does anyone know why these forms are due twice a year (in April and October)? The question mark belongs to the sentence (not to the words enclosed in parentheses); thus the question mark is placed *after* the second parenthesis.

The general manager needs the statistics by Monday afternoon (before 2:00)! The exclamation point belongs to the entire sentence; thus it is placed *after* the second parenthesis.

It would be best if we met in the next month (by April 10 would be most convenient); by then we will have all the data we need. The semicolon belongs *after* the second parenthesis.

When your three-year lease ends (on December 31), you have the option to renegotiate another one. Note the comma *after* the second parenthesis.

BRACKETS

Use brackets to insert remarks, additions, or corrections (especially misspellings) made by another. Also use brackets as a substitute for parentheses within parentheses.

He said, "We have identified the winners [names were not given] of the New York lottery."

The headlines read as follows: "ITS [sic] A SELLOUT!" (Note that *sic* is used to indicate a quoted misspelled word. In this case, *ITS* should be *IT'S*.)

She purchased her first car (a Roadrunner [sedan model]) for $4,000.

EXERCISES

EXERCISE 1   Insert dashes where necessary in the following sentences.

1. The officers of the association the president, the vice president, and the executive director met in Vancouver, British Columbia, to plan the convention.
2. Two of our offices the one in Los Angeles and the one in San Francisco are closing.
3. That book the one lying on the desk is the one Dr. Rivera recommended.
4. In our marketing class we learned about promotional devices free samples, coupons, and discounts.

EXERCISE 2   Insert parentheses where necessary in the following sentences.

1. They inadvertently set the meeting date on a holiday Memorial Day.
2. The contract said to pay eighteen hundred dollars $1,800 for the installation of two electrical outlets.
3. According to the New York Stock Exchange NYSE, your stock is now selling for $42 a share.
4. The study guide lists the course syllabus see page 15.
5. The new provost a summa cum laude graduate, received her doctorate from Harvard University.

EXERCISE 3   Insert brackets where necessary in the following sentences.

1. Patricia last name not given volunteered to help shelter the homeless after the tornado.
2. Only one of the architects (Susan Campbell or Paul Judd Nita's brother) will be working on the Housman plans.
3. The newspaper headline read "There's sic Too Many Unanswered Questions."
4. The operator said, "It the crane will not start."
5. All the workers (over 50 of them mostly veterans) attended the meeting.

EXERCISE 4   Insert any missing punctuation marks (commas, dashes, parentheses, brackets, colons, and semicolons) in the following sentences. In the spaces at the right, indicate how many punctuation marks are necessary (a pair of parentheses or brackets counts as two marks).

1. These are the qualities we are looking for in applicants loyalty dependability and honesty.   1. _____
2. When your contract ends this month on July 31 you may renew it if you wish.   2. _____
3. The report read, "Alot sic of work was completed by a construction firm."   3. _____
4. Howard told us his adopted parents now living in Arizona would be in town when he received his degree.   4. _____
5. The department chairperson as well as the city manager was in favor of the proposal submitted by the city commissioners.   5. _____
6. Her first computer a Zany III cost only $2,000.   6. _____
7. The contest rules said that entries had to be postmarked no later than June 30 by midnight.   7. _____
8. Two of the bank branches the one in Melbourne and the one in Clearwater are expanding their services.   8. _____
9. Sylvia the manager in accounts receivable is asking for a transfer to our department.   9. _____
10. The purchase price of the house was seventy-five thousand dollars $75,000.   10. _____

11. The Organization of Petroleum Exporting Countries OPEC is meeting to decide whether to raise oil prices again.

12. Three of our products all the new ones were developed by Bob Dunham.

13. You can place your order by calling our toll-free number 800-555-2312.

14. Clarence is happy extremely happy about winning the Outstanding Researcher Award from the National Association of Researchers.

15. The answers can be found in the appendix see page 95.

16. The new coordinator of faculty development an Illinois graduate begins work on June 3.

17. We were to leave before noon in fact we were to leave by 1030 a.m.

18. We had 300 miles about six hours to drive before we would arrive in Cincinnati Ohio.

19. Our purchasing agent placed the order on Monday consequently we should have the equipment tomorrow.

20. The accountant has the original report a backup copy is in the files.

11. _____

12. _____

13. _____

14. _____

15. _____

16. _____

17. _____

18. _____

19. _____

20. _____

EXERCISE 5

Circle the punctuation error in each of the following sentences. Then in the space provided, indicate why each sentence is incorrect. If a sentence is correct, write *OK*.

1. Janet is—late always late! for our meetings.

_____

2. Dan asked the firm Fletcher Enterprises to bid on the project.

_____

3. Sharon had three requests: a she wanted to take her vacation in December, b she wanted an assistant, and c she wanted a laser printer.

_____

4. Sunscreen lotion, sunglasses, and books to read these are the items you'll need when you go to the beach.

_____

5. All requests should be submitted in triplicate (see Office Procedures Manual page 42).

_____

EXERCISE 6

Periods, commas, dashes, parentheses, colons, and semicolons have been omitted from the letter below. Use a caret (∧) in the body of the letter to show where each mark belongs. Write each required mark in the letter and also in the corresponding space at the right. For each line that is correct, write *OK* in the space at the right.

Dear Ms Freeman	1.
Yes the three departments in our College Accounting	2.
Management and Marketing have applied for federal	3.
grants	4.
Dr Melford wrote the draft of the proposal Dr	5.
Isau wrote the final draft They were not interested at least	6.
at the present time in having the proposal published	7.
The cost for preparing the proposal for The Federal	8.
Bureau of Banking FBB was two thousand	9.
dollars $2 000 The doctors received a check for five	10.
hundred dollars $500 in advance for their work	11.
Sincerely	12.

Quotation Marks, Underscores, and Apostrophes

QUOTATION MARKS   Use quotation marks (" ") to show that the words within the marks are someone's exact words. As you read the following examples, note that commas and periods always go *before (never after)* the second quotation mark.

Ms. Kaufmann said, "Prices were effective as of July 1, 1991." The quotation marks show Ms. Kaufmann's exact words. Note how the period is positioned *before* the end quotation mark.

"Prices," Ms. Kaufmann said in her report, "were effective as of July 1, 1991." Here Ms. Kaufmann's exact words are interrupted, so the quotation marks are "detoured" around the clause *Ms. Kaufmann said in her report.*

Besides showing a person's exact words, quotation marks serve other purposes. Quotation marks are used for words and phrases following such introductory words as *labeled, marked, signed,* and *stamped.*

The package was stamped "Urgent."

Also use quotation marks to enclose titles that represent part of a complete literary work such as magazine articles, newspaper columns, chapters in books, essays, and songs.

Magazine article: The article "The Elements of Effective Communication" was written by Claudia Grant.

Chapter in book: Students were asked to read Chapter 7, "The Seven Secrets of Success," for Monday.

Essay: Dr. Farley wrote an essay entitled "Subjective Versus Objective Thinking."

Newspaper column: Stan Greeley writes the advice column, "In and Out," for the local newspaper.

Song: We sang "God Bless America" at the end of the program.

Question marks and exclamation points may go before or after the end quotation mark—it depends on whether the mark belongs with the speaker's exact words.

In her report Peg asked, "What is the difference between the two models?" Note that the question mark belongs with Peg's exact words, so it goes *inside* the quotation marks.

Why did Sam mark this "Confidential"? Does the question mark belong with Sam's exact words? No, it belongs with the entire sentence. Thus the question mark goes *outside* the second quotation mark.

After working five hours on the problems, Debbie shouted, "I've got a solution!" The exclamation point belongs with Debbie's exact words, so it goes *inside* the second quotation mark.

Please don't forget to mark this box "Fragile"! The exclamation point goes with the entire sentence; thus it is placed *outside* the second quotation.

"Did You Say 'Quotation Marks'?"   When a quotation appears within another quotation, use single quotation marks (' '), as shown in the following examples:

I heard Frank ask, "Why did Margo label this 'Confidential'?" Note the position of the question mark: it does not belong with the word *confidential;* it belongs with the entire sentence.

When Beth returned, she said, "After working five hours on the problem, Debbie shouted, 'I've got a solution!'" Here, the exclamation point goes before the single quotation mark because it belongs with the words enclosed in the single quotations: *I've got a solution!*

Periods and commas always go before the single quotation mark.

"He should label the file 'Confidential,'" said Mr. Pinkham.

Ms. Badra said, "Yes, label the file 'Confidential.'"

CHECKUP 1   Insert punctuation marks where necessary in the following sentences.

1. Our assignment was to read Chapter 5, "Special Techniques for Reports."
2. Please mark the envelope Registered Mail
3. I remember Cherry saying We should get together for lunch next month before she left

UNDERSCORES   Use underscores for titles of books, magazines, newspapers, operas, and movies or plays.

Book: Have you read Joseph Mitchell's Successful Management Techniques?

Magazine: Here are this week's issues of Secretarial Studies and Business Ventures.

Newspaper: He has a subscription to The Daily Courier.

Opera: They went to see The Marriage of Figaro in New York City.

Movie: They are planning to do another remake of Carnival Times.

Underscores are also used for emphasis and for words used as words (usually preceded by phrases such as *the word, the term,* or *the expression*).

We must be in absolute agreement before the negotiations can end.

The word accommodate is quite frequently misspelled.

APOSTROPHES   The apostrophe is used to show that a letter has been omitted from a word. Words with apostrophes in place of omitted letters are called *contractions*.

There's no reason for us to accept the wrong merchandise. Note the apostrophe in *There's* (short for *There is;* the letter *i* in *is* has been omitted). *There's* is a contraction.

He'll be happy to forward the invoice copies to you. Note the apostrophe in *He'll* (short for *He will;* the letters *wi* in *will* have been omitted).

Here is a list of some frequently used contractions:

it's (it is, it has)	I'm (I am)	doesn't (does not)
we'll (we will)	who's (who is, who has)	she'd (she had, she would)
I'd (I had, I would)	that's (that is, that has)	we've (we have)

The apostrophe is also used to form the possessive of nouns. Note the apostrophes in the sentences below.

Jessica's preparations for the presentation were quite a success.

The *manager's* operating manual included some confusing instructions.

CHECKUP 2   Decide where the apostrophes are missing from the following sentences. Underline each word that needs an apostrophe. Then write the words correctly in the space at the right.

1. Tims car was sitting in the parking lot for over two hours.
2. Whos going to proofread the proposal for us?
3. Well sign the lease for the apartment tomorrow morning.
4. If it werent for her father, Jayne wouldnt have the job.

1. **Tim's** _____
2. _____
3. _____
4. _____

EXERCISES

NAME _____ DATE _____ SCORE _____

EXERCISE 1   Insert punctuation marks where necessary in the following sentences. Be sure to include end punctuation marks. In the space at the right, indicate how many punctuation marks are necessary.

1. Our manager said Well have a meeting tomorrow afternoon at 330

1. _____

2. As we left the office Tanya said Lets go out for dinner tonight

2. _____

3. In jubilation Robert cried out We found it

3. _____

4. Computers said the director will be with us for a long time

4. _____

5. The National Parcel Service carrier delivered a package marked Fragile

5. _____

6. Her latest article Writing Positive Messages was accepted for publication in The Journal of Business Communication

6. _____

7. The professor assigned Chapter 3 Making Oral Presentations for reading

7. _____

8. Will we be singing America the Beautiful after the ceremonies

8. _____

9. Why was this letter marked Personal

9. _____

10. Lillian said No do not mark the envelope Personal

10. _____

EXERCISE 2   Insert apostrophes where necessary in the following sentences. In the spaces at the right, indicate how many apostrophes are necessary.

1. Heres the information you requested on Mike Graves account.

1. _____

2. Youre sure well have that information before we leave the office?

2. _____

3. Clares hobbies are biking, hiking, and swimming.

3. _____

4. Dont forget to confirm Stacys presentation at next Mondays meeting.

4. _____

5. Thats the reason were moving to Montana.

5. _____

6. Barrys transcript showed that he received two perfect scores.

6. _____

7. Were all going to the concert tonight at Woodbury Auditorium.

7. _____

8. How many references to Hollers theory do you have in that report?

8. _____

9. According to the invoice, Sarahs order was sent in two shipments.

9. _____

10. Who has Jeffs car keys?

10. _____

EXERCISE 3   Insert underscores where necessary in the following sentences.

1. Because Alec frequently misspelled the words receive, mortgage, and maintenance, he wrote them on the inside cover of his dictionary.

2. May I borrow your copy of News Review.

3. Dr. Sorenson serves on the review board for The Journal of Marketing.

4. Many business people subscribe to The Wall Street Journal.

5. Here's the March 5 issue of Times that you asked for.

6. His columns have appeared in The Washington Post and The New York Times.

7. Mother loved to watch the movie The Quiet Man starring John Wayne and Maureen O'Hara.

8. Each assistant should have a copy of the Office Reference Manual.

9. When will we be going to see Puccini's Madame Butterfly?

10. He often misspells the word successful.

EXERCISE 4

Insert punctuation marks where necessary in the following sentences. In the space at the right, indicate how many punctuation marks are necessary. Be sure to include end punctuation marks.

1. Will you please give this package to Ms Albright   1. _____
2. Don received his Ph D from the University of Illinois in
   Urbana Illinois   2. _____
3. Ms Wasserman applied for the job was interviewed and was hired   3. _____
4. Heres the sample let me know what you think of it   4. _____
5. Hal signed the contract and then gave it to Mr Balwinder 5. _____
6. As you know Terry Paul and Phil will not be at todays meeting   6. _____
7. While we were in San Antonio Texas our neighbors looked after our
   house and picked up the mail   7. _____
8. The problem in my opinion is that they dont have enough expertise   8. _____
9. We too believe that the work can be done however we dont believe
   that it can be done on time   9. _____
10. Please refer to our catalog see pages 34-39 for a full description
    of the wood paneling   10. _____

EXERCISE 5

Each of the following sentences contains at least one punctuation error. Circle each error. Then in the space provided, correct the error, and indicate why it is an error.

1. Whos in charge of Plant C now that Mr. Avery is on medical leave?

_____

2. Aida by Verdi is one of the most popular operas.

_____

3. The chapter titled Developing Business Writing Skills contains excellent ideas on how to improve one's writing.

_____

EXERCISE 6

Use each of the following punctuation marks correctly in a sentence.

1. an apostrophe in a contraction

_____

2. an apostrophe to show the possessive of a noun

_____

3. an underscore for the title of a book

_____

4. an underscore for the title of a magazine

_____

5. an underscore for the title of a newspaper

_____

6. single and double quotation marks for a quotation within a quotation

_____

7. double quotation marks to show someone's exact words

_____

8. an underscore for the title of a play

_____

9. an underscore to show emphasis

_____

10. an underscore for a word used as a word

_____

CAPITALS

FIRST THINGS FIRST!   Three "firsts" that must be capitalized are (1) the first word of each sentence, (2) the first-person pronoun *I*, and (3) the first word of the salutation in a letter and any noun or title in the salutation and the first word of a complimentary closing, such as *Sincerely yours*. In addition, always capitalize proper nouns—the names of specific persons, places, and things.

Their business, *The Outrigger*, is 5 miles south of the intersection on *Main Street* in *Boulder, Colorado*. Note that *The* is capitalized because it is part of the actual name of the business. *Main Street* is capitalized because it is the name of a specific street. *Boulder, Colorado* is capitalized because it names a specific place.

While touring the *West Coast*, we visited the *San Francisco State College* campus, the *Golden Gate Bridge*, and *Disneyland*. *West Coast* is capitalized because it designates a specific region. *San Francisco State College*, *Golden Gate Bridge*, and *Disneyland* are capitalized because they name specific places.

Capitalize adjectives that are derived from proper nouns with the exception of a few (*french fries, india ink,* and *roman numerals*) that are now considered common.

We sang the national anthem as the *American* flag was raised.

Capitalize trademarks and brand names. Do not capitalize the common noun following the name.

Yesterday they purchased an *Aida* dishwasher and a *Tundro* snowblower.

> **CHECKUP 1**   Underline any letters that should be capitalized in the following sentences. Then in the spaces at the right, indicate how many letters should be capitalized.
>
> 1. on our way to the east coast we stopped to see niagara falls.   1. __5_____
> 2. the salutation in your letter should read "dear mr. haley."   2. _____
> 3. mom, we are out of puro soap and softee tissues.   3. _____

FAMILY RELATIONSHIPS   Capitalize family titles such as grandmother and uncle when they stand alone or when they are followed by a personal name.

I'll ask *Uncle Jim* if I can go.   Did you say that Grandmother will be here next week?

Do not capitalize a family title when a possessive (*his, my, our*) precedes it. Capitalize the family titles *uncle, aunt,* or *cousin* when they are used with a first name, even when they are preceded by a possessive.

Be sure to ask *your dad* if you can go.   Send *your Aunt Nora* a card.

ABBREVIATIONS   Some abbreviations are always capitalized.

FCC   CPA   IRS   YMCA   NASA   UCLA

SEASONS, POINTS OF THE COMPASS, DAYS, AND MONTHS   Capitalize the days of the week and months of the year. The seasons and points of the compass are usually not capitalized.

spring   summer   fall   winter   north   south   east   west
Monday   Sunday   Thursday January   December April

Underline any letters that should be capitalized in the following sentences. Then in the spaces at the right, indicate how many letters should be capitalized.

1. ask mother or dad if we can stay overnight at aunt mary's house.

1. __5_____

2. when he was only five years old, my grandfather came to the united states from germany.

2. _____

3. when the children were growing up in chicago, illinois, they all belonged to the y m c a.

3. _____

4. this summer—probably july or august—we'll be traveling to washington, d.c., and then on to maryland and virginia.

4. _____

IN TITLES

In titles of movies, books, articles, and so on, the first and last words are always capitalized. In addition, all important words are also capitalized. Do not capitalize articles *(a, an, the)*, conjunctions *(and, but, or, for)*, and prepositions *(in, of, off, to, at)* with fewer than four letters unless they appear at the beginning or the end of the title.

The editor approved the revisions of two popular textbooks: *How to Write the Effective Letter* and *The Nuts and Bolts of Car Repairs.* Note that *to* and *the* are not capitalized in the title of the first book. *The* is capitalized in the second book because it is the first word in the title. *And* and *of* in the second title are not capitalized because they have fewer than four letters.

IN PERSONAL TITLES

When a title is used in place of *Mr., Miss, Mrs.,* or *Ms.,* capitalize the title. The titles *Mr., Miss, Mrs.,* and *Ms.* are always capitalized as well.

Regional Director Baylor is in England. The title *Regional Director* is used in place of another title such as *Mr.* or *Ms.*

Bea Baylor, *our regional director,* is in England. Here *regional director* does not replace a title such as *Ms.* or *Mrs.*

ACADEMIC SUBJECTS AND DEGREES

Capitalize titles of specific academic courses but not names of subjects, except for proper nouns and their derivatives. Languages are always capitalized because they are derivatives of proper nouns.

The college student was taking *Management 370, Marketing 340,* and *Accounting II. Management, Marketing,* and *Accounting* are capitalized because they name specific courses.

Next semester Deborah wants to take a *management course,* a *marketing course,* an *accounting course,* and *a Spanish course. Management, marketing,* and *accounting* are not capitalized because they are names of subjects; they do not name specific courses. *Spanish* is capitalized because it is the derivative of the proper noun *Spain.*

Capitalize the abbreviations of degrees when they are used after an individual's name.

James Girgourd, Ph.D.   Alvina Brennan, D.D.S.   Nicholas Byers, M.D.

Underline any letters that should be capitalized in the following sentences. Then in the spaces at the right, indicate how many letters should be capitalized.

1. have you read stephen r. covey's book the seven habits of highly effective people?

1. __10_____

2. research director collins will be returning from paris, france, this fall.

2. _____

3. the vice president in charge of sales, mr. c. l. hammond, has expanded our territories.

3. _____

4. our english professor, dr. patricia kelleher who studied at yale, also taught italian and polish.

4. _____

EXERCISES

NAME _____ DATE _____ SCORE _____

EXERCISE 1 In each of the following pairs of sentences, select the sentence in which capitals are used correctly. In the space at the right, write the letter of the sentence that is correct.

1. a. Dr. Floyd Delano received his degree from the University of Michigan in Ann Arbor, Michigan last summer.
   b. dr. floyd delano received his degree from the university of michigan in ann arbor, michigan last summer.

   1. _____

2. a. My Sister Irene will be visiting us in august.
   b. My sister Irene will be visiting us in August.

   2. _____

3. a. Brian Daly, the academic vice president and provost, is due back this spring.
   b. Brian Daly, the Academic Vice president and Provost, is due back this Spring.

   3. _____

4. a. Before we began painting the roman numerals on the boards, we stopped for some french fries.
   b. Before we began painting the Roman numerals on the boards, we stopped for some French fries.

   4. _____

5. a. Did you visit your uncle Andy this summer?
   b. Did you visit your Uncle Andy this summer?

   5. _____

EXERCISE 2 Underline each letter that should be capitalized in the following sentences. Then in the spaces at the right, indicate how many letters should be capitalized.

1. people sat in their homes and watched news reports of unrest in asia, latin america, and the persian gulf.

   1. _____

2. as a cpa, ms. rose fountain worked for president mitchell at industrial supplies, inc., in dayton, ohio.

   2. _____

3. the new management trainee took management 200 and accounting I when he was at boston college.

   3. _____

4. dr. steinbach, who received her d.d.s. degree from wayne state university, has been my dentist for several years.

   4. _____

5. karen checked the ads in *the main street journal.*

   5. _____

6. dr. harvey gold's latest article, "the importance of physical examinations," appeared in the july issue of *medical review.*

   6. _____

7. this summer several of us plan to take such courses as history, economics, english, and spanish.

   7. _____

8. we'll be leaving the end of october for our winter vacation.

   8. _____

9. regional vice president sampson is responsible for increased sales.

   9. _____

10. when writing a business letter to an organization, you should use the salutation ladies and gentlemen.

    10. _____

11. the next time we're in new york, let's plan to go to yankee stadium.

    11. _____

12. her aunt and uncle will be here from indianapolis, indiana, this summer.

    12. _____

13. students were asked to read the autobiography of benjamin franklin.

    13. _____

14. his new address is 459 west monroe street, crest hill, illinois 60435.

    14. _____

15. while shopping for victorian furniture in austin, we stopped and had a danish roll and coffee.

    15. _____

EXERCISE 3   Underline any letters that should be capitalized in the following sentences.

1. she and her family were vacationing at lake powell, utah, in august.
2. in june 1991, dr. robert b. marks graduated from northwestern university medical school in chicago.
3. mother and dad will be attending the graduation at clifford high school.
4. after taking english, latin, and spanish courses, I was happy to be enrolled in an economics class.
5. on monday, august 15, we'll be going to visit yosemite national park.
6. during the summer my cousin mary lou will be taking two language classes—french and german.
7. on a family vacation with my parents and grandparents, we went to san francisco and had chinese food in chinatown.
8. a student at colorado state university took a three-day hiking trip through colorado's 1,200-square-mile roosevelt national forest.

EXERCISE 4   Rewrite each item listed below correctly in the space at the right. If an item is correct, write *OK*.

1. United States senate   1. _____
2. jefferson memorial   2. _____
3. arabic numbers   3. _____
4. an experienced cpa   4. _____
5. Sincerely Yours   5. _____
6. spring   6. _____
7. far east   7. _____
8. thursday   8. _____
9. *The Taming Of The Boar* (book)   9. _____
10. mr. and mrs. r. c. bridge   10. _____
11. Summer   11. _____
12. finance 402   12. _____
13. history   13. _____
14. a Law class   14. _____
15. a french custom   15. _____
16. Uncle Ben   16. _____
17. professor Smith, ph.d.   17. _____
18. regional manager Hale   18. _____
19. September 1   19. _____
20. the west coast   20. _____

EXERCISE 5   Write five sentences following the directions given below.

1. Use a day of the week.

_____

2. Use a month of the year.

_____

3. Use the name of a public building.

_____

4. Use a street address, including the city and state.

_____

5. Use a compass point.

_____

6. Use a personal title.

_____

Numbers

In business letters, memos, and reports, you will sometimes have to choose between using figures or words for numbers—should it be *9* or *nine*? In general, use words for numbers one through ten, and use figures for numbers above ten.

May I please have *five* copies of this report. (NOT: *5* copies.)

We expect about *50* replies to our mailed questionnaire. (NOT: *fifty* replies.)

ABBREVIATIONS Use figures for numbers used with abbreviations.

During our travels, we saw many road signs such as *SR 405, US 66, I-80, and Hwy 31.*

ADDRESSES In addresses, express house numbers in figures except for house number one. Spell out street names that are numbered one through ten.

Bill's address is *One Brookline Drive,* and Dawn's address is *398 Tenth Street.*

Use figures for street names that are above ten. When figures are used for both the house number and the street name and there is no intervening word, such as *East* or *West,* use the ordinal form (1st, 2d, 3d, 4th) for the street name to avoid confusion.

The Dawsons were moving to *324 South 22 Street;* the Millers were moving to *211 75th Street.*

ADJACENT NUMBERS When two numbers are adjacent and one is part of a compound modifier, use a figure for one number and spell out the other one.

Send the *20 ten-page* reports to the director.   Hal bought *ten 29-cent* stamps.

When two numbers come together, and both appear as words or as figures, separate them with a comma.

On page 25, 14 suggestions are given for making an oral presentation.

DATES Use cardinal numbers (1, 2, 3) for expressing the date after the month. Use either ordinal figures (1st, 2d, 3d, 4th) or ordinal words (first, second, third) for expressing the date before the month.

We're leaving for Colorado on the *twenty-ninth of June* and are returning the *sixth of July.*

We're leaving for Colorado on the *29th of June* and are returning the *6th of July.*

AMOUNTS OF MONEY Always use figures for amounts of money. Whole amounts of money are expressed without the decimal and zeros.

We spent *$25.75* on supplies and *$10* on stamps. (NOT: *ten dollars.*)

For amounts under a dollar, use numerals and the word *cents.*

She has *25 cents* left for a phone call. (NOT: *$ 0.25.*)

DECIMALS AND PERCENTAGES   Use figures to express decimals and percentages.

Tad's car averaged *22.5* miles a gallon on the *500-mile* trip.

Clare was pleased when she learned she earned a *95* percent on her history exam.

FRACTIONS   Spell out fractions when they stand alone (without a whole number). Use figures for fractions when they are part of a mixed number (a whole number and a fraction).

To pass the resolution we need a *two-thirds* majority. (NOT: ⅔)

The presentation is scheduled to take *3½* hours. (NOT:three and a half)

Use figures for fractions when the spelled-out form is long and awkward.

The fabric for the drapes is short by ¾₂ of an inch. (NOT: three thirty-seconds)

TIME   Use figures to express periods of time.

The Sullivans took out a *30-year* mortgage on their house.

Use figures with *a.m.* and *p.m.* Omit the colon and zeros when only the hour is given.

We'll be open from *7:30 a.m. to 5 p.m.* (NOT: 5:00 p.m.)

AGES   In general, express ages in written form.

Pauline will be *twenty-five,* and Norman will be *twenty-nine.*

Express ages in figures when the age appears directly after a person's name, when age is used in a technical sense, and when age is expressed in years, months, and days.

Gary Carpenter, 56, was named president of the company.

The voting age is *18;* the driving age is *16.*   The child is *3 years and 2 months old.*

ANNIVERSARIES   Spell out ordinals to express anniversaries except when more than two words are required.

The store is planning a grand celebration for its *175th* anniversary.

WEIGHTS, DIMENSIONS, AND OTHER MEASUREMENTS   Use figures for weights, dimensions, and other measurements.

We stored *2 tons* of paper in bins that measured *16 yards by 50 feet.*

FIRST OR 1ST?   Spell out ordinal numbers—*first, second, third,* and so on (rather than *1st, 2d, 3d*)—that can be expressed in one or two words. Hyphenate compound ordinals (twenty-first to ninety-ninth).

We expect our biggest gain in the *fourth* quarter. (NOT: *4th* quarter.)

Beware!   Avoid beginning a sentence with a numeral. Reword the sentence in such cases or change the numerals to words.

We expected 500 people to attend the national convention. (NOT: *500* people were expected to attend the national convention.)

EXERCISES

NAME _____ DATE _____ SCORE _____

EXERCISE 1   Underline any errors in number usage in the following sentences. Then write your corrections in the spaces at the right. If a sentence is correct, write *OK*.

1. We planned to take I-eighty when we go out West. 1. _____
2. Type the date as May 15th, 1992. 2. _____
3. Mr. Harper would like 8 copies of this letter. 3. _____
4. The room measured fifteen feet by twenty feet. 4. _____
5. Her plane is due to arrive in Atlanta at eleven thirty-four a.m. 5. _____
6. More than five hundred dollars was collected for the homeless. 6. _____
7. I would appreciate the return of the fifty dollars you borrowed last month. 7. _____
8. The company's address is 1 South Park Drive, Fayetteville, Arkansas. 8. _____
9. By 1995, two hundred more employees will have been hired. 9. _____
10. Our taxes were due April 15th. 10. _____
11. Please place an order for one hundred twenty five light bulbs. 11. _____
12. Dick lives at 2327 10th Street; Myrna lives at 989 64 Street. 12. _____
13. 15 checks were mailed this afternoon. 13. _____
14. The company is moving its headquarters from 201 South 43 Street to 112 Seventy-eighth Street. 14. _____
15. Ann was delighted with her new car because it was averaging about twenty-four miles to the gallon in the city. 15. _____
16. Sonny saves about fifteen percent of her payroll check every week. 16. _____
17. Are you sure that it costs only $.79 cents? 17. _____
18. Her children surprised her with a party on her 68th birthday. 18. _____
19. The rug measured eight feet by twenty feet. 19. _____
20. 12 of us are planning to attend the writing workshop at the Fetzer Center. 20. _____
21. The price of the pen was only ninety-eight cents. 21. _____
22. Our manager asked us to work until six fifteen p.m. 22. _____
23. The company's stock was selling for two dollars and 40 cents a share. 23. _____
24. Marlene was happy with her eighty-five percent on the statistics exam. 24. _____
25. Our new officers are on the 55th floor. 25. _____
26. The open house began at 2:00 p.m. 26. _____
27. The organization was celebrating its 75th anniversary. 27. _____
28. On January 21st we'll start interviewing the applicants. 28. _____
29. We were advised to take route I-sixty-nine to Indianapolis. 29. _____
30. On Flight 407 to Spokane, Washington, ten passengers were sitting in the first-class section. 30. _____
31. I had hoped to get at least fifteen and a half miles a gallon on my trip to the West Coast. 31. _____
32. About ⅔ of the audience gave the speaker a standing ovation. 32. _____
33. Robert is in his 60s; Cheryl is in her 40s. 33. _____
34. Cookston's Department Store will be celebrating its 25th anniversary this spring. 34. _____

EXERCISE 2   Rewrite correctly each incorrect item listed below. If an item is correct, write *OK*.

1. ten dollars
2. fifteen percent
3. two-ounce bottle
4. July 21
5. June 30th
6. thirty-five cents
7. one hundred twenty-fifth anniversary
8. five tons
9. fifteen dollars and fifty cents
10. the legal age is twenty-one
11. 7:00 p.m.
12. payable in fifteen days
13. twenty-one two hundredths of a second
14. .025 inch
15. twenty and a half gallons
16. fifty million dollars
17. ⅔ majority
18. seventy-nine degrees
19. January 15th
20. five twenty-nine cent stamps
21. sixteen yards of material
22. 2d quarter of the game
23. 33d performance
24. 50th anniversary
25. 750 1st Ave.
26. 24 and a half miles
27. seventy-nine cents
28. 2 $10 bills

1. _____
2. _____
3. _____
4. _____
5. _____
6. _____
7. _____
8. _____
9. _____
10. _____
11. _____
12. _____
13. _____
14. _____
15. _____
16. _____
17. _____
18. _____
19. _____
20. _____
21. _____
22. _____
23. _____
24. _____
25. _____
26. _____
27. _____
28. _____

EXERCISE 3   Rewrite the following sentences to correct errors in number usage.

1. 350 people plan to attend the convention in Dallas, Texas.

_____

2. I'll need fifteen dollars for the membership fee.

_____

3. The Diamonds plan to return from their trip on August 10th.

_____

4. Would you believe that Cecilia spent four hundred fifty dollars for a computer?

_____

5. We expected a return rate of at least forty-five percent.

_____

6. A local call costs twenty-five cents.

_____

7. We had a huge increase in sales in nineteen ninety-one.

_____

8. With a student ID card, tickets are only four dollars.

_____

Word Usage

Many words have similar spellings or similar sounds but very different meanings. These words cause many business writers a lot of confusion. Learn how these words are used so that your business writing is clear and unconfused!

Accept means "to take." Please *accept* my sincere thanks.

Except means "to exclude." All *except* you may go.

Ad is short for *advertisement*. See the *ad* in the classified section.

Add means "to join." *Add* the figures.

Advice is a noun meaning a "suggestion, a recommendation." What's your *advice?*

Advise is a verb meaning "to recommend." We were *advised* not to go.

Affect is a verb meaning "to influence, to change." How will these prices *affect* your income?

Effect is a verb meaning "to bring about." The operator managed to *effect* a change in the procedure.

Effect is also a noun meaning "a result." The change in prices had an *effect* on our buying power.

All right means "okay." It is always two words. There is no such word as *alright*. The children who were found were *all right.*

Already is an adverb meaning "previously." They have *already* gone.

All ready means that "all are prepared." They are *all ready* to go.

Amount refers to items that cannot be counted. A large *amount* of trash was thrown in the woods.

Number refers to items that can be counted. A great *number* of concerned citizens came to the meeting.

Anxious means "worried or concerned." He was *anxious* about his grades.

Eager means "intensely desirous." She was *eager* to see the movie.

Assure is a verb meaning "to promise." I *assure* you that I will finish the report by noon.

Ensure is a verb meaning "to make certain." To *ensure* that you receive the merchandise, please enclose your check.

Insure is a verb meaning "to protect." Please *insure* your car before you drive it out of the dealer's lot.

Capital is a sum of money, a city that is the seat of government, or an uppercase letter. Lansing is the *capital* of Michigan.

The *capitol* is the building where the state legislature meets. Students toured the *capitol*.

Choose is a verb meaning "to select." We were able to *choose* the kind of computer we wanted.

Chose is the past tense of the verb *choose*. He *chose* to have his picture in the newsletter.

Complement means "to complete." His red suspenders *complemented* his outfit.

Compliment means "to praise." Teachers should *compliment* their students frequently.

Continual means "in rapid succession." The telephone rings *continually.*

Continuous means "without interruption." The river flows *continuously.*

Desert is a noun meaning "barren region." On our way to California, we crossed the *desert.*

Dessert is a noun meaning "the last course of the meal." We thoroughly enjoyed the cheesecake that we had for *dessert.*

Disinterested is an adjective meaning "impartial." Ms. O'Riley was a *disinterested* judge.

Uninterested is an adjective meaning "not interested." The teacher had a class of *uninterested* students.

Farther means "at a greater distance." **They plan to travel *farther* than 600 miles a day.**

Further means "additional." **Do you have any *further* information?**

Fewer refers to items that can be counted. *Fewer* modifies a plural noun. **Jane purchased *fewer* items than Jake did.**

Less refers to the degree or amount of something that cannot be counted. *Less* modifies a singular noun. **We made *less* progress today than we did yesterday.**

Hear means "to perceive by ear." **Can you *hear* me?**

Here means "this place." **Bring the book *here*.**

Imply is a verb meaning "to suggest." **The speaker *implied* that he would be happy to return for another speaking engagement.**

Infer is a verb meaning "to deduce." **The listener *inferred* from the speaker's comments that the speaker would be cutting back on speaking engagements.**

It's is a contraction for *it is* or *it has*. ***It's* raining. *It's* easy. *It's* been hectic.**

Its is a possessive pronoun, which never takes an apostrophe. ***Its* charter expired. *Its* owner has left.**

Loose means "free." **The strings are *loose*.**

Lose means "to mislay." **Please don't *lose* your tickets.**

Passed is the past tense of the verb *pass*. **She *passed* her exam.**

Past means "over with" or "time gone by." **That's in the *past*.**

Personal means "private." **These are my *personal* papers.**

Personnel refers to a group of people. **Please notify all *personnel* of these changes.**

Precede is a verb meaning "to go before." **What *preceded* the incident in the locker room?**

Proceed is a verb meaning "to continue." **We will *proceed* with our plans for the new building.**

Principal refers to a school official, a chief, a sum of money, or something main or primary. **Mr. Enz is *principal* of Calumet High. He's paying interest on the *principal*. The *principal* reason is lack of funds.**

Principle is a general truth, a rule. **What are the *principles* for good writing?**

Stationary means "fixed." **The chairs in this room are *stationary*.**

Stationery refers to writing materials. **I need to buy some *stationery* so I can write to my friend in Australia.**

Then means "at that time." ***Then* there were only five left.**

Than is used to complete a comparison. **Sue is older *than* Kathleen.**

There is an adverb indicating direction. ***There* it is.**

Their is a possessive pronoun. ***Their* book is on the desk.**

They're is a contraction for *they are*. ***They're* going to class.**

Though means "although, as if." ***Though* I am a first-year student, I have over 30 credits.**

Through means "done with" (and also "into and out"). **I'm *through* with that assignment.**

Thorough means "complete or perfect." **The word processing expert did a *thorough* job.**

To is a preposition. **We went *to* the office.**

Too is an adverb that emphasizes or intensifies. **I had *too* much to eat that day.**

Too is also an adverb meaning "also." **Nancy came to the meeting *too*.**

Two is a number. ***Two* of us were applying for the job.**

We're is a contraction for *we are*. ***We're* in Ms. Smith's class.**

Were is the past tense of the verb *are*. **We *were* in the office.**

Where implies a place. ***Where* did you go?**

Who's is a contraction for *who is* or *who has*. ***Who's* there?**

Whose is the possessive of *who*. ***Whose* book is this?**

EXERCISES

NAME _____ DATE _____ SCORE _____

EXERCISE 1   Read the following sentences carefully. Select the word from each pair in parentheses that better conveys the meaning of the sentence. Underline the correct word.

1. How much *(further, farther)* do we have to walk?

2. If it is *(all right, alright)* with you, I'll finish this project first.

3. After studying grammar for two weeks, the students made *(fewer, less)* errors on their assignments.

4. Mary Ann is very *(though, through, thorough)* as an editor, so I always ask her to proofread manuscripts.

5. The company had a great *(amount, number)* of applicants for the job.

6. *(It's, Its)* not an easy job to put a new roof on the house.

7. The phone in the office rang *(continually, continuously)*.

8. Their *(capital, capitol)* was tied up in stocks and bonds.

9. The company placed an *(ad, add)* in the local newspaper for an engineer.

10. What *(advice, advise)* do you have for a person who does not like speaking to large groups?

11. All factory *(personal, personnel)* were invited to submit their recommendations.

12. Please order a ream of office *(stationary, stationery)*.

13. As a career counselor, her job was to *(advice, advise)* students.

14. Will you be driving across the *(desert, dessert)* at any time during your travels in the Southwest?

15. The announcement from the president was *(preceded, proceeded)* by a memo.

16. She, *(to, too)*, wanted to read the best-selling book during her vacation.

17. *(There, Their)* have been many requests for our article.

18. The furniture *(complemented, complimented)* the decor in the office.

19. Several of the screws were *(lose, loose)*, so Walt had to tighten them.

20. *(We're, Were, Where)* have they put the office supplies?

21. The machine is broken, and *(it's, its)* warranty has expired.

22. The speaker seemed to *(imply, infer)* that we should be exercising more.

23. Our president will serve as a *(disinterested, uninterested)* mediator.

24. Several weeks had *(passed, past)* since we heard from her.

25. Take my *(advise, advice)* and increase your life insurance.

26. Larry *(choose, chose)* to have the operation during the Christmas holidays.

27. We will *(assure, ensure, insure)* the building for its full value.

28. Most of the money they are paying on their home mortgage is being applied to the interest; very little of it is going toward the *(principal, principle)*.

29. Tom *(already, all ready)* purchased five raffle tickets.

30. Because he missed several classes, he was *(anxious, eager)* about the exam.

31. Do you *(accept, except)* the terms of the contract?

32. How will the merger *(affect, effect)* your company?

33. First, we code the orders, and *(then, than)* we file them.

34. I am so *(anxious, eager)* to hear about your trip to Australia.

35. *(Were, We're)* signed up for the computer seminar.

36. *(Hear, Here)* is the information you requested.

37. *(Who's, Whose)* keys are these lying on the desk?

EXERCISE 2   Underline the correct word from each pair of words in parentheses. Then write your answer in the space at the right.

1. A huge *(amount, number)* of work was waiting for us after our return from a two-week vacation.

2. We used *(fewer, less)* gasoline on this trip than we did on our last trip.

3. High school counselors give *(advice, advise)* to students who seek their help.

4. The Calverts plan to *(ad, add)* another bedroom to their existing house.

5. Even *(though, through, thorough)* she was a new sales representative, she made her quota before the end of the year.

6. It's *(all right, alright)* with me if you would like to take the afternoon off.

7. While in Washington, D.C., we toured the *(capital, capitol)*.

8. The water in the sink was running *(continually, continuously)*.

9. Let me know when we can *(further, farther)* discuss my qualifications.

10. The bank received *(it's, its)* approval from the federal government.

11. The *(principal, principle)* of the school had been there for over 25 years.

12. Because it was a *(personal, personnel)* matter, Rex did not want to discuss it.

13. If you *(lose, loose)* your passport, you'll be unable to continue the tour.

14. We were planning *(to, too)* vote for the school board members at next week's meeting.

15. My sister knows how to accept a *(complement, compliment)*; she always says "Thank you."

16. We were not able to turn our chairs around for a discussion because the chairs were *(stationary, stationery)*.

17. *(There, Their)* proposal was accepted for the program at the national convention in Montreal.

18. The Browns should arrive soon; we just *(passed, past)* them on the road.

19. May we *(precede, proceed)* with our plans, Ms. Taylor.

20. After that enormous meal, no one wanted *(desert, dessert)*.

21. Claudia had heard good things about the book, and she was *(anxious, eager)* to read it.

22. I *(assure, ensure, insure)* you that I will be at the meeting on time.

23. Because he was preoccupied, he seemed *(disinterested, uninterested)* in what the teacher was saying.

24. I *(imply, infer)* from your statement that you would like a transfer.

25. *(Accept, Except)* for John, the entire class attended the concert.

26. Employees were able to *(choose, chose)* their vacation dates.

27. This *(passed, past)* winter we had very little snow in the Midwest.

28. *(We're, Were, Where)* thinking of purchasing a new car this summer.

29. *(Who's, Whose)* going to volunteer for registering participants at the Corporate Olympics?

30. I would rather work in the exhibit booth *(then, than)* in the refreshment booth.

31. What *(affect, effect)* will the layoffs have on the company?

32. They were *(already, all ready)* to leave when we arrived.

33. I *(hear, here)* you had a very exciting trip to China.

34. We have all the necessary equipment and supplies *(accept, except)* for the lumber.

35. Please *(accept, except)* my compliments for a job well done.

1. _____
2. _____
3. _____
4. _____
5. _____
6. _____
7. _____
8. _____
9. _____
10. _____
11. _____
12. _____
13. _____
14. _____
15. _____
16. _____
17. _____
18. _____
19. _____
20. _____
21. _____
22. _____
23. _____
24. _____
25. _____
26. _____
27. _____
28. _____
29. _____
30. _____
31. _____
32. _____
33. _____
34. _____
35. _____

Index

a, an, the, 2, 101–102
Abbreviations, 162, 189, 190, 193
Abstract nouns, 25
accept, except, 154, 197
Addresses, 174, 193
Adjective clauses, 146
Adjectives, 2, 101–112, 130
  absolute, 110
  adverb-adjective choice, 114, 122
  comparative and superlative, 109–110
  compound, 106, 162
  demonstrative adjectives, 102
  descriptive, 102
  double, 105
  irregular, 110
  limiting, 102
  nouns disguised as, 101
  positive degree of, 109
  possessive, 102
  prepositional phrases as, 130
  pronouns disguised as, 101
  proper, 105, 106
  punctuation with, 105–106, 174
Adverb clauses, 146
Adverbs, 5, 61, 113–120
  adjective-adverb choice, 114, 122
  comparative and superlative, 117–118
  conjunctive, 126
  irregular, 118
  positive degree of, 117
  prepositional phrases as, 130
affect, effect, 97–98, 197
Agreement
  of pronouns, 38, 85
  subject-verb, 85–88
among, between, 133
Antecedents of pronouns, 37–38, 49, 85
Apostrophes, 186
Appositives, 173
Articles, 2, 101–102
as I said, 154
Auxiliary verbs, (see Helping verbs)

bad, badly, 122
because, where, that, 154
beside, besides, 134
between, among, 133
borrow, lend, 97–98
both/and, 142
Brackets, 182
bring to, take away, 97–98

Capitalization, 22, 189–192
Clauses, 49, 50, 145–148, 166
  adjective, 146
  adverb, 146
  dependent, 145–146, 165–166

independent, 126, 145–146, 165,
  177, 178
  misplaced, 150
  noun, 146
Collective nouns, 26, 85
Colons, 178
Commas, 165–176
  with adjectives, 105, 174
  in dates and addresses, 174
  with descriptive expressions, 169
  in direct address, 174
  with interrupters, 169–170, 173
  with introductory expressions, 166
  joining clauses, 165–166
  with parenthetical elements, 169
  in series, 166
Comma splices, 154
Comparatives, 109, 110, 117, 118
compare to, compare with, 134
Compound adjectives, 106, 162
Compound nouns, 26, 34
Compound subjects, 14, 85–86
Compound verbs, 14
Compound words, 162
Concrete nouns, 25
Conjunctions, 6, 141–146, 157
  common errors with, 153–156
Conjunctive adverbs, 126
Contractions, 186
Coordinating conjunctions, 141–142
Correlative conjunctions, 142
could have, 134

Dangling participles, 149–150
Dashes, 181, 182
Dates, 174, 193
Declarative sentences, 17
Definite articles, 101–102
Demonstrative adjectives, 102
Dependent clauses, 145–146, 165–166
Descriptive adjectives, 102
Descriptive expressions, 169
different from, different than, 134
Direct address, commas with, 174
Direct objects of verbs, 41, 58
Double adjectives, 105
Double comparisons, 110, 118
Double negatives, 121

each, every, 54, 86
eager, anxious, 197
effect, affect, 97–98, 197
either/or, 142, 157
else, other, 125
Enumerations, 158
Essential elements, commas with, 169,
  173
every, each, 54, 86

except, accept, 154, 197
Exclamation points, 18, 161, 162,
  185
Exclamatory sentences, 18

from, off of, 133
Future perfect tense, 82
Future progressive tense, 66, 74, 78
Future tense, 66, 74, 78

Gender, 38
Gerund, 42, 138, 166
Gerund phrases, 42, 138, 166
good, well, 125

Helping verbs, 58, 61
her, she, 45
Hyphens, 105–106, 162

I, me, 45
identical with, identical to, 134
Imperative sentences, 18
Indefinite articles, 101–102
Indefinite pronouns, 54, 86
Independent clauses, 126, 145–146
  punctuation with, 165, 177, 178
Indirect objects, 42
Infinitive, 129, 137
Infinitive phrases, 129, 137
Interjections, 6
Interrogative pronouns, 53
Interrogative sentences, 17–18
Intransitive verbs, 58
Introductory expressions, 166, 185
Irregular adjectives, 110
Irregular adverbs, 118
Irregular verbs, 69–72
it's, its, 198

lay, lie, 89–92
learn, teach, 97
leave, let, 97
lend, borrow, 97–98
let, leave, 97
lie, lay, 89–92
Limiting adjectives, 102
Linking verbs, 62
Lists, 158

Main clauses (see Independent clauses)
Main subjects, 13
Main verbs, 13
Measurements, 194
me, I, 45
Misplaced modifiers, 121, 149, 150
more (or less), 109, 110, 117, 118

neither/nor, 142, 157
Nominative pronouns, 41, 49
Nonessential elements, commas with, 169
not only/but also, 142, 157
Noun clauses, 146
Nouns, 1, 9, 21–36
  abstract, 25
  collective, 26, 85
  common, 22
  compound, 26, 34
  concrete, 25
  disguised as adjectives, 101
  plural, 29–32, 33–34
  possessive, 33–34, 186
  proper, 22
Numbers, 162, 193–196

Objective pronouns, 41–42, 49
off of, from, 133
other, else, 125
Outlines, 158

Parallel structure, 153–154, 157–160
Parentheses, 181–182
Participial phrases, 138
Participles, 61, 69–72
  dangling, 149–150
Past participle, 61, 69–72
Past perfect tense, 81–82
Past progressive tense, 66, 74, 78
Past tense, 61, 66, 69–74, 77–78
Perfect tenses, 81–84
Periods, 17, 18, 161, 162, 182
Phrases, 137–140
  gerund, 138, 166
  infinitive, 129, 137
  introductory, 166
  participial, 138
  prepositional, 129–130, 137
Plural nouns, 29–32, 33–34
Plural pronouns, 38
Possession, separate and joint, 34
Possessive adjectives, 102
Possessive nouns, 33–34, 186
Possessive pronouns, 42
Predicate, 9, 10, 137, 145
  predicate adjective, 62
  predicate noun, 62
  predicate pronoun, 62
Prepositional phrases, 129–130, 137
Prepositions, 5, 129–136, 154
  common errors with, 133–136
Present participle, 61
Present perfect tense, 81
Present progressive tense, 65, 73, 77
Present tense, 61, 65, 69–72, 73, 77
Progressive tenses, 65, 66, 73, 74, 77, 78

Pronouns, 1, 9, 37–56
  antecedents of, 37–38, 85
  disguised as adjectives, 101
  gender of, 38
  indefinite, 54, 86
  interrogative, 53
  nominative, 41, 49
  objective, 41–42, 49
  plural, 38
  possessive, 42
  self-ending, 53–54
  troublemakers, 45–48
Proper adjectives, 105, 106
Proper nouns, 22
Punctuation, 161–188 (*see also* specific marks of punctuation)
  apostrophes, 186
  brackets, 182
  colons, 178
  commas, 165–176
  dashes, 181, 182
  exclamation points, 18, 161, 162, 182, 185
  hyphens, 105–106, 162
  parentheses, 181–182
  periods, 17, 18, 161, 162, 182, 186
  question marks, 17, 161, 162, 182, 185
  quotation marks, 185–188
  semicolons, 177
  underscores, 186

Question marks, 17, 161, 162, 185
Questions, 17–18
Quotation marks, 185–186

raise, rise, 94
real, really, 125
Regular verbs, 69–72
Repetition, unnecessary, 121, 133
retroactive to, retroactive from, 134
rise, raise, 94
Run-on sentences, 154

Salutations, in business letters, 178
self-ending pronouns, 53–54
Semicolons, 177, 182
Sentences, 9–12, 17–20, 133, 194
  declarative, 17
  exclamatory, 18
  imperative, 18
  interrogative, 17–18
  run-on, 154
  subjects of, 9–10, 13, 14, 85–88
Series, punctuation of, 166, 177
set, sit, 93
she, her, 45
speak to, speak with, 134
Subjects, 9–10, 13
  agreement with verbs, 85–88

compound, 14, 85–86
  main, 13
  understood, 10
Subordinate clauses (*see* Dependent clauses)
Subordinating conjunctions, 145–146
Superlatives, 109, 110, 117, 118
sure, surely, 122

take away, bring to, 97–98
teach, learn, 97
Tenses, of verbs, 61, 65–68, 69–84
that, because, where, 154
that, these, those, this, 53, 102
that, which, 50, 53
the, a, an, 101–102
Time, 194
Titles, 186, 189, 190
to, too, two, 198
to be, tenses of, 73–76
to do, tenses of, 77–80
to go, tenses of, 77–80
to have, tenses of, 73–76
Transitive verbs, 58
try to, try and, 154

Underscores, 186
us, we, 46

Verbs, 2, 10, 57–100 (*see also* specific verbs)
  agreement with subjects, 85–88
  compound, 14
  direct objects of, 58
  helping, 61
  intransitive, 58
  linking, 62
  main, 13
  principal parts of, 61, 69–72
  regular and irregular, 69–72
  tenses of, 61, 65–68, 69–84
  transitive, 58
  use of, 57

we, us, 46
Weights, 194
well, good, 125
where, that, because, 154
whether/or, 142
which, that, 50, 53
who, whom, 49, 53
whoever, whomever, 49, 50
whose, which, that, 53
without, 154
Word placement, 121, 149
Word usage, 197–200 (*see also* individual words)